The Life and Times
of Sir Goldsworthy Gurney

The Life and Times of Sir Goldsworthy Gurney

Gentleman Scientist and Inventor

1793–1875

Dale H. Porter

Lehigh
University
Press

Bethlehem: Lehigh University Press
London: Associated University Presses

Associated University Presses
440 Forsgate Drive
Cranbury, NJ 08512

Associated University Presses
16 Barter Street
London WC1A 2AH, England

Associated University Presses
P.O. Box 338, Port Credit
Mississauga, Ontario
Canada L5G 4L8

The paper used in this publication meets the requirements of the American National Standard for Permanence of Paper for Printed Library Materials Z39.48-1984.

Library of Congress Cataloging-in-Publication Data

Gurney, Goldsworthy, Sir, 1793–1875.
  The life and times of Sir Goldsworthy Gurney : gentleman scientist and inventor, 1793–1875 / Dale H. Porter.
    p.   cm.
  Includes bibliographical references and index.
  ISBN 0-934223-50-5 (alk. paper)
  1. Gurney, Goldsworthy, Sir, 1793–1875. 2. Mechanical engineers—England—Biography. I. Porter, Dale H. II. Title.
TJ140.G87G87   1998
621'.092—dc21
[B]   97-31833
                                                            CIP

PRINTED IN THE UNITED STATES OF AMERICA

To the memory of Robert Thompson

Contents

Illustrations

Preface

DURING HIS LIFETIME, SIR GOLDSWORTHY GURNEY WAS A SURGEON, AN EXPERI-
mental researcher and lecturer in chemistry, an architect and builder,
a local leader in scientific agriculture, a consultant and contractor
for the Houses of Parliament, and an inventor of laboratory equipment, steam locomotives, gas lights, musical instruments, heating
stoves, and ventilating systems. His name was well known to contemporary scientists, government officials, and journalists. When he
approached retirement at seventy years of age, Queen Victoria recognized his many contributions to the public by granting him a knight-
hood. Yet, even before his retirement, his most significant invention
had been credited to a rival, and after he died, his large and varied
body of work was largely forgotten. An entry in the *Dictionary of
National Biography,* based on obituaries prepared by his daughter
Anna Jane and by the Institution of Civil Engineers in London, was
the only enduring record of his life.

In 1975 the Trevithick Society, dedicated to preserving the memory
of Cornish inventors and their part in the early industrial revolution,
commissioned a local historian, T. R. Harris, to write a centenary
biography of Goldsworthy Gurney. After a painstaking search of local
archives, old newspapers, and Parliamentary papers, Mr. Harris produced a brief memoir remarkable for its thoroughness and fidelity
to the sources. Although my biography revises and expands the late
Mr. Harris's work in many ways, I wish to acknowledge my debt to
him. I have set many of the facts he gathered into their relevant
social, political, and scientific contexts; added material on contemporary inventors, rivals, and associates; and explained scientific and
technical terms that were used in the early nineteenth century, but
whose meaning is opaque today. I have also corrected some errors
and confusions that arose from Mr. Harris's use of Gurney's testimony before various Parliamentary committees, in which Gurney
recalled his early life and career under circumstances that encouraged inconsistency and hyperbole.

The personal papers required for an understanding of Gurney's
personality and of his relationships with his family and associates
were lost or destroyed long before 1975. My biography, like Mr. Har-

ris's memoir, is therefore limited to matters of public record. Comments and quotations in the memoir suggest that Mr. Harris had seen some fragments of private correspondence, but these are not cited in his notes. In fact, because the memoir was published for a general audience, Mr. Harris quite reasonably decided to reduce his reference notes to the bare minimum. He thus omitted most of the citations needed to verify or to expand upon his statements, and the notes from which he prepared his text are no longer filed with the manuscript in the archives of the Trevithick Society. I have rechecked almost all of his quotations from newspapers and journals, and report his comments on Gurney's personal life with appropriate qualifications. I reread all of the Parliamentary papers listed by Mr. Harris and unearthed other sources, such as the Society of Arts committee notes on Gurney's inventions and the files from his employment by Her Majesty's Office of Works, which Mr. Harris did not see.

The present book is a collaborative effort. I first encountered Gurney's Parliamentary testimony while writing a research paper in graduate school, and mentioned him from time to time in classroom lectures on British history. Early in 1986, one of my students with Cornish connections, Ms. Dawn LaPlante, searched the local archives while on an extended visit to her family. She brought back a suitcase full of books, pamphlets, maps, photographs, and photocopies.

While I was making preliminary plans to exploit this material in a book, members of the Bude-Stratton Council in Cornwall decided to renovate their meeting hall, which Gurney had built as his own residence in 1830. To give the project and the local "forgotten genius" their proper historical perspective, Councillor Bryan Dudley Stamp and regional museum curator Stephanie Meads gathered drawings, maps, photographs, and original documents related to Gurney's life and achievements. These were exhibited, with appropriate textual material, in April 1993, when the new council chambers were dedicated. Having read my letters of inquiry in the council's "Gurney" file, Mr. Stamp had initiated an exchange of information, and he incorporated sundry details from my sources in the exhibition. He also issued an invitation to attend the opening ceremonies, hardly imagining that I would actually show up. Thanks to his hospitality, I enjoyed "Gurney tours" to Wadebridge, Padstow, Treator and Launcells.

My research was made possible by a sabbatical leave from Western Michigan University, supplemented by grants from the W.M.U. Faculty Research Fund and the Burnham-Macmillan Endowment Fund. For assistance in locating archival material on Gurney, I wish to thank

Lady Alexandra Wedgwood, architectural archivist at the House of Lords Record Office; Mr. Michael Chrimes, librarian at the Institution of Civil Engineers; Mrs. Susan Bennett, librarian at the Royal Society of Arts; and Mr. Bill Newby, Honorary Secretary to the Trevithick Society. The staffs of the Greater London Record Office in Clerkenwell, the Public Record Office at Kew, the Science Museum in Kensington, and the British Library were immensely helpful. Mr. Peter Gurney of London kindly supplied information about his family, read the first draft of the manuscript, and, with his brother Michael, commissioned a splendid scale model of the 1828 Gurney steam carriage for the Bude museum. I owe thanks to Ms. Jean Chapman for her energetic bibliographical assistance, and to my longtime colleague, Dr. Michael Swords, who critiqued the chapters on Gurney's chemistry lectures. Dr. Cecelia Porter, my sister-in-law, explained the nuances of early nineteenth-century keyboard instruments, and Ms. Christine Porter, my daughter-in-law, created many of the original illustrations. Needless to say, none of these people is responsible for mistakes or misinterpretations in the text.

Goldsworthy Gurney, ca. 1820. By permission of the Bude-Stratton Town Council.

Introduction

LIFE AND TIMES IS A RATHER OLD-FASHIONED TITLE FOR A BIOGRAPHY, BUT IN THE case of Sir Goldsworthy Gurney, I think it appropriate. Born in 1793, Sir Goldsworthy was raised in an extended network of aunts, uncles, cousins, and family friends, comprising several strata of Cornish provincial gentry. In many ways he remained all his life a country gentleman. However, at the age of twenty-seven he set out for the great capital of London to seek his fortune in the realms of medicine, science, and invention. The personal, Cornish parts of his life remain largely obscure because he left behind few personal papers and artifacts. For that reason, his *Life* is shaped mostly by the investigations, discoveries, and controversies of his career.

That career was shaped by two great developments in British culture: the "chemical revolution" of the late eighteenth and early nineteenth centuries, and the application of steam power to industry. The chemical revolution involved the discovery of oxygen, chlorine, and other elements, along with the secrets of chemical combination and combustion. It was set off by the work of Joseph Priestley and Antoine Lavoisier in the generation before Goldsworthy Gurney was born, and was then led by Gurney's contemporaries and erstwhile associates, Humphry Davy and Michael Faraday. While other fields of scientific investigation remained the province of amateur gentlemen, who typically carried out experiments without benefit of a systematic theoretical framework, chemistry began the process of institutionalization and professionalization that would eventually create modern scientific disciplines.[1] Meanwhile, the application of steam power to industry was proceeding by the efforts of entrepreneurs, such as Josiah Wedgwood and George Stephenson, who combined a keen interest in scientific experiment with the ability to organize traditionally skilled craftsmen into new forms of enterprise. Although such men were pillars of local and regional "scientific" societies, and eagerly applied new ideas to their particular ventures, there remained a vague but important boundary between their community, social class orientation, and style of thinking, and those of the gentleman scientist.

A quarter-century ago, historians debated whether science, or "natural philosophy," as it was called before 1830, had any appreciable effect upon the progress of industrialization. A consensus of sorts was established by A. E. Musson and Eric Robinson, whose detailed investigations showed that while practical craftsmanship remained vitally important to industry, frequent, substantive exchanges between experimental scientists and industrialists, often fostered by local societies, provided significant intellectual capital.[2] Indeed, it proved difficult to distinguish between "intelligent empiricism" and "applied science," especially because the scientific institutions emerging around 1800 tended to dedicate their resources to utilitarian improvements in such endeavors as bleaching, agriculture, and metallurgy.[3] British scientific practice for the eighteenth and most of the nineteenth century was resolutely empirical; theoretical speculations, like the atomism of John Dalton or Michael Faraday's electromagnetic "lines of force," met with suspicion and criticism.[4]

Musson, Robinson, and their colleagues appear to have argued the question of science's impact on industry without noticing Thomas Kuhn's contemporary essays, which undermined the image of scientific inquiry as a series of progressive intellectual breakthroughs.[5] Kuhn pointed out that the great, paradigmatic discoveries made by Lavoisier, Davy, and Faraday were exceptions to the rule that most "scientific" activity, in most times and places, consists of extending the application of known principles and properties of subject matter, devising apparatus to improve the reliability of measurements, and confirming details suggested by general hypotheses. He added that "the invention, construction, and deployment of new experimental apparatus demanded first-rate talent," an observation borne out by Goldsworthy Gurney and his London associates. In addition, most scientific experiments seldom resembled the neat, logically progressive steps laid out in published reports and textbooks. Even today, a good deal of guesswork, random exploration, and intuition may also be involved, even though scientists usually work within a historically circumscribed set of expectations and practices absorbed during their apprenticeship.[6] Finally, we must not judge earlier periods of intellectual work by present standards; even Musson and Robinson agreed that people in the early nineteenth century, although expressing attitudes and terminology later discarded, had "scientific" knowledge.[7] If Gurney had remained a gentleman surgeon-cum-scientist, we would therefore be able to say that his energetic pursuit of new ideas, and the experimental apparatus he so ingeniously contrived, placed him at the heart, if not at the head, of the chemical revolution in Britain. But in 1824, Gurney took the fateful step of giving up his medical practice and his scientific lectures to devote his entire time to the invention of a new steam locomotive. That brought him into the world of mechanics, engineers, and technology, which for him was new territory. It is true that chemistry, more than other fields of research, involved analyzing industrial materials and constructing mechanical apparatus. But the engineers, who were gradually emerging from traditional craft occupations, had two qualities that Gurney lacked and never really learned to appreciate. They knew how to convert trial-and-error contraptions into efficient, reliable machines by applying systematic design principles, and they could envision the technological, financial, and even political conditions for the systematic exploitation of inventions. They learned these skills by apprenticeship in the growing community of engineers. Although they were aware of relevant scientific data, they did not think scientifically.[8] Thus Gurney's relative success in one field did not carry over to the other.

Biographies of scientists and inventors tend to be written according to a formula so well known that readers accept it as historical truth. In that formula, an exceptional youngster, displaying early curiosity and analytical cleverness, eventually targets a particular area of current debate or incredulity. His ability to recognize the significance of work by lesser colleagues, or to revive and exploit knowledge considered useless by authorities, plus a dogged perseverance in pursuit of truth, leads to a breakthrough discovery. Then, the hero is either rewarded by inclusion in the scientific establishment, or must challenge that establishment in order that truth many prevail.

There is a corollary formula for inventors of the second rank whose career and achievements never matched their early promise. Their relative lack of success is blamed either on diversions—professional, political, or social—which took their eyes off the prize at crucial moments, or, more commonly, on vested interests and unscrupulous competitors who sabotaged or stole the hero's work for their own gain.

These two formulas share a common fallacy, which, in recent studies of the social history of science and technology, is termed the fallacy of asymmetrical explanation.[9] Simply, this means that the types and combinations of conditions, forces, and people used to explain the *success* of discovery and invention ought to be the same types and combinations used to explain its *failure*. It is obvious, from a close study of any inventor's life, that successes and failures frequently occur to the same "genius," under virtually the same conditions, with similar associates and resources. It is not usually the case, in other words, that breakthroughs happen by reason of lonely, feverish investigations of unpopular hypotheses, whereas disappointments are due to nasty competitors or idiotic patrons. It may be useful for inventors and their biographers to make such arguments, but it does not help us understand the reality in which they lived and worked.

The career of Sir Goldsworthy Gurney was fashioned according to the standard formula, not only by himself and his friends, in testimony before public agencies, but in memorials written shortly after his death. These accounts naturally emphasized Gurney's personal achievements, without much reference to the often substantial work being done in the same fields by contemporaries, and they lamented his loss of recognition and financial rewards, caused by the interference of vested interests, without giving equal consideration to the influential friends, mentors, and patrons without whose help Gurney might well have remained an obscure provincial surgeon.

This book explores the "times" of Gurney's life, then, as a way of constructing a meaningful, symmetrical account of his career. Looking at what other inventors were doing and what other scientists were publishing helps us make reasonable inferences about Gurney's own goals and methods, even where direct evidence is lacking. We cannot, unfortunately, extend such inferences to other aspects of his world. Although Gurney spent endless hours and days dealing with politicians, including Lord Palmerston and Benjamin Disraeli, he himself had no Parliamentary ambitions and, sadly, not much political acumen. He arrived in London just as the Prince Regent was raised to the throne as George IV, only to have his much-traveled queen return from her Continental liaisons to claim her royal rights. Queen Caroline's divorce proceedings were a pretext for outrageous partisan campaigns by both Whigs and Tories and months of screaming headlines in the local press, but we know nothing of Gurney's reaction to it, nor of his reactions to the Great Reform Bill of 1832, the Irish famine, or the Crimean War. For similar reasons, we cannot penetrate the veil of his marital and family relations, even when it seems crucial to do so. The anxieties of his first wife, watching her husband tinker with noxious chemicals and explosive steam boilers, are only hinted at in a couple of anecdotes. The mystery of his second marriage, at age sixty, to a farmer's daughter of twenty-four; the birth of a second daughter; and the disappearance of both of them within five years, has never been solved. His lifelong attachment to his first daughter, Anna Jane, who eagerly watched his early experiments and became, at various times, his confidant and companion, secretary, and nurse, could be explored adequately only in a novel.

One aspect of his social life can, however, be filled out and evaluated with a fair amount of assurance. So much of Victorian culture has been examined and written about in recent years, especially by experts on family and class relations, that Gurney's attitudes and resources as a member of the Cornish gentry can be identified and drawn out of the volumes of offical testimony in which they were usually embedded. So, too, can we extract the contrasting feelings and assumptions that he developed as an ambitious competitor in the scientific, commercial, and political arenas of London. This part of his "life and times" was not separate from the other, more technical part. They were intertwined, and only by studying how they interacted can we understand his successes, his failures, and his uniqueness as a person.

The Life and Times
of Sir Goldsworthy Gurney

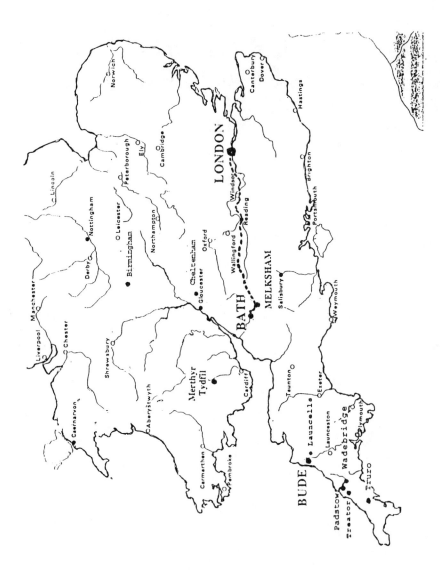

Goldsworthy Gurney's Britain, 1793–1840. Porter collection.

1

Gurney's Cornish Background

CORNWALL HAS BEEN LIKENED TO A FISHERMAN'S SEA BOOT. IT EXTENDS, CRIN-kled and slightly buckled, from the southwest of England. Fringed by rugged seashores and marked off from Devon and the rest of England by the river Tamar, Cornwall is almost an island. Seafarers from the Mediterranean settled here before England was overrun from northwest Europe. Until recent times, the Cornish people remained more closely connected by language and by commerce to Brittany than to Essex or Yorkshire.

The great cliffs of the westward coast push the slate shelf of land upwards in steplike plateaus to the high, level moors. The upland soil is thin and poorly drained, but underneath it lie great seams of tin, copper, and other minerals, alongside massive uprisings of granite. In places the granite has metamorphosed into kaolin, called china clay, exported round the world in the nineteenth century. The deep, picturesque river valleys are lined with sediment washed down from the moors. They offer possibilities for agriculture on small farms fertilized with sea-sand lime and seaweed. Shoals of herring and pilchards swarmed the coastal waters until the Victorian era. The geography of Cornwall gave its residents but three choices of livelihood, all precarious: seafaring, mining, and farming. Queen Elizabeth said of her Cornish gentlemen that they were "born courtiers, with a becoming confidence." Their reputation for cheerful hospitality, however, was tempered with a suspicion of outsiders and a tendency to exaggerate and prolong slights and injuries. Claude Berry, the antiquarian of Padstow, says, "We are given to brooding over wrongs until they assume unwarranted, sometimes even fantastic, proportions"—a sensitivity resonant in the career of Goldsworthy Gurney.[1]

Cornwall's sharply indented coastline promises many small harbors, but gives few that are safely navigable. It is a ships' graveyard. In the early modern period, the Cornish gained as much from salvaging as from shipping. Along the northern coast, the most secure harbor was at Bude Haven, where Goldsworthy Gurney would spend much of his later life. Farther south, at the estuary of the river Camel, lay Padstow, an ancient but silt-threatened port. Padstow traded with Wales, Ireland, and ports in the Bristol Channel, transshipping timber and ores to the English Channel and exporting its own good Cornish slate, copper ore, and tin. Emigrants to America were beginning to take ship from Padstow in the early nineteenth century. Today fishing boats share the harbor with pleasure craft, and the old quay buildings have been renovated as tourist shops, renewing the town's proverbial motto of "Good Fellowship." But in the streets leading up from the water, one can discover houses and shops that look much as they did two hundred years ago.

Goldsworthy Gurney was born 14 February 1793 at Treator (pronounced "Traitor"). Treator occupied a bend in the hedge-bound lane that follows the coast southward, about two miles outside Padstow, beyond the great Elizabethan mansion of Prideaux. It was neither a crossroads nor a market, merely a collection of slate-sided houses and outbuildings overlooked by a modest manor house. The Gurney family arrived in Cornwall at the beginning of the eighteenth century. They traced their lineage from Sir Hugh de Gournay, who came to England with William the Conqueror. Sir Hugh's descendants, anglicizing the surname to Gurney, had flourished near London until the seventeenth century. Then, Gregory Gurney, Captain of the Foot Guards under Charles I, chose loyalty to his king in the Civil War and lost both life and property. A tradition claims that the Restoration brought marks of favor from a grateful king. In the early eighteenth century, however, the Gurneys were living in reduced circumstances, though still among the gentry. Around 1700, Goldsworthy's great-grandfather, John, an elegant classical scholar, became domestic chaplain to Theophilus Blackall, Lord Bishop of Exeter. In the usual style of preferment, the Bishop rewarded John Gurney with the vicarage of St. Merryn, near Padstow. It was not a rich living, but John decided to settle there until a better position presented itself. His patron, however, shortly passed to his reward, leaving the young vicar to serve the parish for the next fifty years.

John apparently made the best of it, assuming the role of gentleman scholar and pillar of his community, like so many other provincial vicars. His respectability was rewarded. He drew his youngest son, Gregory, into the church, obtaining for him the rectorship of St. James and the vicarage of Tregony, some fifty miles away. He then arranged a marriage between Gregory and a local heiress of distinguished family, Mary Peter, of the parish of St. Merryn. They were soon established in his new wife's residence at Trevorgus.[2]

Goldsworthy's father, John, was the second son born to Gregory and Mary Peter Gurney. The eldest having died in infancy, John succeeded to the estate. His younger brothers, Gregory and Thomas Peter, took orders and found livings in the usual way. Born and raised a gentleman, John married Isabell Carter, the daughter of yet another clergyman, and settled into the Peter mansion at Treator, an original part of the family estate. The "Gurney house" identified today by local residents may or may not be his. A square, slate-sided structure typical of the region, it looks too common for a man of John's position and probable income, and certainly too small for a family of six. The mansion, overlooking the road from the rise opposite, was built in 1700 and would still have been serviceable.[3]

Goldsworthy's Christian name came from his godmother, a daughter of General Goldsworthy who served Queen Charlotte as maid of honor. The name was passed to his son, Goldsworthy John, who died without heirs. It was also given as a middle name to his nephew, Elias, whose family remained at Trevorgus, and to one son in each succeeding generation, right down to the present.

Goldsworthy related many anecdotes from his youth during his later testimony before Parliament, but we know almost nothing of his everyday life. He grew up when boiled beef and onions, goose and parsnips, squab and leeks were common fare among the middling classes, and clotted cream was poured over pasties of every description. He no doubt attended church, perhaps more than once a week, and the whole region from Padstow and Wadebridge down to Truro was filled with relatives to visit. If the Peter family was wealthy, the Gurneys were prolific: his father's seven brothers and sisters provided Goldsworthy with extensive family connections that were to prove advantageous to his early education and later career. He was cousin to the Vivians, a prominent local family, and related on his grandmother Peter's side to the headmaster of Truro school, where he and the Vivian boys would be educated. Through them and through his uncle, Samuel Gurney, he was introduced to Andrew Vivian of Camborne and to Davies Giddy (later Gilbert), both of whom helped Richard Trevithick build the first high-pressure steam locomotive. Goldsworthy, in fact, frequently met Trevithick himself, whom he described as "a plain unpretending man of great genius."[4] Gurney was only seven years old when Trevithick drove the first model of his steam carriage, without rails, around the garden of his cottage at Camborne, with Davies Giddy acting as stoker and Lady De Dunstanville of Tehidy as engineer.[5] In the next decade, the young man would witness Trevithick's invention of the high-pressure steam boiler and his experiments with railway engines.

Despite such experiences, Goldsworthy remained innocent of important aspects of the industrial revolution. Signs of extensive mining and quarrying are still visible in western Cornwall, but there are no comparable landmarks of "industry" as one is apt to think of them in nineteenth-century terms. The granite quarries and china-clay pits that developed around 1800 were organized in hundreds of companies, all modest in size. The typical production factory was really but a workshop, rarely employing more than ten people, and usually tucked into a converted building in the back street of a market town. This was the kind of enterprise that Gurney would set up after he moved to London and began experimenting with steam carriages.

References in later life indicate that he participated in the customary holidays and amusements of the region. Some were religious, some vaguely pagan. Most were a mixture, born of the church's accommodation of traditional agricultural rituals. In Padstow, May Day was still celebrated (despite Methodist preachers) by the dancing of the Furry, a line of people parading hand in hand through the streets with pipes and tambourines, stopping periodically to perform a set of fancy steps. Then came the blanket-clad, stick-riding Hobby Horse, led by a prancing guide with mask and club, weaving through the town with a crowd singing "Summer is acome in."[6] Goldsworthy might have been forbidden the latter ritual, since it generally ended in drunken brawls, and he would have been held back from the old sport of hurling—a kind of massive, daylong rugby match, played between groups of young toughs from competing villages over a two-mile pitch. But even a gentleman's son would join the wrestling matches that marked many feast days and for which the Cornish, including Richard Trevithick, were famous.

Most sons of gentlemen were schooled at home, during their first years, in the rudiments of arithmetic and geometry, some Latin, a bit of geography, and history. The Bible, church traditions, and theology were commonplace topics in family conversation. If Goldsworthy had a natural bent for mechanical and scientific subjects, as Harris suggests, these were pursued informally. He later recalled that he kept notes on local farming practices, the movements of tides and beach sand, atmospheric conditions, and engines of all kinds. Padstow, only a few miles distant, combined the coastal and Irish shipping trade with commerce overland to the Channel ports. Goods from all over the world passed along its wharves, and a boy could see sailing ships of many varieties.

By the age of ten or eleven, Goldsworthy was prepared to matriculate at the reputable Truro grammar school. Truro was the political center and cathedral town of all Cornwall, grown wealthy on trade and tin coinage, an annual fair, and overseas trade. Its leading families enjoyed horse races and balls, carriages and stately Georgian homes, theaters and a Philharmonic Society. The houses in Padstow clammed together up the narrow streets leading from the harbor; in Truro they were typically detached. The streets were wide, well cleansed by watercourses, and bordered by foot pavements. Lemon Street, home to the Lemons of Carclew, had recently been graced by a row of unified Georgian buildings, and the Assembly Rooms presented one of the most attractive features of a civilized country town.[7] Here, as elsewhere in Cornwall since the Wesleyan revival, there was a sharp division between church and chapel. Church people, like the Lemons, Vivians, and Gurneys, being in a minority in the region, if not in Truro itself, were apt to be more militant than elsewhere in the kingdom. When Gurney arrived to take up his studies, the school reflected that attitude.[8]

Truro School liked to compare itself to Westminster, Eton, and Winchester as a training ground for political and religious leaders. Its curriculum was strictly traditional: for two guineas a year, the student received board and lodging along with Greek and Latin, Roman antiquities and classical literature, writing, grammar, and the principles of religion. French, music, and dancing lessons could be added for a few shillings more. Flogging and caning were regular practices. The school's primary function was to civilize the sons of gentry, but it also sent scholars to Oxford, mostly for religious training. The large, high-ceilinged schoolroom was appropriately fitted with Corinthian pillars. A small library sat in one corner; a large playground spread outside at the back. For teaching an average of sixty boys a year, the schoolmaster received the sum of £25 from an endowment founded by the Borlase family, and £25 from the Truro borough corporation.[9]

At the beginning of the century, Truro School sailed in difficult waters. The veteran headmaster, an Oxford graduate named Cornelius Cardew, won accolades from at least one former pupil for giving equal attention to dull and bright students, and for keeping his considerable temper under control. Possessed of a substantial fortune and a large family from two marriages, he enjoyed a wider recognition and higher status than the usual schoolmaster. But his reputation was compromised by his behavior as a magistrate for Truro, in which role he showed a clear preference for relatives and friends. His partisan decisions outraged rival families and political cliques, and the reputation of the school declined along with his own. After several years of controversy, he was forced to resign not only the bench but the schoolhouse as well.[10]

When Cardew left, in 1805, Gurney was thirteen—old enough to have suffered a year or two under the traditional curriculum, but too young to graduate. Fortunately for him, the mayor and corporation of Truro decided to hire Thomas Hogg as the new headmaster. Hogg was a decided novelty: he was a layman, and a talented disciple of the Scottish Enlightenment. He had imbibed the new scientific curriculum at Edinburgh University, which brought practical mechanics and agriculturalists together with academic theorists and introduced such novelties as laboratory experiments in chemistry. He had already written a text, *The Institutes of Mathematical Geography.* In the autumn of 1805, he introduced geometry and navigation, astronomy and mathematics, modern geography and map projection to his students at Truro. Hogg then advertised in the local paper that after the Christmas holidays, he would offer a course of evening lectures in "Natural and Experimental Philosophy" to the public for a subscription fee. Classics were still the primary part of liberal education, he assured readers; his lectures were intended only "to afford the rising generation an opportunity to acquire practical knowledge; to exhibit a few of the improvements that have accrued to the arts of civilization, by recent discoveries in various branches of Experimental Philosophy, and to demonstrate that literature and science can advance together."[11]

Thomas Hogg moved into a residence next to the schoolhouse to devote himself to his students. It should not be surprising that Goldsworthy Gurney became one of his favorites. The curriculum was tailor-made for his natural curiosity and mechanical turn of mind. He was encouraged to experiment, to read beyond the curriculum, to link the principles of science to the world around him. In 1807 Hogg presented his pupil with a copy of his *Institutes* as a reward for his enthusiasm and acumen.[12]

Upon leaving school Goldsworthy was apprenticed to a practicing surgeon, Dr. Avery of Wadebridge. It might seem odd that a gentleman's son should be articled as an apprentice, especially into a trade that had not yet attained the status of a profession. At the beginning of the eighteenth century, surgeons were considered fairly low-ranking craftsmen on the level of barbers or mechanics. They generally treated external ailments, leaving the prescription of internal medicines to apothecaries or folk practitioners. They were disdained by the learned physicians, who gave advice based on classical texts without ever actually touching bodies. However, in the course of the century, the "sick trade" flourished in a growing consumer market, and the old hierarchy disintegrated. Medical knowledge increased, requiring more extensive training for every rank of healer. New medical courses, offered at Edinburgh, London, and other centers, together with an extremely vague set of criteria for distinguishing physicians from practical healers and quacks, meant that a medical man could treat a great variety of ailments, mix his own medicines, and depend on his patients to evaluate his skill. Besides, surgeons and apothecaries could be found everywhere in Britain, whereas physicians were rare and served only small groups of wealthy patients in large cities. Dr. Avery was probably the only reputable medical man in Wadebridge. Gurney, trained in chemistry, could well act as his apothecary.[13]

The apprenticeship would also have suited Gurney because medicine was probably the closest ally of scientific investigation at the time. "Natural philosophy" was, and would remain for some time, a gentleman's pastime; the devotee without an independent income usually secured a medical practice to support it. Humphry Davy, son of an old established Cornish family and, like Gurney, a graduate of Truro School, was apprenticed to the apothecary-surgeon Bingham Borlese, the mayor of Penzance, for exactly the same reason.[14]

After Truro, Wadebridge must have seemed a sleepy backwater. It was located up the River Camel, about five miles southwest of Padstow. About fifty houses clustered on either side of the river, joined by "the longest, strongest, and fairest bridge the Shire can muster." There were a few respectable shops, a comfortable inn, the standard church, and numerous warehouses and timber yards for river commerce. The roads connecting Wadebridge to nearby towns had suffered two centuries of neglect.[15] Since the 1760s, however, a new turnpike linked it to Launceston and Truro, the first of a series of improved roads that gradually brought carriage traffic to most of the Cornish towns and great colorful mail coaches thundering down from London.[16]

Most medical apprentices in the early nineteenth century received precious little instruction for their fees. They usually found themselves stuck with "capping bottles and rolling pills." But Dr. Avery was preparing to retire from his practice, so he gave Gurney closer attention and more responsibility than might otherwise have been the case. Harris states that the young man invented "several ingenious contrivances" for Dr. Avery's professional use. He also wrote several original papers on chemistry, heat, and electricity while still an apprentice. When his master retired in 1812, Goldsworthy, not yet twenty years old, succeeded to his practice.

Cornwall was reputed to be a healthy region of the kingdom. Even before the railways made it easily accessible, people from England came there to recover from consumption and other respiratory ailments. Germ theory was still a half-century away; the prevailing belief was that disease came from miasma ("bad air"), so the strong winds that blew off the sea across the uplands were thought salubrious. Common folk, on the other hand, kept their windows shut against the open air, since a robin or other bird entering the house signaled impending death. They believed wholeheartedly in omens, spells, and fairies. Gurney, as a young surgeon, would have found pieces of the hangman's rope from Bodmin Gaol carried around his patients' necks like amulets, believed to cure ulcers as they rotted. In a celebrated case, a drunken man died "instantly" from lockjaw after yelling in a seditious and blasphemous manner in the local tavern.[17]

A contemporary chronicler claimed that because the Cornish tended to be "sanguine or irritable" rather than "choleric" or "melancholic," they presented the physician with a mixture of debilities rather than with clear cases of specific disease. The acrid, moist air caused surprisingly little ague, but a local type of pleurisy, called "suffocative catarrh," became endemic in winter, causing many deaths. Sore throats and croup threatened the children at all times. Dropsy, gout, and rheumatism, often combined with worms, spread widely among the lower classes due to the cold, wet conditions in which they often worked, and to their excessive drinking. Their steady diet of fish and salt pork also left them prey to scurvy. Small-pox, fatal in the past, was now being reduced by the practice of vaccination, introduced by Jenner in 1798. The consumption, fevers, and injuries specific to miners, which killed them off at an early age, would not have been part of Gurney's regular practice, since the underground tin and copper mining region was to the south of Wade-bridge, and an infirmary had been recently established in Truro expressly for those ailments.[18] He did record a case of the well-known "Devonshire colic," which invaded Cornwall for a time. The medical world had never ascertained the origin of this colic, but Gurney's observations of farming and his knowledge of chemistry led him to guess correctly that it must be due to the ingestion of lead, sometimes used to line the region's many cider vats.[19]

What could he do for his patients? The practice of medicine at the turn of the century was still a mixture of folk remedies, confounded with medieval philosophy, unreformed by the revolution in chemistry emerging all around it.[20] The *Lancet* admitted as late as 1840 that "the information of the medical profession, generally, on matters of natural science, is very little greater than that of the people at large." Medical examinations of the body were perfunctory, since the doctor did not know what to look for. Dissection and the study of anatomical pathology would not become common for half a century. The stethoscope, though invented, was held to be useless. Thermometers were too large to insert in the usual orifices and took at least twenty minutes to register a body temperature. Under the circumstances, Gurney, like most doctors, was content to ask about previous illnesses and habits, appetite, and the appearance of urine and feces. For diagnosis and treatment, he relied on the same kind of common sense and local custom that his patients did, but dressed it up with Latin or the latest scientific jargon. Doctors commonly believed in the number seven, for instance: a fever would crest on the seventh day and disappear on the fourteenth. Cases of epilepsy or dyspepsia in men were attributed to sexual excitement, for which abstinence and hard labor were prescribed. Bleeding with leeches, violent purges, liquid diets, and "cupping" to suck the poison from sores or joints were the most common remedies for illnesses and malfunctions of every kind. Patients were liberally dosed with opium or its mild derivative, laudanum; with quinine, creosote, mercury, and calomel; or better yet, with a mixture of these and other substances. Doctors routinely criticized the homeopathic remedies offered by midwives and other folk healers, but since those were given in relatively small doses, they at least allowed the sick some chance of spontaneous recovery.[21]

Gurney's medical techniques probably differed little from those of Dr. Avery. However, he was certainly better trained in chemistry and understood the principles of scientific thinking. He was, moreover, a habitually curious observer and note-taker, fond of diagnosing problems. If the evidence of his later life is any indication, he was also loquacious and enthusiastic about his inquiries. This quality, coupled with his classical learning and friendly disposition, undoubtedly helped establish his reputation in Wadebridge. At any rate, he took over the practice at the age of nineteen and managed to keep all of Dr. Avery's patients under his own care for the next eight years.

In the course of professional and social engagements, he made the acquaintance of a Wadebridge solicitor, Richard Symons. In the manner of country society, the eligible bachelor was soon introduced to Richard's older sister. Elizabeth Symons lived at Cann Orchard, a prosperous farm outside Launcells, near Bude Haven in northern Cornwall. The farm had been in the family for at least ten generations. Elizabeth was already thirty-three years old, an age when single women of her class would normally resign themselves to spinsterhood, when she agreed to Gurney's proposal of marriage. Her parents, Thomas and Grace Bray Symons, had died earlier; her five brothers and sisters were married. No descriptions of Elizabeth appear in the few private records left by Gurney. Judging from the photograph of her daughter, taken at roughly the same age, she must have been attractive enough. In the 1820s, when Gurney was experimenting with steam engines, Elizabeth was depicted as somewhat skittish and fretful, but she had good reason to be: the machines had a habit of killing or maiming their operators. Regardless of her age and personality, she had two qualities that made her a very satisfactory bride for an ambitious young surgeon. She came from a respectable family, and she had a substantial dowry.

Gurney, as a younger son with a provincial practice, could not offer much wealth or property to Elizabeth. But the few extant drawings render him as slender and well proportioned, slightly taller than the average, with regular features and a friendly, open expression framed by dark, curly hair. He was gregarious and intelligent, could converse (or hold forth) about a variety of subjects, and was well connected in Cornish society. Elizabeth married him in the family church, at Launcells, in March 1814. The following January, domiciled at Wadebridge, she bore their first child, Anna Jane.

The Gurneys lived five more years in Wadebridge while Goldsworthy consolidated his practice and pursued a variety of scientific studies and inventions. He developed into an accomplished pianist, constructed a small pipe organ of his own design, and even invented a way to combine the two instruments so that they could be played together by a single performer. Knowing that the sea sand at Padstow was rich in carbonate of lime, from the many shells smashed against the rocky shoreline by wave and wind, he analyzed the sand at Wadebridge and found it likewise rich enough to be used as fertilizer. As it was dug out and hauled away, he noted that the tides, carrying silt from the mouth of the Tamar fourteen miles away, filled in the holes but did not deposit additional amounts. He also observed the swirling of the sand along the edge of the river as the tides moved upstream—a phenomenon he would recall later, when investigating mine ventilation and the problem of pollution in the Thames River at London.[22]

Such amusements and investigations could not satisfy Gurney's natural ambition. Even with his family connections and Elizabeth's dowry, he was bound to feel the limitations of life in a provincial town. Changes in British society after 1815 created additional inducements for moving to a larger, more cosmopolitan city. In the first place, Gurney had lived his entire life during the French revolutionary and Napoleonic wars, which had brought prosperity to the farmers, miners, and seafaring people of Cornwall, along with an artificial dampening of political and social divisions. When peace came in 1815, these conditions changed rapidly, mostly for the worse. The summer of 1815 produced a record harvest just as the army was disbanded, leaving farmers without a market for their grain. Shipping dropped off, and the need for tin and copper fluctuated. Thousands of soldiers returned to civilian life looking for work. The next three years were unusually cold and wet, ruining crops, and thus driving the price of bread up, while the landowning classes reaped profits from the steep import tariffs imposed by the Corn Laws. The laboring classes clamored for relief. They agitated for tariff and Poor Law reforms, and flooded the countryside with political pamphlets attacking the landowning gentry. A country town doctor like Gurney would see his poorer patients grow sicker but less able to pay for medical services, while people of his own class rallied together against what they perceived as a conspiracy of dangerous agitators. The contrast would have been particularly disturbing for a young man who fashioned himself as a member of the liberal scientific reform movement, but lived among friends and relations who were mostly Tory country gentlemen or Church of England clergy. Gurney himself rarely expressed political views of any kind; yet the members of Parliament with whom he associated in the following two decades tended to be more liberal, even radical in a Reform Whig sort of way, than his former provincial connections.

Changing professional standards also made relocation attractive. Like many other general practitioners in Britain, Gurney would have supported the movement to improve medical education and regulate medical practice as a way of combating the charlatans and "irregulars" who flooded the market with cheap patent remedies and marvelous mechanical devices. The first trophy won by this movement was the Apothecaries' Act of 1815, which made it illegal to dispense medicine in England and Wales without a license from the Worshipful Society of Apothecaries. In one sense a thoroughly retrograde measure that attempted to restrict competition, the Apothecaries' Act was also a harbinger of reform. Its authors attacked the privileged ignorance of the medical elite as well as the purveyors of pills and phrenology. They demanded, among other changes, a thorough grounding in chemistry for all medical students. Gurney must have felt vindicated and encouraged by this movement. As a provincial surgeon, he would hardly be affected by the Apothecaries' Act, since it was ineffectually enforced in rural areas. But if he moved to London, paid the requisite fees, and passed the licensing examination (widely regarded as a complete sham), he might then invade the ranks of society doctors. He could never hope to join the prestigious Royal College of Surgeons, because he lacked the requisite university degree. But he could combine a reputable practice with scientific investigations in association with some of the most eminent men of the time.

Individual relationships may have played a part in Gurney's decision to move. Richard Trevithick, with whom he had continued to correspond, left Cornwall in 1812 for an ill-fated venture in South American mining. Trevithick's associate, Davies Gilbert, was now a member of Parliament and served on the Board of the Royal Institution, the premier scientific research establishment in London. Humphry Davy, who preceded Gurney at Truro school, had become the Royal Institution's most popular and influential researcher. Thomas Hogg's classmates from Edinburgh were challenging the traditional hierarchy of physicians and surgeons in the metropolis with their new concepts of scientific medicine. The Lemons, Gilberts, Molesworths, and other Cornishmen, with whom Gurney was linked by kinship, class, and old school ties, held seats in Parliament. In a society still operating by kinship connections, by patronage, and by regional loyalties, these changes created a network of opportunity, drawing Gurney toward the capital.

The route they took can only be conjectured. Packing their belongings for shipment, they presumably set off by coach to Bodmin, south of the moor, and then through Lostwithiel to the port of Fowey on the south coast. Taking passage on a coastal packet with their furniture and baggage, they proceeded eastward along the south coast of England, angled northeasterly through the Strait of Dover to Margate, and sailed with the tide up the River Thames to the great port of London.

2

London, 1820–1824: Lectures on Chemistry, Part I

To pass up the Thames on the incoming tide and dock at the "Pool" below London Bridge, in 1820, was to enter a turbulent forest of ships' masts, barges, lighters, and ferries. The noise of thousands of sailors, dockers, agents, warehousemen, and customs officials surrounded arriving passengers. Hawkers of food, clothing, and sundries assaulted them as they went ashore. Running this dockside gauntlet and securing their furniture and belongings would have sapped the Gurneys' courage. Escaping the crush of the City would leave them exhausted. A million people crowded London, and more were arriving every day. The Gurneys carried themselves westward toward the newly expanding suburbs, where a congenial young surgeon might hope to attract progressive, affluent patients. When they passed St. James's Palace and turned toward Kensington, they would have been astonished to find close-packed housing estates gobbling up open fields; new construction; and traffic everywhere. The medieval city boundaries had been outflanked long ago; the uniform, classical Georgian houses that spread outward, row by row, from the crowded confines of older neighborhoods could not keep up with the burgeoning population.

During the Napoleonic wars, the high cost of materials, labor, and credit had slowed the pace of expansion. After 1815 there was a new burst of energy, a celebration of victory, coupled with a determination to give London the elegance and grandeur befitting the capital of a world empire. George III, the homely "farmer king," had been judged insane in 1810, this time for good. The Prince Regent was free to express his flamboyant tastes through architecture and urban planning. Under his patronage, John Nash laid out the great horseshoe-shaped gardens of Regent's Park, as large as the old City itself, and the Prince encouraged his aristocratic friends to build mansions around its perimeter. To the south of the new park, he leveled acres of slum dwellings to make room for a dramatic new thoroughfare, sweeping down across Oxford Street and curving through Piccadilly Circus all the way to Carlton House Terrace. Other men planned to extend its line of elegant colonnades along the Thames River on a palatial embankment stretching from Westminster to St. Paul's. London Bridge, 700 years old and truly falling down, was to be replaced with a span of graceful arches. On the flanks of Regent Street and in the new suburbs of Belgravia and the Grosvenor Estates, aristocratic landlords had dignified the modest terrace houses with wide streets and spacious squares. Critics of London, traditionally hostile to urban life, for once applauded the new neighborhoods. Foreigners and provincial visitors thought them clean and fashionable.[1]

But the overcrowding, misery, and pollution that were to outrage Victorian reformers were not far away. Although Regent's Park mansions displayed walls of imported stone, most of the new dwellings were built of plain London clay brick. They soon blackened. The heavy smoke and soot from thousands of coal fires and factory chimneys, mixed with the effluvia from tanneries and gasworks, overflowing cesspits, open drains, and the droppings of a million horses, coated every surface with grime. The old thoroughfares between the City and Westminster—Fleet Street, the Strand, Whitehall—were jammed with twenty thousand carriages and wagons each day, competing with countless pedestrians and droves of cattle. Spoils of empire and international commerce flooded into the warehouses and wharves along the muddy, sewage-strewn banks of the River Thames. The size, wealth, and energy of the capital—the dominant arena of political, financial, commercial, and cultural life in Britain—was equaled only by its noise and squalor.

The Gurneys obtained a lease at Number 7, Argyll Street, a short residential lane just southeast of Oxford Circus near Regent Street. It was an ideal location for attracting society patients to the new surgery. Like other medical men, Goldsworthy sought contracts to analyze commercial chemical products and to assist in the occasional postmortem. More important, he began offering public lectures on subjects connected with chemistry and medicine. Advertised in subscription series of five or six, the lectures attracted a sizable audience. Sir Anthony Carlisle, Dr. William Hyde Wollaston, and "many other eminent surgeons and physicians then in extensive practice" attended. They regarded his views on chemistry as "original and valuable."[2] After two years, his reputation earned him a nomination as Lecturer in Chemistry and Natural Philosophy at the Surrey Institution, an endowed school located at the south side of Blackfriars Bridge and "established to afford the working classes the means of self-culture." The Surrey, one of several imitations of the Royal

Institution, offered evening classes for skilled workers and lower-middle-class students hoping to break into one of the professions, and for educated members of the public. After a probationary presentation in which, Harris reports, the "novelty and aptness of his illustrations delighted his large and discerning audience," he was hired for a course of twelve lectures in the elements of chemistry.[3]

The Surrey Institution lectures offer an interesting survey of scientific knowledge during an important period of chemical discovery. They were neither the first survey, nor the most popular, published in the first quarter of the nineteenth century, but for Gurney's career they were absolutely crucial. To understand why, we need to look at the world of public science in 1820 as it was understood by practitioners and by the audiences at their public lectures.

One feature of this world was the astonishing popularity of chemistry among all classes of people, who regarded it both as an extremely useful science and as a key to the secrets of nature. Readers who recall struggling through a required chemistry course in school may not believe that the subject could ever be considered fashionable, fascinating, or fun. But in the early nineteenth century, it was all three. Public lectures attracted audiences of both sexes and all ages. Home "experimental" kits found a ready market among the middle classes. Pamphlets and textbooks on chemistry sold widely.

One reason for its popularity was a utilitarian one. The new industrial and agricultural methods introduced during the eighteenth century required a practical knowledge of metallurgy, of gases and combustion, of soil chemistry. Such knowledge had to be accessible to farmers, industrialists, geologists, and mechanics, who often lacked specialized training and equipment. These men and their wives formed a rapidly expanding market for public science.

Chemistry was also attractive because its leading intellects were pioneering a dramatic reconstitution of every field of scientific knowledge. The "chemical revolution" of 1760–1820 encompassed the use of heat, electricity, and reactive agents to isolate and identify new elements; the invention of more sophisticated and effective equipment for conducting experiments; and the development of a systematic nomenclature for elements and compounds. These three transformations began simultaneously and developed in response to one another. By 1770 Joseph Priestley had decomposed air (although he interpreted the results in terms of "phlogiston," a type of "heat matter" supposedly released by combustion). Then, Antoine Lavoisier named oxygen as an element, isolated it from water, and proclaimed it the agent of combustion, rust, acidity, respiration, and chemical composition. His *Méthode de Nomenclature Chimique* (1787) showed how all compounds could be named so as to indicate their elementary composition. Like the *Encyclopédie* of his contemporary *philosophes,* Lavoisier's work was much more than a set of new names for old knowledge. Built into it was a whole complex of ideas and methods antithetical to classical tradition. This self-proclaimed "revolution" was further systematized in a textbook, *Traité Elémentaire de Chimie* (1789), which combined the system of nomenclature with descriptions of the relevant experiments, standards of instrumentation, and theoretical principles. By 1800 Lavoisier's paradigm was almost universally accepted in Britain as well as on the Continent.[4]

The second phase of the chemical revolution was centered on the development and application of the galvanic or voltaic pile, a primitive electric battery. Sir Anthony Carlisle and William Nicholson first described it in 1800. Voltaic piles could be made from all sorts of materials, but there was little agreement as to how they worked or how to interpret the results of experiments that used them. Humphry Davy, however, immediately realized their potential for decomposing compounds and mixtures into their constituent elements. Through his research at the Royal Institution, and through lectures for the Royal Society, he established the pile as a reliable instrument for chemical analysis, isolating sodium, potassium, and chlorine.[5] The French and the British were soon competing to build the largest apparatus: the "voltaic pile war" paralleled the Napoleonic wars. By 1820 the competitors had jointly established iodine and fluorine as additional elements.[6] Gurney himself assembled a voltaic pile and demonstrated its effects at the Surrey Institution.[7]

Davy's work made the analysis of inorganic compounds the most important field for technical development. But electricity was not the only method used. Equally important were decomposition by fire and by a whole range of reagent solutions. Techniques developed for mineralogy and for the analysis of mineral waters at Britain's popular spas were extended to soil analysis and other fields.[8] Older methods of mineral analysis were gradually integrated with the new chemistry. The German A. G. Werner (1750–1817) had developed a system whereby miners and geologists, working in the field, could identify the constituents of mineral ores by combinations of smell, texture, hardness, weight, color, crystalline form, degree of transparency, and other external characteristics. Werner gained a following in Britain, and, though he admitted that chemical analysis was more suitable for laboratory research, many men who came to chemistry from other endeavors continued to use his descriptive approach for preliminary investigations.[9] Gurney, who had grown up in mining country and trained as a doctor, mixed Wernerian descriptions of color, taste, and texture with his enumerations of chemical properties when introducing the metallic elements and compounds. For instance, he said that the base metallic oxides "have a characteristic taste, are caustic to the skin, reduce animal bones to jelly, facilitate the union of oil and water, and change vegetable blues into greens."[10]

Another adjunct to chemical analysis was crystallography. The French philosopher René-Just Haüy (1743–1822) argued that each mineral possessed an underlying primitive geometric form, revealed by the cleavage planes of the crystal and the angles between them. Haüy's theory was made practical by the invention of a simple, cheap, and portable instrument for measuring crystalline angles. Like the Wernerians, Haüy's advocates came to accept the use of chemical analysis as a complement to their own system, and in 1820 the different approaches were shown to be scientifically compatible.[11] When Gurney devoted parts of two lectures to crystals, therefore, he was reflecting some of the very latest developments in chemical theory and practice.[12]

The newest and most controversial theory claimed that the structure of matter was atomic. This theory had been proposed by John Dalton as early as 1804 and expounded, with diagrams, in his *New System of Chemical Philosophy* (1808). The idea that each element had a characteristic weight, and that it combined with other substances in certain proportions, was not new. It had been incorporated in eighteenth-century tables of "elective affinity" and "equivalences" between types of matter. The tables were compiled by trial and error and periodically amended and refined as further experimental data became available. From his work in chemistry and meteorology, Dalton derived a law of constant proportions that applied to all types of combinations. Many chemists accepted this law, in principle, and set about testing it on various substances. But Dalton went further: he argued that elements were really made up of atomic particles too small to measure by ordinary sensations or instruments. Almost nobody accepted this idea, because it was simply too speculative for the evidence available at that time.[13] William Hyde Wollaston, a leading chemist who at first supported Dalton, withdrew his endorsement in 1814 and published a "Synoptic Scale of Chemical Equivalents," showing how Dalton's data could be applied to chemical analysis without entailing any commitment to atomic theory. He then devised a logarithmic slide rule for making the necessary calculations, and this became an almost universal item of laboratory and manufacturing equipment for the next forty years.

Wollaston's slide rule was the perfect instrument for its time: it facilitated the advancement of analytical chemistry as a specialty, but was widely available to the public and relatively simple to use.[14]

Gurney was undoubtedly adept at the use of the slide rule; it is hard to imagine him ignoring such an ingenious gadget. He did introduce the idea of an atomic structure in his chemistry lectures. However, he sided with his friends Wollaston and Davy against Dalton. The price of doing so may be judged by his attempt, in his second lecture, to explain crystals as hypothetical collections of tiny spheres with differential weights and possibly, even, electrical charges, organized into particular patterns on purely mechanical grounds. Reading the lecture today, one is distressed to realize how close he came to a really fundamental insight into the nature of matter. Had he not been diverted by other pursuits, it is quite likely that he would eventually have recognized the similarity between his atomic theory and Dalton's. He might have got it right after all.

It is easy to see why Gurney should have been so deeply interested in chemistry in 1820. But why would a young surgeon, arriving in London to begin a new practice, spend time and energy preparing a series of public lectures about it? There are three answers. In the first place, lectures were the accepted way to show the London medical establishment that one was not just another country doctor. Back in the 1760s, graduates of Edinburgh University's new, enlightened medical curriculum, finding themselves excluded from London's prestigious hospitals and science faculties, won acceptance by giving public lectures on chemistry. Their success inspired a regular flow into London of Scottish and provincial practitioners hoping to establish themselves in the capital through a combination of teaching and well-publicized research. Lecturers in general science followed regular circuits through provincial towns and spas. Their programs typically included statics, mechanics, hydrodynamics, physical pneumatics, and perhaps also heat, light, and electricity. Chemistry, however, was usually reserved for physicians, surgeons, or apothecaries. Gurney was thus following a well-marked path to career advancement when he promoted his classes in London.[15]

In the second place, his teaching a public course in chemistry attracted prospective patients. The medical profession had not yet achieved its later reputation for Godlike authority. Private practice was still fashioned according to the prejudices of the patient, and doctors had to establish their credentials in public. Lectures were therefore a convenient method of advertising, especially by doctors new to London. Women were often in attendance, and the usual fee of one guinea for men, half a guinea for women, ensured an audience with the income to patronize private physicians.

In the third place, as a consequence of the popularity and professional mystique of chemistry, lecturing and publishing textbooks in the field was far more profitable than the ordinary surgeon's practice, especially for a surgeon new to London. By 1820 the London market for such lectures was large and highly competitive. The range of scientific and medical institutions, coupled with London's preeminence in chemical manufacturing, machine-tool and clockmaking works, gas lighting, and several branches of engineering, not only provided a ready audience for chemistry and metallurgical information but offered specialties not available in most provincial cities.[16] In addition to the teaching hospitals that hired physicians, surgeons, apothecaries, chemists, and botanists on a freelance basis, there were research and instructional faculties at the Royal Institution (established 1799), the Russell Institution (1808), the Surrey Institution (1810), the expansive and wealthy London Institution (1805), and the Philosophical Society of London (reorganized and renamed in 1811). The City Corporation of London had its own institutions, and the expanding suburbs developed a second tier of scientific, philosophical, and literary societies (much like those already operating in the provinces), which tapped the fund of talent available in the metropolis.[17]

Gurney claimed that his freelance lecturing before 1822 yielded between £300 and £400 per year in an age when £150 could establish a person comfortably in the middle class. Compared to prevailing rates for London lecturers, such an amount was, as Harris comments, "very lucrative," and the claim should be accepted with caution.[18] Humphry Davy earned £500 per year, but he was the Royal Institution's leading fund-raiser and had other duties as well. His successor, William Brande, was paid £200 at first, and later only £150, as was his successor Michael Faraday. Moreover, the London Institution rewarded Richard Phillips for a particularly pleasing set of chemistry lectures in 1823 with a gratuity of £10, over and above his fee of £80.[19] Men like Phillips and Gurney might give single lectures on their own premises or in rented halls, but they preferred the security of a series or course of lectures at an institution, advertised for prior subscription and offered only if the returns, supplemented by sales at the door, promised to be adequate. A contract was drawn up for the series on a flat per-lecture fee, usually £4 to £6, and lecturers could present essentially the same course at more than one institute, sometimes simultaneously.[20]

Around 1800, lecturers had often tried to cover everything then known in the field of "natural philosophy" in marathon series of fifty to a hundred sessions. But by the 1820s, so many lecturers were spread among so many institutions that they had to offer a variety of shorter, cheaper, more specialized packages. The twelve-lecture class Gurney presented was probably standard in 1822; by 1830 the norm would be six. By that time, too, the style of lecturing had changed. Humphrey Davy made rhetorical excursions into natural theology, poetic inspiration, and moral injunctions a part of his public presentations. Michael Faraday, who followed him at the Royal Institution in 1820, introduced a detached, objective persona. His lectures emphasized clear expression, careful organization, and steady focus on the material phenomena of his subject.[21] Gurney fell somewhere in between these two. He was certainly inspired by Davy, but by 1822 he had already become associated with Faraday. Except for an occasional paean to the divine inspiration and perfection of nature, his rhetorical flourishes seem quite modest. When he was concentrating on difficult chemical matters, he was all business. However, he mixed in plenty of entertaining experiments, amusing anecdotes, and suggestions for applying knowledge outside the lecture hall.[22]

The question of style was not just a matter of personal expression. Behind Davy's and Faraday's performances at the Royal Institution stood a distinct philosophy of public science, in which the natural philosopher played the part of Olympian genius, delivering the results of highly sophisticated research to docile, appreciative audiences. This philosophy was diametrically opposed to the Enlightenment tradition in which Gurney was trained at Truro, one aimed at educating the public for democratic participation in politics and society.

The Enlightenment tradition was fostered by William Cullen (1710–1790) and his successor Joseph Black (1728–1799), professors at Edinburgh University in the second half of the eighteenth century, who led the reform of medical education that made chemistry lectures so necessary.[23] Practical laboratory experience for all science students was one of their more controversial innovations. One of their students, as mentioned earlier, was Gurney's Truro schoolmaster, Thomas Hogg.

The hero of democratic science, however, was not a professor but a radical philosopher. Joseph Priestley (1733–1804) believed that scientific thinking would lead to political freedom. His avowed aim was "to provide the population with direct experience of the providential powers of nature in order to liberate them from the ignorance on which corrupt authority was founded."[24] Priestley conducted experiments in public, using the simplest possible equipment. He described them, both in lectures and in illustrated texts, so that any intelligent person could replicate them. His presentations became wildly popular and he trained a host of disciples in the art of public lecturing. Although remembered for his discovery in 1775 of "dephlogisticated air" (subsequently named "oxygen" by his rival, Lavoisier), he was essentially a writer and publicist who also published works on metaphysics, theology, politics, and history. He described his scientific discoveries, not in the guise of an Olympian, but through factual narratives, written in an informal analytical style so that readers could "think through" the explanations for themselves. He presented himself as a character in these narratives, often surprised by accidental discoveries, wary of theoretical speculation, a bit naive, generous in giving credit to others. These "marks of candour" were deliberate attempts to build credibility. Gurney, who would have obtained Priestley's works at school or from the many lending libraries around Truro and Wadebridge, used such techniques in 1822, to great effect.[25]

Humphrey Davy was closely allied to Priestley and to his associate Thomas Beddoes during the 1790s. But "democratic science" became identified with the radical politics of the French Revolution and was roundly condemned by conservatives like Edmund Burke.[26] Davy was so unnerved by the campaign of ridicule and invective directed against Priestley and Beddoes that in February 1801 he accepted a position at the Royal Institution in London. There he established a laboratory, where he perfected applications of the new voltaic pile. He began to present his findings in a style clearly calculated to be undemocratic. His public lectures, filled with "convenient and spectacular experimental demonstrations," were designed to persuade the audience of his unique command over nature, not to help them to participate in the generation of knowledge. The voltaic pile was ideal for this purpose. It could produce mild shocks, showers of sparks in different colors (depending on the metal used), and explosions. The Royal Institution's program had originally been aimed at skilled workers, provincial agriculturalists, and businessmen who were excluded from the older societies. Davy reoriented it toward middle- and upper-class men and women in London. His presentations were soon popularized in all kinds of periodicals, pamphlets, and books.[27] A short, dark, handsome young man with a forceful personality and carefully cultivated oratorical skills, Davy used his lectures and textbooks to celebrate his own achievements and surrounded the voltaic pile with a kind of aura.[28] At the same time, he competed aggressively within the international science com-

munity to garner superior research resources and establish the reliability of his experimental results. His style required greater
specialization within each field as well as greater separation from
the lay public. Amateurs and outsiders found it difficult to challenge
his combination of expensive equipment, institutional support, and
polished rhetoric.[29]

In the two decades before Goldsworthy Gurney gave his lectures
on chemistry to the Surrey Institution, Humphry Davy provided a
model for presenting chemical science to the public. Michael Faraday, who followed him into the Royal Institution, eliminated Davy's
moral rhetoric and theological flourishes but worked equally hard
to transfer experimental effects from the private conditions of his
laboratory to the public space of the lecture theater, exaggerating
the phenomena while masking the time and effort required to produce them, so that he would appear as an "expert mediator" between
his audience and nature.[30]

Gurney generously cited Davy's achievements in the fields he discussed. Like his fellow Cornishman, he was adept at using new
technology to show himself as a specialist in the eyes of his audience. When explaining how he had devised a particularly significant
piece of equipment, he followed Davy's model of presentation, making a smooth, analytical narrative out of what must originally have
been a tangle of trials and errors. Nevertheless, most of his lectures
engaged his audience as active participants in the search for knowledge. The Surrey Institution, after all, was not the Royal Institution.
It catered to a mix of amateur scientists; students of engineering,
metallurgy, or medicine; and curious men and women of the local
gentry and commercial classes. These students were more interested
in the practical application of chemistry to their intended fields of
work or study. They expected to be addressed as if they were capable
of replicating Gurney's experiments on their own, whether they actually could or not. He therefore described his techniques simply and
carefully, so that his experiments could be reproduced in home labo-
ratories, and suggested inexpensive substitutes for the equipment he
used in the lecture hall. The legacy of Enlightenment science fostered
by the graduates of Edinburgh and the disciples of Priestley was a
lasting one.[31]

The course in general chemistry had been introduced at the Surrey
Institution in 1808 by Friedrich Christian Accum (1769–1838), a
chemical analyst and manufacturer of coal gas, who had been an
assistant to Davy but disdained his imperial approach. Accum wrote
successful textbooks on analytical methods and mineralogy, subjects
which Gurney included in his lectures, and even published a collec-

tion of simple but exciting experiments, entitled *Chemical Amusements* (1817), for amateurs to perform at home.[32] As Accum had done, Gurney included some topics of personal interest that would be regarded as extraneous today, such as music, weather, steam engines, and electricity. He also took care to discuss commercial applications for various techniques and substances. At the core of his lectures, however, were the principles of chemistry as they were understood in 1822, that is, near the end of the "revolution" but before its theoretical implications were fully worked out. It was a time when the relationship of chemical reactions to electricity, magnetism, and the physics of steam power was still an arena for ingenious, speculative, and often wildly misdirected hypotheses.

Chemistry Lectures at the Surrey Institution: F. C. Accum, ca. 1810. From R. Ackerman, *The Microcosm of London,* **reprint, London: Methuen, 1904; vol. 3 (ca. 1810), 154.**

3

Lectures on Chemistry, Part II

IN THE PREFACE TO *A COURSE OF LECTURES ON CHEMICAL SCIENCE,* PUBLISHED in July 1823, Gurney confessed that when he began preparing his lectures, he intended only to review what was already known. But as he devised and rehearsed experiments to be used in the lecture hall, he was caught up with the discovery of new information and the construction of new or improved laboratory apparatus to assist his inquiries. (In fact, he said, he was forced to set aside several lines of inquiry because they were leading him away from the basic course of lectures.) His scientific friends thought this work sufficiently novel and interesting to warrant publication. He realized (in words that were to echo through his career) that "I ought not carelessly to abandon any claims that I may possess." In spite of "the unavoidable engagements attendant on an arduous profession," which prevented him from applying himself to "the niceties of literary composition," he committed them to print. Thus, with a characteristic mixture of self-deprecation and self-advertisment, Gurney introduced an edited version of what he had presented in lectures the previous year.[1]

The "Introductory" lecture Gurney included in his book may, in fact, have been the probationary presentation he gave to obtain the contract.* It projected his restless imagination and amiable personal-

---

*We have no way of knowing how closely the book follows the lectures, but it may be assumed that Gurney worked from some sort of script or extensive notes, and there are enough diagrams in the book to indicate that many of the experiments and the apparatus he explains there were actually used by way of illustration. I have therefore assumed the position of a reporter at the original lectures, describing experiments that were probably demonstrated at that time. Modern terms and/or formulas for the various chemical substances mentioned in the lectures are given in brackets. The numbers in parentheses refer to the corresponding pages in the published lectures. The book is over 300 pages long, and we may assume that each of the lectures, with time given to experiments, must have lasted several hours. Reading them straight through does not give a true picture of how the audience experienced them, since they were given in a weekly or twice-weekly schedule.

ity and blended humor with hard science in measures nicely adapted to the Surrey Institution audience. As Davy had done for two decades, Gurney began by claiming that chemistry was the most important and interesting branch of natural philosophy, whose task it was "to follow the ultimate particles of matter through their most secret changes of state, and wring from them a knowledge of those invariable qualities and habits, those affections and dispositions, with which their Creator endowed them." Chemistry, he said, was indispensible for all those material arts that make life better, from domestic aids to fermented liquors and medicines, agriculture, bleaching and dyeing, leather tanning and printing. He then broke away from these traditional claims to urge an open-minded approach to chemical experimentation. He argued that "the highest achievements of human wisdom have had their root in the lowest absurdities of human weakness; and that the severest truth has sprung from the most ludicrous and exaggerated fictions of mingled folly and fanaticism." He illustrated this argument by a series of anecdotes from the history of astrology and alchemy, introducing Alonzo the Astrologer of Castile, who claimed to know how to turn base metals into gold, and Roger Bacon, whose *Opus Majus* "may be regarded as the work of a high intellect, swayed and moulded by a vast fund of uncertain knowledge" (14). Gurney's homage to the alchemists was taken almost directly from Davy's *Elements of Chemical Philosophy*, but it undoubtedly expressed his own attitude toward science and technology. He thought, typically, through images and analogies rather than through logical syllogisms, and preferred hands-on, trial-and-error manipulation of materials to systematic, theoretically based experimentation.[2]

The second lecture began with an Aristotelian version of Dalton's atomic theory. Every substance, said Gurney, is constituted of absolutely unchangeable and indivisible atoms, endowed by their Creator with certain dispositions to unite according to invariable laws and, through union, to constitute the world as we know it. Atoms of similar kind display homogeneous attraction; dissimilar atoms display hetereogeneous attractions, which are further modified, by force and intensity, to produce cohesion, solution, crystallization, and other chemical actions. A piece of sealing wax represented the class of substances in which cohesion was weak; a bar of iron represented cohesive strength. Aeriform substances [gases] had no cohesion, since, if allowed to escape, they became dissipated, as Gurney demonstrated by opening a flask of sulphureted hydrogen [chlorine] in the lecture hall. He also mixed spirits of wine with aqua-fortis [nitric acid] in a wide-necked jar and sent the gas flaming outward for several feet, showing the path of dispersal. He then warned people who wanted to try this experiment at home to keep the proportions exact, and the mouth of the flask very wide, to prevent explosions!

Gurney commented, at this point, that "cohesion" did not mean actual contact, but simply that particles are held more closely together than humans could measure. They stay together in an "elective affinity," unless overcome by one or more mechanical forces (e.g., filing, grinding, pulverizing), by heat, or by solution. He went on to demonstrate each of these forces with solutions and mixtures that fizzed, boiled, exploded, vaporized, or (by contrast) remained inert.

The rest of Lecture Two was devoted to crystallization, which Gurney thought "the most striking aspect of cohesion." After demonstrating the regularity of crystal formation in camphor and salt, he showed how crystallization could be precipitated by dropping a solid object into a supersaturated solution of Glauber's Salt [a colorless crystalline sodium sulfate used as a cathartic and in textile dyeing]. Any solid substance can serve as a nucleus, he pointed out: short threads are used to start sugar candy, verdigris [copper patina], and other products. He crystallized alum on the surface of a common blacksmith's cinder, in perfect imitation of natural quartz, commenting that alum solutions were also used to "decorate" miniature wire baskets, which became studded with crystals in five or ten minutes (46).

He then turned to the external forms of crystals, noting that research in this area was weak. René-Just Haüy, a leading French philosopher, had decreed that all crystals were combinations of three basic forms: the tetrahedron, the simple prism, and the cube. Gurney's friend William Wollaston argued, in contrast, that they must be spheres, spheroids, and ellipsoids (47–48). However, the forms of some substances were not explicable by either theory. Gurney therefore devoted all of Lecture Three entirely to crystallization, because he felt that if a true law could be discovered in that area, it would lead to the solution of many other problems. "I shall not apologize," he began, "for laying before you the result of some investigations which I have lately been engaged in, on this most difficult and interesting subject." He hoped to show that all known forms of crystals could be derived from one primitive form by the operation of one fundamental law. Given the constraints of a public lecture, Gurney did not go into the calculations that led him to distrust the prevailing theories and adopt a new one, but proceeded to state the assumptions upon which a successful theory would have to be grounded (52). These assumptions indicate how strongly science was still influenced by scholastic precepts, despite the revolution in some areas. First, said Gurney, every atom must be a sphere, the simplest and most perfect possible shape. Second, atoms are indivisible and unchangeable. Third, every primary atom is of the same size and mass. Fourth, the properties of a given atom never change, regardless of circumstance; what changes is the order of juxtapostion or aggregation. In other words, combinations of atoms must be the result of some mechanical process, rather than of some qualitative change in the atoms themselves (55).

Gurney then described, in considerable detail, a system for arranging perfectly spherical atoms, according to rules of attraction and repulsion, into a variety of crystalline forms. He noted that his principles bore a striking resemblance to the recently discovered principles of electrical charges, and he predicted that the two phenomena would someday be proved interchangeable (63).

He also found a significant analogy in the pattern of vibrations on the surface of water in a glass that was rubbed to produce a musical tone. He had observed, he said, many other phenomena in nature which fit the same pattern. He could not delve deeper into the subject at present; but, he advised his audience, "the laws which I have laid down are so simple, and at the same time so comprehensive, that any one acquainted with the subject is capable of examining their validity" by experimenting for himself (64).

Gurney's hypothesis on crystallization led him to the brink of modern atomic theory. He had grasped the reductive principles that all such forms depended upon mathematical ratios of their constituent atoms, and that rules governing combinations of atoms derived from a single law. He also surmised that the atomic ratios in some way determined the geometry of the crystals. He had then, with the help of William Wollaston, made the imaginative leap to the idea that the atoms could be spheres with space between them, held together not by friction or gravity but by some other kind of attraction, probably electrical. He realized that, in the process of combination, some elements "cancelled out" the action of others. This, too, fitted what was known about electricity. Yet he could not overcome the classical assumption that atoms, as the ultimate substance at the foundation of Creation, must be indivisible, immutable, and perfectly spherical.

Lecture Four centered on "elective affinity," that is, the forces underlying chemical reactions. Elective affinities had been the subject of intense empirical investigation since the 1750s. Many chemists had derived tables of affinities without committing themselves to any fundamental theory. Gurney confessed that it was impossible for anyone to remember all the possible combinations in the tables, so he showed his audience a way to diagram the basic reactions (82–

84). Using various combinations of oil of vitriol [suphuric acid], phosphorus, potassium, camphor, copper nitrate, and water, he showed how reactions could generate heat. Those that generated cold temperatures were ignored, as they were not so visible or dramatic as hot ones. He did produce, and reverse, changes of color and taste in such common substances as ink, Epsom salts, and various homeopathic remedies (80–81).

To demonstrate the effects of external forces on affinities, Gurney used mechanical pressure to combine hydrogen and oxygen into water and then carbonated it to make it effervescent. He placed a few grains of an explosive called "fulminating mercury" on an anvil and hit it with a hammer, making a loud explosion. The same was done with phosphorus and with a mixture of chlorate of potassium with sulphur. "It is prudent in this case," he warned his audience, *"never* to exceed *one grain of phosphorus,* and to cover the chemical with a cloth, or wrap it in paper," as otherwise the explosion might "occasion mischief."

At the end of his lecture on affinities, Gurney explained the chemical nomenclature developed by Lavoisier, an "admirable and beautiful invention." The names given to the new compounds being discovered daily indicated not only their elements but the proportions of which they were constituted. For example, there were probably no less than fifteen hundred kinds of salts the chemist needed to know about, but could hardly be expected to remember. With the new nomenclature, he could determine the composition and many of the affinities of any given salt as soon as he heard its name, even if it was entirely new to him (98–101).

Gurney's lectures show that he was in touch with the latest scientific developments in Great Britain and on the Continent. He was an avid reader of scientific journals and obviously took delight in replicating the experiments described in published papers. By giving generous credit to other scientists, especially those of France, Belgium, and Germany, Gurney fashioned himself as one of their number, a member of a progressive international community. He was interested in a wide variety of phenomena, and his intuitive cast of mind led him to make interesting, if not always correct, connections between different lines of research, following the rule that the most promising scientific hypothesis was the one explaining the most phenomena with the fewest principles.

His lecture on heat and cold was based on Lavoisier's supposition that all changes of temperature, and the sensations arising from them, derived from a fluid called "caloric." Caloric had replaced Priestley's hypothetical substance "phlogiston" and would in turn be replaced by the modern concept of the calorie as a unit of heat measurement.[3] "I call caloric *matter*," said Gurney, "because, though we are not at present capable of demonstrating it to be such, the preponderance of evidence arising from its effects is in favour of this supposition" (104). Caloric, he said, has the power to radiate from one body to another, and expands all bodies that it enters. "Hence arises the evening breeze under the Tropics, the delightful zephyrs of our summer days, the shoots of the various tribes of plants and trees, and animation of the torpid and slothlike tribe of certain animals" (105–7). Explaining how heat can be used to create a vacuum in a jar, he commented: ". . . cupping in surgery is now performed in this manner, instead of using an exhausting syringe, as was formerly practised" (109). Metals, too, respond to cold, causing clocks and watches to keep irregular time. He remarked on the insulating qualities of eiderdown, double windows, and the walls of icehouses, which utilized the poor conductivity of air (117). He also suggested that the various animals inhabiting the far north have mostly white skins because white resists heat, whereas black conducts it readily. This was a bit confusing, because he added that dark clothes, spread on the snow, would conduct more heat than light-colored ones, and would sink into the melted snow. The idea of *absorbing* heat from the sun did not seem to be a part of this argument (119).

The Enlightenment influence in Gurney's education was reflected in several comments that echoed the philosophic optimism of Dr. Pangloss in Voltaire's *Candide,* and perhaps deserved the same satirical treatment. In his discussion of "caloric," he pointed out that water, when freezing, releases heat, so that the water surrounding the ice actually warms up. And because water has a greater specific gravity than ice (an exception among fluids), the ice remains on top, and the lower parts of our rivers and oceans never freeze. "It was of the utmost importance to the well-being of our world," he pronounced, "that the general law, which would necessarily cause the above state of things, should be made, and therefore such a law was made. But it was of equal importance that the above single exception to that law should exist; and therefore that was made also" (121–22). Likewise, in a later lecture on nitrogen, Gurney called attention to "two beautiful provisions of nature." Since nitrogen was a noxious gas, inimical to animal life in its pure form, and since all animals exhale it, there must be some arrangement made for expelling it from the immediate region in which we breathe, lest the air become contaminated and unable to support life. And so there is! First, there is always a short interval between respirations of animals, which allows the gas to escape into the atmosphere above us. Second, nitrogen is lighter than regular air, so it evaporates automatically (200). He might have added, "Thus everything works for the best in this best of all possible worlds."

In his sixth lecture, Gurney explained and demonstrated the galvanic pile, invented by Sir Anthony Carlisle and exploited so successfully by Humphry Davy. Admitting that electricity was a novel and mysterious force, he still maintained that the laws of attraction and repulsion were "the grand disposing cause of all chemical changes" (129, 133). He showed how the pile was constructed, and demonstrated the electrolysis of various compounds (135–36). Magnetism, only recently discovered, had been proved to be directly related to electricity. Using a coil of "common bonnet wire," hooked up to a voltaic pile, he showed how an iron bar could be magnetized with different polarizations and how a compass needle was affected by the electric charge, observing that it "will instantly start across the current, and point east and west." This statement has been linked by some admirers, chiefly his daughter Anna, with a subsequent remark about the possible use of the needle's behavior for electric communication, to imply that Gurney anticipated, or even originated, the principle of the electric telegraph. That claim, however, will not stand up to scrutiny.[4]

As a doctor, Gurney could not resist the thought that electricity and magnetism were somehow vital to human health. He promised that someday the secret of their relationship would be clear, and ventured two personal conjectures that give us an interesting view of contemporary medical knowledge. He considered that atmospheric electricity, generated by clouds passing over earth, probably energized the skin, which affected the stomach, which was the "chief source" of mental instability. "Can it be considered too fanciful a supposition," he asked, to think that the atmosphere affects people of a nervous and irritable habit of body? His second conjecture likened the body's nervous system to a galvanic battery; this explained why, when a nerve was damaged, the part of the body to which it led became cooler than normal. Following up this analogy, Gurney predicted that artifical electrical impulses would in future be used "with the most beneficial effect" to treat many human diseases (142–44). He would not have been surprised at the hundreds of electrical and magnetic appliances, invented later in the century, that promised miracle cures for every form of debility.

Gurney's seventh lecture was devoted to combustion, again linked to the electrical qualities of chemical affinities. As he had done in earlier lectures, Gurney proceeded from a few demonstrations to the general theory, then used a homely example to effect a transition to the next part of his subject. Having mentioned oxygen, he commented that it was part of the air we breathe, "one might say of *vital* importance;" anything which diminished its proper proportion would be detrimental to health. This was, of course, known to everyone; but yet, Gurney said, people risked their health daily by building fires in their sitting rooms. The fire first creates drafts by drawing cold air from outside. When people try to prevent drafts by making the room airtight, they decrease the available oxygen for breathing and for combustion. The solution to this common problem, he said, was to build the fire *outside* of the room, conveying its heat into the space by way of flues through the walls and under the floors. Then, the room could be made airtight without danger to health or to combustion. Very little additional heat would be needed to keep the temperature up and "a great savings in fuel would be effected." Here Gurney was already expressing the principle of central heating that he would apply thirty years later to the Houses of Parliament and the Law Courts. He realized, however, that although the idea might work in large public buildings, it was not feasible for residences, because fireplaces were built into the fabric of the social order, and possessed (as we still realize) highly symbolic value. "I am afraid we must change all our present habits with regard to domestic life," he concluded, "before we shall consent to part with the cheering sight of a sea-coal fire" (154–56).

Gurney's discussion of burning gases revealed the vague standards of measurement and nomenclature still used by many scientists, and shows us why Lavoisier's campaign for accuracy was so badly needed and so often resisted. Most authorities, for example, agreed that hydrogen would burn at about 1,000° Fahrenheit. Published research reports, however, regularly employed terms like "glowing red hot" or "bright red hot" instead of thermometric degrees, and the composition of the gases used in research could not be regulated closely enough to ensure repeatable results. In one case, a chemist reported blowing on a piece of burning charcoal to make it "white hot," so that it would inflame the hydrogen, as if temperature alone were the consideration (156–57). Gurney himself used the terms "pale blue flame" and "white flame" to indicate variations in temperature, but he also described how, by preheating gases in several ingenious instruments of his own design, he had burned hydrogen at 428° F.

The matter of flame itself was of special importance to Gurney. His innovations regarding this apparently simple phenomenon were to outlast most of his other ideas and inventions.[5] He had come to the view that flames are hollow, with nothing burning in the middle, and have a conical shape because of atmospheric pressure. They are hollow because the flame burns on contact with the atmosphere, forming a film around the matter within and sealing it from contact with oxygen. Gurney illustrated this by sticking his finger up into the middle of a puddle of burning brandy floating in a large glass of water. The flame, he observed, is simply where the atoms of the combustible substance meet the atoms of oxygen. "Here they saturate each other, change their electrical states, become condensed, part with their light and heat, and their places are instantly supplied by the series of elementary atoms next in succession, both from within and without [the flame]" (168). This fact explained why air, forced into the middle of a flame through a blowpipe, a technique used in metallurgy since the 1750s, created intense heat and light: it provided the oxygen needed to burn the whole of the flammable material at once. Devising a reliable blowpipe to regulate the flow of air would therefore facilitate the development of apparatus for lighting and for specialized heat processes.

Because flame requires a certain shape and volume, it will not pass through holes of very small diameter. This was the principle behind the miners' safety lamp, an invention attributed to Davy, although claimed by others. The Davy lamp was basically a candle encased in a lamp with a wire gauze or screen covering. The hundreds of tiny apertures allowed light out and air in, but prevented the flame from reaching the explosive atmosphere of the mine. The metal wire also served to dissipate the candle's heat. Athough carbureted hydrogen [methane] in the mine would explode at a spark, it would not explode on contact with red-hot iron. Davy lamps had even been observed to turn red-hot from methane burning *inside* the screen, while the volatile gases *outside* remained unchanged. Explosions did happen, of course, but Gurney attributed these to defects in the lamp's construction, or to the accumulation of flammable material on the outside of the wire gauze, which required frequent cleaning. He demonstrated how the lamp worked and how it could fail with appropriate, but controlled, explosions (173–74). His experimental knowledge of this subject eventually proved highly useful when, in the 1840s, he took a leading role in the ventilation of coal mines.

In the next two lectures, Gurney covered the elements that supported combustion—oxygen, chlorine, iodine, and fluorine—and the elements they combined with to make acids—hydrogen, nitrogen and carbon, phosphorus, sulphur, and boron. By this point in the course, he had introduced most of the known elements and had demonstrated many of their properties in his experiments with combustion, crystalization, and electricity. Members of the audience who lacked the background, diligence, or wit to keep up would have ceased to attend; the remainder would have been well prepared to deal with more specialized material.

He reviewed the various compounds of oxygen with hydrogen and nitrogen in water and air, with a few discrete observations on nitrous oxide, the "laughing gas" which Priestley and Beddoes had made notorious. He recounted the history of chlorine research[6] and performed a set of sensational experiments, full of flames and sparks, to show how chlorine combined with such metals as copper, antimony, and zinc. The properties of hydrogen were listed as a Wernerian might have given them: extinguishes flame, but is highly inflammable; fatal if inhaled; has no affinity for water; invisible and nasty smelling; fourteen times lighter than air, so that it is useful for raising balloons. This last property was illustrated with hydrogen soap bubbles, which he blew through a tobacco pipe and let float out over the audience (198–99). He also demonstrated that hydrogen, when burnt in a glass tube under certain conditions, or even in a wine bottle, gave out a "clear and distinct musical sound." He claimed that he had even replicated the lowest note of a violoncello by directing a jet of burning coal gas into the neck of a large stone jar. It is evident, from his detailed comments, that he had made numerous experiments on this unique method of creating music. One can only wonder what his neighbors in Argyll Street imagined was going on at Number 7.

On a more practical level, he indicated that hydrogen, mixed with carbon, was the gas that lit all the streets, houses, and theaters of London. Moreover, when these two gases were mixed with oxygen and forced through a jet in a given direction, they could burn or fuse all known substances (197). This was a direct reference to the "oxyhydrogen blow-pipe" he had perfected during his laboratory experiments and would introduce at the end of the lecture series. Gurney discussed nitrogen* and the various compounds of carbon (charcoal, sugar, gums, resins, fuels, mineral waters) and projected the discovery of a process, one day, that would produce artificial diamonds. In this respect, he added, if all the alchemists of the past who had tried to turn base metals into gold had concentrated on forming diamonds instead, they would have been less ridiculous and unscientific, even if they had failed (203–4).

---

*Gurney believed that nitrogen was not a simple element, but "a peculiar compound" of hydrogen and oxygen in equal proportions, produced by animal organs. He was carrying out a series of experiments based on this hypothesis.

By this time Gurney was facing a problem encountered by most institutional lecturers. A systematic survey of basic elements was required, not only to acquaint the audience with their properties, but to demonstrate the nature of the system itself. However, the material was generally tedious to go through, and experiments, designed to enliven a session, would not be appreciated without a basic background in chemistry. Moreover, experimental demonstrations could easily use up the entire lecture, as some of Gurney's expansive anecdotes had already done. He was therefore reduced to describing mere lists of applications, hoping that the audience would know enough about one or two of them to figure out the rest by extension. He discussed a few of the more attractive items, such as gold, silver, mercury, and silicone, but hardly mentioned other metallic ores and oxides, "as their uses and properties are at present but little known." In addition, Gurney did what other teachers have done: he advised his audience to purchase one of the "numerous extensive and excellent works which we at present possess on chemical science" (210–11).

The eleventh lecture, which concentrated on the acids, their salts, and the alkalies or bases, was significantly more thorough and better organized than the previous two. Research on acids and salts had progressed rapidly during the previous two decades (chemists now identified between thirty and forty of them), and Lavoisier's nomenclature, which Gurney again reviewed with appropriate examples, had created a systematic framework for inquiry. The chemical reactions among these substances provided an array of literally colorful experiments for the lecture hall. Some of the salts and acids had medical applications. Gurney noted, for instance, that carbonic acid [carbon dioxide, CO_2] was suffocating to the lungs, but beneficial and stimulating to the stomach when dissolved in beverages, antiseptic when applied to the skin, and useful in preventing putrification (239). Sodium carbonate and ammonia, in the forms of purgatives and smelling salts, were also therapeutic.

For his last scheduled lecture, Gurney returned to the theme illustrated by alchemy, that many brilliant discoveries and important theories have arisen from happy guesses in the pursuit of dubious goals. Reasoned experiment may eventually prove the hypothesis and show its utility, he said, but "I have seen enough of experimental philosophy in the hands of others, and have had enough practice in it myself," to know that such hypotheses often originate by accident or conjecture (256). In that spirit, Gurney proposed "to consider a few of the grand phenomena of nature, as they are connected with chemical causes." He acknowledged that his text would be full of conjectures, and if his audience was dissatisfied with these, he would not complain, since he was not convinced about them himself. He then unleashed a flood of speculative hypotheses that fluctuated wildly between scientific ingenuity and fanciful associations. Light, for example, must be a modification of electricity, like heat and magnetism. It was essential to vegetation, and the various colors of flowers derived from light-produced metallic oxides. Because blood also contains metallic oxides, which help regulate the organic system, light must be necessary to animal health. Without it, people grow pale and sallow, then sicken and die. Tropical birds are more colorful than those in frigid areas, no doubt because color was a better conductor of heat than white and would eliminate body heat faster, whereas birds covered with white feathers would enjoy better insulation. Trees displayed different colors on their sunny and shaded sides, a fact that enabled Indians to find their way through the American forests. And so on. His most audacious speculation, based on supposed relationships among electricity, combustion, and sunlight, was that the planets might be formed by giant electromagnetic currents that converged at the sun, creating its intense light and heat. Of course this was only an opinion, he cautioned, and he had only recently formed it. It was supported by many other facts, but "the subject is one of such overwhelming grandeur and sublimity, that it must be approached by all with an awe-inspiring modesty, much more so by one whose pursuits and habits have not given him those adventitious advantages which others possess for such inquiries" (264–67).

Gurney did not go on to talk about storms, volcanoes, or other natural occurrences, and he omitted a treatment of agriculture and animal life which had been promised in the syllabus. He considered it evident by now that all these phenomena were due to chemical reactions of one kind or another. But this conclusion was accompanied by a religious disclaimer, perhaps exorcising the spirit of Joseph Priestley that remained in his teaching. "The ultimate and actual cause of all things must be referred to a higher origin, and into the minutiae of which it is not our present business to inquire." Mischief usually attends such inquiry, he warned, and "with respect to ultimate causes, perhaps the best and only true philosophy is to love, admire, confide in, and be silent. And the silence of humility well becomes us, when we know that the Being who created all beings, and all things, who is in fact the cause of all effects, has left us (the lords of his creation, and the pride of all his works) in no less actual ignorance of his operations, than the meanest insect that peoples the dust beneath our feet" (268–69). With that, he closed, reminding his audience of the novelty of his experiments, and thanking them and the Surrey Institution for indulging his introduction to the London scientific community, "my first attempt to address a public audience of any description" (270).

Gurney's published lectures were favorably received by reviewers for *The Times, John Bull,* and *The Literary Museum.* The critic of the *Quarterly Journal of Science, Literature and the Arts,* however, took exception to some of the arguments regarding previously accepted theories. In general, the public seems to have appreciated the lectures, while a minority with specialized knowledge opposed his attempts to revise traditional ideas in their areas of interest.[7]

The Surrey Institution lectures capped a three-year period of professional growth for Gurney. He had established his surgery in one of the most fashionable parts of London, and his lecturing brought him to the attention of some of the most eminent medical and scientific men of the day. He was in communication with experimenters in chemistry, electricity, magnetism, and steam power in England and on the Continent, and kept abreast of the latest scientific journals. Had he continued on this course, he might have enjoyed a long, modestly reputable, and lucrative career. Instead he turned back to those paths of inquiry uncovered but left unexplored during his preparations for the lecture demonstrations. These paths engaged his mechanical ingenuity as well as his scientific knowledge, a combination which he would find irresistible throughout his life.

4

New Directions

WHEN GURNEY WAS PREPARING HIS LECTURE DEMONSTRATIONS, IN THE SPRING of 1822, he made a number of experiments, which (as he told his audience) threatened to lead him into lines of investigation far outside the limits of his syllabus. He was also completing some inquiries initiated in Wadebridge. Having successfully presented the lectures and found a number of valuable friends and colleagues in the London scientific community, he decided to continue these investigations. A few of them yielded immediate and practical results. Those that failed are equally significant, however, because they anticipated Gurney's later accomplishments and illustrate his unique blend of theoretical and mechanical skills. It is often assumed that technical improvements depend upon, and are preceded by, scientific analysis. The sequence is seldom so straightforward. As Gurney would show again and again, scientific knowledge can be gleaned from solving technical problems.[1]

To give himself the necessary time for experimentation, Gurney employed a surgeon named Campbell as an active partner in his medical practice. It was evident to him that surgery was a relatively routine activity with modest social pretensions, whereas scientific discovery could lead to fame and fortune. Chemistry was a popular and fashionable subject. As a contemporary text exclaimed, "Not only are treatises of Philosophy and Chemistry met with in every quarter, but beaux, ladies, all are now chemists, or pretend to be so. All are vying with each other in the ardour of experimenting and communicating. Monthly and even weekly journals are teeming with experiments, and with real or supposed discoveries."[2] In this climate Gurney's reputation, established at the Surrey Institution, was bound to give him a great advantage.

His family responsibilities were also growing. Elizabeth returned to Launcells, some time in 1822, for her lying-in, and was delivered of a boy, named Goldsworthy John. Anna Jane, now seven years old, was no doubt given lessons at home, as was customary at that time for daughters of gentlemen. She would learn the basics of reading, writing, and arithmetic, together with Bible lessons, perhaps a bit of French, some children's history, and such domestic skills as embroidery. These lessons would normally be Elizabeth's responsibility, but among the gentry and members of the rising professional classes, fathers sometimes supervised home education, even of daughters, or added lessons on special subjects.[3] It is evident from Anna's later comments that when she returned to London with her mother and new brother, she had frequent access to her father's surgery and laboratory and followed his experiments with great interest. Although her brother proved later to be a brilliant student, in the 1820s he was but an infant. Anna was old enough to respond to her inventive, gregarious father and, as often happens in such cases, to be treated as an "honorary" son, a familiar apprentice. There was certainly plenty to see and learn at Number 7, Argyll Street, where Gurney assembled equipment, made numerous experiments, and gave lectures.[4] Even when he leased a building in Albany Street, by Regent's Park, in May 1825, to construct full-scale locomotives, the residential quarters were barely separated from the laboratory and manufacturing areas. Anna recalled watching the first trial run of the steam carriage from a nearby window.

We have seen that in his youth, Gurney did not confine himself to the regular course of study for medical students. He wrote papers on heat and electricity, studied tidal movements, and discussed with local agriculturalists the use of sea sand for soil conditioning. At Wadebridge he also became an accomplished pianist. True to his nature, he began experimenting with the internal mechanism of his pianoforte and studying other keyboard instruments. Sometime before 1819 he constructed a pipe organ, making and assembling all the parts himself, on the basis of theory alone.[5] In one of his lectures at the Surrey Institution, he told a story about it to illustrate the effects of heat upon various metals. He said that people who heard the organ told him it had a very fine tone. "Flushed with this success, I did not see any reason, in *theory*, to prevent my connecting a pianoforte with my organ." In fact, he thought that the two would improve each other: the sudden stops of the organ notes would be covered, in great measure, by the modulation of the pianoforte strings, and the mixed tone would be pleasing and harmonious. He finally managed to combine the two instruments with a single set of keys, and attached pedals to enable the performer to play piano and organ either separately or together, "as might please his fancy." Again, the effect was delightful. Then, said Gurney, he invited his friends over to witness this marvel, and "after waiting in anxious expection," he sat down to play.

> Commencing with a fine slow movement, [I] began presently to change my modulation and time into what musicians call an "allegro." Now, then, was the moment to introduce the lively notes of the piano; accordingly I removed my foot from the silent pedal, expecting to entrance my audience, and receive 'showers of applause.' But judge of and pity my feelings when I tell you that instead of a 'concord of sweet sounds,' my instrument poured forth the most frightful discords that ever fought together for the especial discomfiture of musical ears! You may easily conceive my chagrin and disappointment. The mischief (as you will perhaps have anticipated) was occasioned by this property of heat which we are now considering. The number of persons in the room, added to a better fire, perhaps, than was usual, raised the *temperature;* and, consequently, the metallic strings of the piano were *expanded* by it, their tension became diminished, and of course the notes were all flattened; while those of the organ pipes were rather affected in the opposite way, so that they produced together a complete separation and discord. The next morning, when the temperature of the room was reduced, the instrument was again in perfect tune.

What a marvelous tale to tell his audience! Aside from its instructive value, Gurney's confession must surely have secured his reputation as a "boy genius." Whether the story was strictly accurate or not, we may never know. It has an aura of hyperbole, which was common enough among Gurney's contemporaries and may perhaps be excused in the furtherance of instruction. But the idea of linking an organ and a piano is so typical of Gurney's inventive curiosity and enthusiasm that one has to believe that he did it. Members of the audience surely thought so, regaling their friends and families with the story for days afterward. In fact, it was reported in the *Royal Cornwall Gazette,* 17 September 1819, without mentioning Gurney by name.[6]

At the time he recounted this episode, he was still working on keyboard inventions (he mentions using harpsichord wire for an experiment with gases). In his lectures he demonstrated the mathematical ratios of sound waves by drawing silk ribbon across wine goblets, and afterward he adapted this technique to an upright grand piano, replacing the wires with spherical glasses and attaching ribbons to the key mechanisms. He also contrived ways to extend the notes and regulate the volume. This "glass piano" was said to possess an organlike tone, but the sound produced, lacking the vibrato produced by strings, was "so affecting that persons of nervous habits could not bear to hear it." Gurney obtained his first patent for this "improved finger-keyed musical instrument" on 11 January 1825. He displayed it in the Regent's Park Colosseum, a popular commercial exhibition of the day, until that enterprise failed.[7]

For his lecture on "Caloric," he made extensive inquiry into the nature of fire damp or coal damp [methane, CH_4], and constructed an apparatus through which the gas could be drawn from one to 500 feet per minute. He used this apparatus to test the Davy lamp under various conditions and communicated his findings to Davy, and in a letter to the *Times* in the summer of 1824, without generating any response.[8] From what we know of his later work, it is certain that this apparatus was an early version of the steam jet, which increased the power of steam engines by creating a powerful draft through their boilers. It was apparently utilized for ventilating his Albany Street workshop as early as 1827, and then installed in the steam carriages he built there. In the late 1830s, it would again be applied to the problems of fire damp and mine ventilation.[9]

In the same lecture, he discussed the problem of measuring the effect of heat on the expansion of metals at temperatures higher than a mercury thermometer would register. This had always been an uncertain procedure, and there were several devices for the purpose. Lavoisier and LaPlace had developed a "calorimeter," consisting of a triple-walled chamber packed with ice, which, they claimed, gave extraordinarily accurate measurements. Other scientists were unable to replicate their results, and by the 1820s the device was regarded a failure.[10] A "pyrometer," invented by Josiah Wedgwood for his pottery works, was favored by Humphry Davy and other British scientists. This machine used delicate gears and levers to turn a pointer on a dial, which amplified and displayed the expansion of heated metal. It was not very accurate, but it did demonstrate relative rates of expansion. Gurney probably used a Wedgwood pyrometer in his early experiments. However, he soon displayed an improved version, of his own design, that was described by a member of the lecture audience in the *Transactions* of the Society of Arts in 1825.[11]

The last and most important of his inventions at this time was a "blow-pipe" of his own design, used in several of his lecture demonstrations. Knowledgeable members of the audience and staff of the Surrey Institution realized that Gurney's apparatus not only was safer than other versions but produced a much hotter flame. They asked him to explain how it worked, so he gave an "encore" lecture, which was published along with the others. This lecture clearly reveals the level of instrumentation and theoretical knowledge possessed by a typical research chemist of the time, who lacked the "adventitious advantages" enjoyed by Davy and his colleagues at the Royal Institution.

A blowpipe was basically a narrow tube through which a steady stream of air could be forced into a candle flame, in the manner of a miniature bellows. The pipe bent the candle flame toward an ore sample, and the extra oxygen produced temperatures high enough to allow analysis of its mineral elements. Blowpipes had been used for a long time to form glass and to work metals. Chemists had adapted them for laboratory use in the last half of the eighteenth century. A blowpipe could be hooked up to a bellows, or to a chamber of high-pressure air, for use in the chemical laboratory. A blowpipe was included in Accum's "closet laboratory" (1818), and a telescoping "pocket" version to be carried by mineralogists working in the field was invented by Gurney's friend, William Hyde Wollaston.[12] Blowing through the device was tricky because one had to exhale continuously while inhaling through the nose, as in playing a clarinet or oboe. But hundreds of people apparently mastered its use and learned to interpret the results consistently.[13]

Even more powerful was the "self-acting spirit blow-pipe," which used high-pressure gas. Gurney claimed that the most intense heat was obtained from this type by burning oxygen and hydrogen gas together, in the proportions that otherwise formed water (H_2O). For this reason, it was called the "*oxy-hydrogen* blow-pipe." The gases were condensed separately into strong metal boxes by a "condensing syringe," or pressure tube. They were then mixed while passing through a separate chamber designed to prevent explosion, and blown out through a small tube, where they produced a jet of flame. In principle it was a precursor to today's acetylene torches.[14]

The man who had done most to develop the oxyhydrogen blowpipe, a Cambridge professor of mineralogy named Edward Daniel Clarke, found it impossible to prevent the intense flame from being drawn back into the gas-filled chambers and blowing up the whole apparatus. Clarke learned from harsh experience to burn very small quantities of gas, and to keep a strong partition between the blowpipe and himself. Other chemists dreaded working with the instrument. Despite its promise, it had had very limited utility.[15] Gurney knew that such instrumentation was a path to scientific discovery and public acclaim. He determined to make the blowpipe safe or to build a different kind of jet altogether. In his lecture to the Surrey Institution, he described his experiments in chronological order, using Priestley's narrative technique, so that his audience could follow and critique his reasoning. At each stage, he commented on the scientific principles that were substantiated or challenged by his research.

He first stripped a standard oxyhydrogen blowpipe down to its essentials and substituted soft materials for hard, so that explosions would not injure him. In place of the heavy copper box used by Clarke, he tried a silk bag to hold the volatile gases, and then a common bladder on a light wooden platform. The bladder was linked by a valve to a horizontal pipe, so that it could be removed and replaced. To add pressure when needed, he laid a piece of pasteboard on top of the bladder and ran small strings from its four corners down through holes in the platform to a small tray, into which he could put a weight. The weight, the only object hard enough to injure someone during an explosion, was sheltered under the stand (278).

The next problem was to burn the gases through a jet without letting the flame reverse through the pipes to explode in the bladder. Gurney first separated the bladder pipe from the jet by a three-inch copper tube with tiny holes in either end, on the principle of the Davy lamp. After trying tubes of all descriptions (plaster of Paris, pipe clay, glass, bamboo, mahogany), and many modifications of wire gauze, Gurney realized that the problem lay elsewhere. Going back to an ordinary blowpipe, he observed that when the pressure on the bladder was raised too high, the gas jet would not ignite at all. He began to suspect that its opposite, namely *low* pressure, caused the explosions. A check of his "improved" apparatus showed that the weights could shift, gradually releasing pressure on the bladder, which virtually sucked the flame back into the device. A few modifications of the tray, with the addition of a pressure gauge, allowed him to vary the pressure by the weight of his hand. After a bit of practice, he found that he could burn gas quite safely through a fairly sizable jet, or extinguish it by raising the pressure.

The end product was simple enough that anyone could build one (see illustration). The gases were mixed in a large, detachable bladder. They then entered the inflatable reservoir through a tube with a stopcock. The reservoir rested on a wooden platform, and pressure was applied to it from above by a plate and cross brace, which could be raised or lowered by pressing on a tray mounted underneath the platform. The plate was made of papier-mâché, so that explosions, which were frequent during the early tests, would prove harmless. The surface of the reservoir platform was exactly one square foot, enabling simple calculations of gas volumes and pressures. As the gases were released through the jet, they were inflamed. So long as pressure was applied steadily, the flame did not regress and explode.

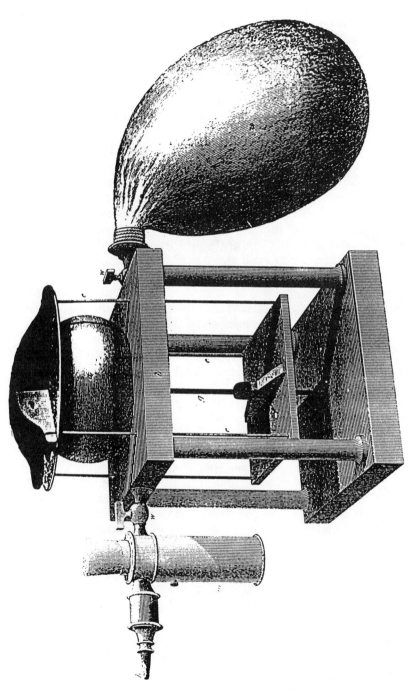

Goldsworthy Gurney's Oxy-Hydrogen Blowpipe, 1823. Transactions of the Society of Arts, vol. 41 (1823–34). By permission of the Royal Society of Arts, Manufactures, and Commerce.

This instrument was reliable enough to test the density of various gases, to experiment with different kinds of musical reeds, to work with metallic compounds, and to establish the true temperatures at which combustible gases would inflame. Still, the danger of explosion remained. Whenever pressure on the gas was released, the flame tended to be drawn back through the jet. However, Gurney also noticed that small explosions sometimes occurred within the jet tubes before the flame reached the bellows. When this happened, the pressure of the explosion extinguished the flame. After a few false starts, he constructed a small triple-chambered tube, mounted directly behind the gas jet, with two sets of wire gauze placed between that chamber and the bellows. Whenever the flame backed into the jet, it exploded the gas in the small chamber, artificially raising the pressure at that point. Since the flame could not pass through the wire gauze at high pressure (the principle of the Davy lamp), it rebounded upon itself and was instantly extinguished. Thus the safety chamber acted as a self-regulating device (286–87).

Gurney never understood why sudden pressure should extinguish the flaming gas. Instead of deriving a theory, he pragmatically tried different sizes of gas tubing, jets, and safety chambers to establish the relative dimensions that would guarantee safety. He realized that other scientists might still be apprehensive about the instrument despite his own investigations, and that it would not be useful until they were convinced that it was safe. He therefore added a second safety valve, which forced the mixed gases through a column of water before they entered the primary safety chamber and were expelled through the jet.[16] He also installed stopcocks at either end of the bellows, so that the experimenter could mechanically shut off the gas. For laboratory use, he made up a set of jets of different sizes and a plaster-of-Paris burning platform into which they could be fitted. The platform could be covered with a large bell jar to collect the products of fusion and combustion. In addition, a long flexible tube could be inserted between the jet and the safety chambers, so that the jet could be moved anywhere in the laboratory. "Such is the facility with which I can handle and direct it," boasted Gurney, "that I can write, or rather burn any sentence through a steel plate with the greatest rapidity." Gurney offered the improved oxyhydrogen blowpipe for sale through a mathematical instrument maker in the Strand (290–96).

What could this instrument do? "The intensity and power of the explosive gases, when burnt by this blow-pipe," said Gurney, "is truly astonishing." Gun flints, rock crystals, and precious stones fused instantly into glass. Porcelain also vitrified. Common china melted

into crystal; diamonds burned; magnesia fused into granular particles hard enough to scratch glass. A large steel file, put into the
flame, produced brilliant fireworks: the fused globulets of metal
jumped several feet into the air, where they burst and sparkled. Jewel-
ers' platina, which generally resisted heat, fused and sparkled even
more readily than copper or gold. In fact, Gurney had to use pipe
clay and china as retorts, instead of the usual platina, to do his
experiments. Other substances burned into gases, which could be
collected in a special jar he had devised.

Gurney claimed that fusing metals with the oxyhydrogen blowpipe
was better than soldering, as it prevented the galvanic action that
often occurred when different metals came into contact (293–94).
He fused a number of objects in front of the audience and explained
that by mixing them with chrome, copper, iron, etc., he could color
them and create artificial gems. He also demonstrated the powerful
"limelight," produced by holding pure lime in a strong flame of nine
or ten inches. "The light from lime is not unlike daylight," he wrote
later; "I am confident that one of our largest theatres might be lighted
by it with the most splendid effect." In fact, one of the audience
recalled that "the whole of the lecture theatre of the Institution became as bright as sunshine and the shadows on the walls startled
me."[17] Gurney predicted that someday it would be used in lighthouses (294–95), and indeed he later developed a similar light for
just that purpose. Before he retired from London in 1863, he would
also see limelight street lanterns installed on Westminster Bridge.

He had observed when burning carbureted hydrogen gas (methane, CH_4) that when pressure was gradually increased on the bellows, the flame turned from its usual white to red, orange, yellow,
green, and then "a most beautiful and permanent blue," in the order
of the prismatic colors. Knowing that the prismatic order also indicated the relative calorific power (red being coolest, violet being
hottest), he inflamed a coil of steel wire while varying the pressure
and found that the flame's heat changed with the colors. He even
discovered, to his surprise, that when the pressure increased enough
to (apparently) extinguish the flame, the wire became even brighter,
and fused. He realized then that the prismatic spectrum included an
invisible band at which the greatest heat was produced, and that
the flame, far from being extinguished, was burning at its highest
temperature (304).

It appears that Gurney was still working within the tradition of
phlogiston, now transformed into "caloric," and so regarded color
as a kind of material, fluid agent, like heat or electrical charge. He
reported to his audience that having moved a bar of platina from the

outer tip of a blowpipe flame gradually back toward the opening of the jet, he observed the metal change colors, again in prismatic order. When it reached the point at which the flame was dark and apparently hollow, the bar fused. He was thus convinced that his description of flame had been backwards. The actual combustion, which was a chemical reaction, took place within the invisible, or dark, center of the flame. The more visible layers were built up as the original heat dissipated into the atmosphere (306–7). Moreover, because he believed that light, heat, and electricity were "members of the same family," if not alternative forms of the same agent, he had tried to discover the particular electrical states belonging to each color of the flaming gas. He reported that he could extinguish the blowpipe flame by passing a strong electrical current through it, and then, to his astonishment, could ignite it again with another electrical charge. The "hotter" colors of flame conducted the electrical current more readily. Gurney arrived at the hypothesis that hotter flames expanded the atmosphere, lowering pressure within the area of combustion, which in turn increased electrical conductivity. It was all very intriguing. Gurney promised to continue his experiments on this subject and to communicate any future discoveries to his audience (310).

Gurney's exhibition of the oxyhydrogen blowpipe solidified the reputation he had established in the scheduled lectures. Because the apparatus was familiar to specialists, the efficacy of the improvements he had made on it could be readily appreciated; the utility of such a torch for metallurgy, jewelry, and laboratory experimentation, needed no argument. He left his Surrey Institution audience literally and figuratively at the cutting edge of scientific inquiry.

When Gurney prepared his lectures for publication, like most first-time authors, he found the editorial demands of the publisher confusing and aggravating. Meanwhile, he applied to the Society of Arts, Manufactures, and Commerce for the opportunity to exhibit his improved blowpipe. The Society's committee on chemistry and mechanics met with him on 11 April 1823. He reviewed the problems of Professor Clarke's apparatus and showed how his own design worked. The committee's opinion was "that Mr. Gurney's Oxy-hydrogen Blowpipe is new, simple, & ingenious, & appears to be perfectly safe, & is likely to be of very considerable use to the public." However, an objection was raised by a Society member, Mr. Gray, who stated that Gurney's blowpipe was "extremely similar" to one invented by another man, one that he had hoped to manufacture. The committee reconvened a fortnight later, examined the competing apparatus, and determined that it was neither as safe nor as maneuverable as Gurney's. They recommended that Gurney receive the Society's Gold Isis medal as a reward for his achievement, on the usual condition that he donate a working blowpipe and a description of it to the Society for the use of the public, and relinquish all claims to a patent.[18] The medal was duly awarded by the Society's president, the Duke of Sussex, and a full account of the blowpipe was published, with illustrations, in the Society's *Transactions* for 1823–24.[19]

It may be wondered why Gurney would give up his patent rights to such a valuable instrument, especially since he was offering it for sale at the same time. Three reasons may be suggested. In the first place, as Mr. Gray's intervention shows, oxyhydrogen blowpipes were in a stage of rapid development. A patent on any given model would quickly become outdated. In any case, the procedure for obtaining a patent was cumbersome and time-consuming. Counterclaims were bound to be raised, and legal redress of patent violations from competitors might take years to resolve.[20] Gurney had solved the most important problem, that of making the blowpipe safe to use, but his technique could be incorporated into a variety of designs. In fact, an "oxy-hydrogen microscope" was advertised a few years later in connection with a popular "anatomical" waxworks museum. This was actually a magic lantern or slide projector that used lime pellets inflamed by a small blowpipe for illumination. Gurney had invented the technique and predicted that it would be used to light theaters. The blowpipe-lighted magic lantern grew common by the 1840s and was widely used until the introduction of carbon arc lamps in the 1890s.[21] Given the difficulty of protecting such a patent, the public recognition afforded by the Isis medal was extremely valuable.

In the second place, it is likely that Gurney's income from his lectures and medical practice, combined with the monetary value of the gold Isis medal itself, was substantial enough to allow him this demonstration of public generosity. Later in his career, he claimed not to need monetary rewards because he had "independent means." Yet he complained often and bitterly that he had been deprived of just compensation for the inventions that contributed so much to the public welfare. This pattern, of generosity alternating with abject pleas for assistance and rewards, was typical of an age when people of Gurney's background were struggling to fashion themselves as independent professionals with claims to gentility, despite the fact that patronage was still the primary means of advancement. It was also typical, perhaps, of the Cornish tendency to act with impulsive generosity, but to bear a grudge when slighted. In 1822–23, Gurney was doing very well for himself and could reasonably look forward to further profits from other inventions and processes under development. He might also have expected that the donation would earn him an invitation to join the Society of Arts, but in this he was disappointed.

A third reason for Gurney's generosity is suggested by the 1823 *Transactions* of the Society of Arts. In addition to a description of the blowpipe (called an "improved Pyrometer"), the *Transactions* included a sketch of another of Gurney's inventions that combined experimental knowledge of chemistry with mechanical ingenuity. This invention promised much greater rewards than the blowpipe, and Gurney was too deeply absorbed in its possibilities to waste time defending the lesser claim. Turning away from the lectures and laboratory instruments that had secured his reputation in the London scientific community, he gave his attention, energy, and money entirely to his new interest. It was a self-propelled steam carriage, designed to run on city streets.

5

Inventing the Steam Carriage

Gurney never forgot his childhood impressions of Richard Trevithick's steam carriages and locomotives. He corresponded with Trevithick throughout the period of his medical pupilage at Wadebridge, remaining "intimately acquainted with all the changes and improvements that were made in his engine." He experimented on his own with various mechanisms for giving power, and in his Surrey Institution lectures, he spent a good deal of time analyzing the expansion and contraction of various gases, including hydrogen, chlorine, and atmospheric steam. He knew by then that such gases expanded exponentially when heated, citing "Mr. Perkins's new steam engine" as evidence of how this principle could be applied. He deduced from these facts that "elementary power [the power of gaseous elements] was capable of being applied to propel carriages along common roads with great political advantage, and that the floating knowledge of the day placed the object within our reach."[1]

Part of that "floating knowledge" was contained in papers, given by Davy and Faraday in 1823, on the use of carbon dioxide and methane as substitutes for steam, to power engines. Upon reading these papers, Gurney immediately set to work experimenting with various gases in models of his own contrivance. After a year or so, he built a small model locomotive that ran on ammonia gas. It required very little alteration in the mechanical design of an ordinary steam engine. This model was tested on the hilly road at Kilburn in May 1825. Its success led him to obtain a patent and venture further into this field.[2]

If his London lectures came near the end of a Golden Age of popular chemistry, his work on steam locomotion was, in every sense, pioneering. His contributions were fourfold. First, he disproved through actual demonstrations the common belief that steam carriage wheels could not maintain traction on a road surface. Second, he radically redesigned the steam boiler, making it much lighter and safer than before. Third, he invented a steam jet to improve the draft of air through the firebox, vastly increasing its heat and power. Fourth, he demonstrated that steam power could be used to propel carriages on common roads safely and consistently.

These great achievements, however, led to an even greater disappointment. As he had remarked in connection with his idea for central heating, any invention that requires people to give up a whole complex pattern of social and economic interaction, with all its vested interests and daily habits, will inevitably be resisted. Hence, all those whose livelihood depended on horse travel, who stood to lose by the introduction of steam—stablers, hostlers, stagecoach companies, turnpike trusts, even the farmers who grew feed grains— organized attacks on the new invention. At the same time, it faced competition from a more ambitious rival, backed by enormous financial and political capital: the railway.

Most of what we know about Gurney's steam carriage comes from a few newspaper accounts of the time, from his testimony before Parliament when he sought compensation for his ruined trade, and from a thorough treatment of his work in Alexander Gordon's contemporary *Treatise on Elemental Locomotion*. We also have his autobiographical accounts of the development of the carriage, published in 1832, and of the steam jet, in 1859.[3] Information from these sources, selectively quoted and condensed in Harris's commemorative biography, gives the misleading impression that Gurney's carriage was almost the only one in operation. The evidence was extensively reworked and amplified by David Beasley in his lively 1988 study, *The Suppression of the Automobile: Skulduggery at the Crossroads*.[4] Beasley was partial to Gurney, but placed his machines in the wider context of innovations in power and transport that characterized the 1820s.

Gurney assumed that if he communicated his theories about the use of steam power in his lectures and displayed a small working model, someone with mechanical ability and financial resources would seize the opportunity to build a steam carriage. He himself would act in the capacity of a scientific consultant, as befitted a man of his social status. As a result of his inquiries, however, he became convinced that he would have to do the job on his own. "Incredible as it may now seem," he wrote later, "at the commencement of my experiments, for want of practical engineers to second or assist my views, I was compelled to turn engineer myself."

He first obtained a partner to take over the bulk of his medical practice. Then, he established a workshop in Oxford Street and built his first full-size carriage. This was driven successfully to Windmill Hill, near Edgware, about eight miles to the northwest. Now firmly convinced of its importance, he expanded his operations. He leased the former Ophthalmic Hospital in Albany Street, a large U-shaped structure designed by John Nash, which was situated near the Royal Life Guards barracks on the east side of Regent's Park. The Gurney family moved into living quarters overlooking the street. The yard in back was enclosed with workshops fronted by colonnaded verandas. A boiler and steam engine were installed under one of the colonnades; the adjacent workshop fitted out with lathes, drills, forges, and other equipment; and mechanics hired. It is worth remembering that at this time, iron was the metal of choice for construction. Steel was rare and expensive; there were no artifical abrasives, standardized screws, mechanized cutting tools, or mineral oil for lubrication. Leather and wood were still used as common construction materials for machines.[5]

Mounting a steam engine on a carriage frame seems, in retrospect, a fairly simple arrangement. It would have a firebox and a boiler, with one or two pistons connected to the drive wheel. In practice, the mechanisms required to regulate water flow, steam pressure, intake and exhaust valves, and articulated drive rods were complex and difficult to synchronize. Despite the achievements of Boulton and Watt, steam engines were still imperfect and idiosyncratic. They required constant attention and maintenance.

It must also be noted that "work in progress" was not protected under patent law in that period. Each time Gurney made a significant improvement on the original design, he had to obtain another patent, at roughly £360 per application, before testing the carriage on public roads, lest his competitors pirate his ideas. Three additional patents were eventually obtained this way, on 21 October 1825, 14 October 1827, and 8 July 1829.[6]

He was neither the first nor the most prominent steam engineer at that time. Once James Watt had proved that the expansion and contraction of a gas could generate power, any number of men tried to adapt the principle to vehicular propulsion. The French military engineer Nicholas Cugnot built a working three-wheeled steam wagon as early as 1769. Watt himself secured a patent for a steam carriage, and his assistant, William Murdock, built an experimental vehicle around 1785.[7] Other engines appeared in Scotland and in Halifax before the turn of the century. The Napoleonic wars put a damper on mechanical development, but in 1821–22, a prototype carriage with tubular boiler, steam condenser, and gear-driven wheels was built in London by Joseph Bramah's sons for a local inventor, Julius Griffith. The Griffith carriage was driven experimentally for several years, providing much information for other inventors.[8] David Gordon patented carriages powered by Samuel Brown's gas-vacuum engine in 1822 and 1824. In 1824 Gordon organized a society of gentlemen "tending to the ultimate establishment of a company for the purpose of contracting to run the mail-coach and other carriages by means of a high pressure steam-engine, or of a gas-vacuum or pneumatic [compressed air] engine, supplied with portable gas."[9] By 1824–25, there were additional patents taken out by W. H. James of London and by Timothy Burstall and John Hill of Scotland. There was also an early hot-air engine devised by Sir George Cayley, a wealthy Yorkshire gentleman with whom Gurney became closely associated, and a number of "philosophical toys" using electromagnetism. Gurney's original model, like Davy's, ran on ammonia gas. The two men, like most of the others, soon realized that steam was the most effective agent.[10]

Many scientists and mechanics doubted that steam could be adapted to road carriages, however. Richard Trevithick's first steam vehicle, which he built for road travel in 1801, had a problem with friction: the wheels tended to slip when power was applied by the piston. This was due in part to the way the vertical connecting rods were attached to the drive wheels, and in part to the abominable state of the turnpike roads at the turn of the century. After a decade of trying to run his locomotive* on roadways, Trevithick gave up and adapted it to rails, as did every other inventor who followed him. His locomotive continued to slip at the slightest incline, however. Other inventors attacked the problem of friction with toothed drive wheels and even with pushrods that acted on the ground like horses' legs. Finally, William Hedley (1813) and George Stephenson (1814) developed double-cylinder engines that gave power to all four wheels at once, by means of cogs or chain drive. Stephenson's engine weighed about seven and a half tons with a full water tank, and pulled twelve loaded carriages, with a combined weight of about fifty-eight tons, up a one percent grade. His 1816 patent for both locomotive and rail design remained the standard until 1830.[11]

Development moved slowly at first. By 1824 less than a dozen locomotives were in operation, and they were all colliery trams. In that year, however, both the Stockton and Darlington and the Stratford and Moreton railway lines were nearing completion.[12] Both would carry passengers as well as goods. In April 1825, Nicholas Wood, Stephenson's former pupil, published *A Practical Treatise on Rail-*

---

*A steam *carriage* has the engine on board with the passengers; a *locomotive* or *drag*, on the other hand, is a separate engine on wheels, used to pull a wagon or carriage.

roads, the first complete work on rail steam locomotion. Wood's enthusiasm for rail transport and his predictions of commercial success coincided with a period of financial speculation in England. Dozens of rail lines were projected, with wild claims of investment opportunities. The bubble quickly burst, however, and the only venture to survive was the Liverpool and Manchester Railway, not completed until 1830.[13]

Gurney's first experimental model was tested only a month after Wood's *Treatise* was published. Although it is obvious that he was keeping close watch on the railway ventures, he deliberately chose the alternative mode of transport. In hindsight this choice might seem misguided or even perverse. In 1825, however, railways and their locomotives were still uncertain novelties. Most had been designed by practical engineers for industrial owners and businessmen, and the future of railways was thought of in terms of short-line "feeder" routes to supplement Britain's extensive canal network.[14] Few people imagined that locomotives would transform long-distance travel within a quarter of a century. Railways required the organization of a whole new infrastructure, including rights of way, coal and water depots, locomotive factories, ironworks, miles of rails, and armies of navvies to put them in place. Steam carriages, by contrast, were intended for small groups of people. They used existing roads and were expected to be serviced by existing, or easily adapted, facilities for horse-drawn vehicles. One or two could be built and tested without building a whole system, so they were more likely to interest the mechanically talented gentleman with a modicum of capital. Throughout his career, Gurney made a virtue out of adopting the odd perspective and approaching problems from new tangents. He had neither the resources to build a railway nor the talent for large-scale organization possessed by men like the Stephensons. But he had plenty of experience riding the stagecoaches between Cornwall and London. He could apply his knowledge of steam power directly to that common and still-brutal means of travel.

In the years between Trevithick's first locomotives and Gurney's carriages, the British turnpike system had spread out from London and provincial cities into a fairly decent trunk system. Parliament approved the formation of local turnpike trusts to raise capital, build roads, and operate them with toll revenues. Other roads were built as private ventures by wealthy individuals or partnerships. Thomas Telford and the McAdam brothers learned how to improve road surfaces by layering different grades of crushed stone, especially Cornish granite, and a complete explanation of the new roadbuilding techniques was written for the *Encyclopaedia Britannica* in 1824.

Horse-drawn coaches, now blessedly equipped with laminated springs and stronger, ironshod wheels, could make the trip from London to Edinburgh in two to three days, compared to ten or twelve in the previous century. The new technology made it possible to develop new kinds of vehicles. In fact, as Gurney's work began to show success, and steam carriages became economically feasible, other engineers experimented with cemented gravel, granite paving blocks, and iron wheel lanes to accomodate them.[15]

The main problem with steam carriages, at least in theory, was that they could not go up hills. As an exasperated Alexander Gordon would later recall, the difficulty of maintaining the adhesion of locomotives on rails of any significant incline led engineers to conclude that the problem would be nearly impossible on roadways. This idea entered into the general "floating knowledge" of scientists and inventors as a proven fact, despite an almost complete lack of evidence. When Gurney consulted Humphry Davy and other experts on the question, he was assured that "experiments" had proved the point. Being at that time preoccupied with the design of a lightweight boiler for his engine, Gurney, like many others, took the principle for granted. He began devising supplementary means of propelling his carriage.[16] He consulted with David Gordon, who in 1822 had taken out a patent for a carriage using toothed drive wheels. Gordon's contraption (there is no better word for it) involved a miniature steam locomotive with cog wheels, mounted inside a nine-foot-diameter drum with toothed inner rims. The engine rolled the drum along rather like a squirrel cage, pushing an attached carriage ahead of it.[17] A similar device was being developed by marine engineers John and Samuel Seaward. They used a small "pusher" drum with exterior cleats, chain-driven by an engine mounted on the back of a carriage.[18] The Gordon drum was huge and ungainly, the Seawards' unreliable and damaging to the road surface. Gurney therefore adopted a different strategy. According to Harris, he replaced the regular carriage wheels with toothed rollers, which were linked together and driven by a revolving chain. The arrangement, although described in vague terms, appears to have anticipated the modern Caterpillar tractor tread. Such a tread was being developed at about that time by Gurney's friend Sir George Cayley, and it is likely that he got the idea from that source.[19]

In 1824 David Gordon tried again with "an arrangement of machinery, by which an action similar to horses' feet could be obtained." Six jointed iron legs, fitted with feet, were connected by brass joints, straps, and keys to a set of cranks, propelled by a pair of steam engines. The legs extended through the floor in the middle of the carriage, analogous to the legs of a horse, and the feet pushed backwards on the road to move the carriage forward. This astonishing arrangement had been tried by other inventors before Gordon. It was regarded as quite promising despite its ungainly, clattering features. After Gordon applied to Gurney for permission to use one of his light tubular boilers, Gurney adapted Gordon's machinery for his own carriage, constructing a set of smaller legs to be used as supplementary traction when going up hills. The legs, or "propellers," were attached to parallel wooden blocks that slid back and forth in metal grooves, in alternate strokes, underneath the carriage. In his first experiment with a full-size carriage, Gurney used the propellers to ascend Windmill Hill. He found them inconvenient and heavy, but still believed they were necessary for the purpose. Indeed, several scientific journals had just published papers demonstrating that "fact" with mathematical formulas. However, "after much thought and experiment," as Gordon reported it, Gurney devised a mechanism that would bring the propellers into action only when the wheels slipped. With this in place, he launched a second run of nine and a half miles between his Oxford Street factory and Edgware. Much to his surprise, the ordinary carriage wheels maintained excellent traction, even when going up considerable inclines. The whole phenomenon of slippage, he discovered, resulted from the sudden impact on wheels by the large cylinders of older high-pressure engines. Because his locomotive increased steam pressure gradually by means of a throttle, it eliminated the shock. Gurney apparently kept the propellers for a while, expecting that they would be necessary in case of mud or snow, but after several more trials, they were abandoned. In later evidence before Parliament, he claimed that he had used his carriage on both snow and ice, with few problems.[20] After the Windmill Hill–Edgware trials, the rear carriage wheels were driven by a crankshaft attached directly to the dual pistons of the engine, and in fact, power was commonly directed to only one wheel at a time.[21] Although hundreds of people witnessed these trials, and although they were reported in the local press, some mechanics still refused to believe the results. One of these was John Farey (1791–1851), a civil engineer experienced with steam engines, who had prepared the drawings for Gurney's original "propeller" patent. Farey evidently changed his mind, because he later adapted the Gurney design to a steam carriage of his own.[22]

The steam for Gurney's first carriage was generated by a large drum boiler, common to most engines at that time. The design had two drawbacks, which he and other inventors worked to overcome. First, the boiler was heavy, especially when filled with water. It added significantly to the weight of the carriage and ate up its own energy in moving forward. This was not a problem on rails, which reduced friction to negligible proportions, but it proved impossible on gravel roads. Second, the boiler was likely to explode. As hot water rose in the boiler, cold water descended along unpredictable pathways. Heat and cold, water and steam were often distributed unevenly around the inside of the boiler, causing "hot spots" to form and burst. Also, the evaporation of the steam left a residue, or crust, called fur, which collected near the bottom of the boiler where the flame struck its surface. The fur caused further irregular heating and eventually ate through the metal. Filtering the water did not solve this problem; the residue was chemically dissolved in the water to start with, and, after it was deposited, it could not be removed except with hammer and chisel or a rough rake. Moreover, Gurney had discovered in the course of his chemistry research that small amounts of water in a hot boiler actually decomposed. Combining with nitrogen in the atmosphere, they formed new, highly volatile compounds. Most inventors of the time simply ignored the problem of safety. They aimed to reduce the weight of the boiler, hoping, as Alexander Gordon acidly commented, that the skill of the engineer, or sheer luck, would prevent explosions, or that if one occurred, it would be "attended by death only to some of those whose situation could be supplied on the morrow at equally low wages."[23]

When Gurney was performing experiments on "caloric" for the Surrey Institution lectures, he studied the currents of water as it was heated in hollow glass tubing. The tubing was bent into various shapes, beginning with a simple circular hoop with a hole in the top for steam to escape. He observed that the hot water rose up one side of the hoop, and after the steam blew off, it descended on the other side, setting up a regular current that maintained the water at a constant temperature and kept it in contact with the surface of the tube at all times . The cylindrical shape of the tubing minimized the deposit of residues, withstood pressure better than other shapes, and was easily cleaned. Because the current moved the water past the flame at a fairly constant rate, more steam could be generated from a smaller volume of water than was the case in a large vat or drum boiler. Thus he discovered the secret of a lightweight, efficient, and safe boiler. Similar boilers had been built before in England, but all had proved defective. There is no evidence to show whether Gurney knew about the pipe boilers built by Oliver Evans and other Americans before this time. In any case, theirs tended to use fewer, larger pipes than his design.[24] For his second steam carriage, built late in 1825, he produced a boiler with a dozen iron pipes, from one-half inch to two inches in diameter, about one-eighth inch thick, wrapped vertically around the firebox in the shape of a figure eight. The pipes were attached at the top to a large horizontal chamber, where steam was separated from the water and drawn off to a second, vertical steam separator before escaping to the engine cylinders. The steam separator prevented water from being drawn into the cylinders along with the steam, a problem that had plagued previous locomotives. The "waste" water returned to the bottom of the boiler through drains from each separator. As this arrangement reminded the workmen in Gurney's factory of the circulation of blood in the body, they called it the "'natomy boiler."[25]

In a third design, used in later carriages, Gurney compressed the main pipes into the shape of a "V," turned sideways. The ends of one set of legs were attached to the cold-water receptacle below, and the other set to the steam separator above. On top of the pipes, he ran a coil of tubing for the cold water supply, which was therefore heated by the fire as it was drawn toward the receptacle. By layering several such coils, separated by thin metal plates, he caused the fire to wind around them. The whole arrangement was encased in a metal firebox.[26] John Farey later testified that the pipes in this third design were too small to keep the water in circulation at all points. Gurney, however, produced a fourth version with larger pipes. In his evidence before a committee of the House of Commons in 1831, he admitted that in his first design, the tubes were not welded together, and sprung leaks when great pressure built up. He found "from practice and experience" that he had to overlap their edges and weld their seams from end to end. After that, few of the pipes ever burst, and those that did merely hissed. They could be repaired with a hammer, a far cry from the damage done by large boiler explosions.[27] The pipes and tubing were proved to withstand 800 pounds of pressure per square inch, but the usual pressure when traveling was between 70 and 130 pounds. With the new tubular boiler, the weight of the steam carriage was reduced from 8,000 to about 3,000 pounds.

To deal with the problem of fur in the pipes, Gurney first injected acid into the water, hoping that it would combine with the residue and carry it away. This apparently worked for him but not for the mechanics who tried it on their own. Consequently, he placed threaded plugs at the corners of the tubes, so that they could be opened and scraped out mechanically.[28] James Stone, engineer for the carriage Gurney built for Sir Charles Dance, said that the boiler tubes needed cleaning once a month, but could go longer, and were blown out with excess steam at the end of a run every two or three days.[29]

Alexander Gordon, writing in 1836, said that Gurney "has made the greatest step towards a light and safe boiler of any others who have yet appeared in the field." His tubular design was adopted by many other engineers, including rival steam carriage designers. It was featured in a stationary boiler patented by Babcock and Willcox in America in 1867, which proved commercially successful for half a century. Later versions, larger in size and built for higher pressures, were used to power steam turbines. In 1832 William Crawshay, a Welsh iron magnate who had purchased one of Gurney's locomotives, wrote: "The favourable opinion entertained by my engineer and myself of the tubular boiler over every other we have yet seen, not only remains unshaken, but is strengthened and confirmed by eighteen months' constant use, and observation of it on our own road; and also by all we can collect from other testimony, of what is doing elsewhere in this neighbourhood with boilers of other descriptions. The ease and economy of first construction; the facility of repair when required; the extreme lightness; the great capacity for raising steam; and the perfect freedom from danger of the tubular boiler, all render it, in our opinion, pre-eminently adapted to locomotive engines."[30]

Having solved the problems of traction and weight, Gurney tried to figure out how to produce enough steam pressure to maintain the speed of the engine. Trevithick had shown that a steam locomotive could run at high speeds (in 1813, on a set of rails laid near Euston Square in London, he had outrun a racehorse), but the speed dropped as the boiler pressure worked off. The draft through the firebox was not strong enough to keep up the volume of steam required for sustained velocity. Subsequent engineers added a mechanical bellows, or "blast," to the boiler; Gurney used one in an 1827 design. The blower, however, tended to blow hot ashes out through every orifice of the engine, and it still did not create the needed power.

Gurney's observations of previous locomotives made him suspect that he could boost the draft by creating a vacuum through the smokestack or chimney. The vacuum could be obtained by rapidly condensing high-pressure steam. As early as 1804, he had seen Trevithick exhaust waste steam up the stack, primarily to make the steam invisible and less frightening to onlookers. The Stephensons also directed steam up their locomotive chimneys, and it was the usual method of exhaust in the 1820s.[31] What Gurney discovered, some time between 1820 and 1824, was that if the steam was discharged at sufficient pressure up the center of the chimney, filling the upper half, it produced a powerful vacuum behind it.

Much later in life, Gurney claimed that the "jet of steam" was inspired by experiments with gases, heat, and atmospheric pressure for his 1822 chemistry lectures. The furnaces used to decompose metallic compounds required a strong draft, he said, and his attempts to provide such a draft led directly to the invention of the oxyhydrogen blowpipe, which in turn inspired the steam jet. The information in his published lectures, however, does not support this statement.[32] The text gives many details of the blowpipe and its application to metallic compound analysis and fusion, but says nothing of any steam jet. It is more likely that as he was experimenting with the various types of jets used for the blowpipe, and with different instruments for demonstrating the behavior of steam, he discovered how to create a draft through a vent pipe.

The basic principle of the steam jet was this: steam forced out through a jet forms an expanding cone, which pushes the air ahead of it, forming a partial vacuum behind. In an open space, or in a chimney where the jet is off center, the air flows back around the cone to fill the vacuum, creating what Gurney rather picturesquely called an "Aërial Flowerpot." But if the jet of steam is blown up the exact center of a chimney, or funnel, of relatively small diameter (about nine inches on Gurney's models, compared to twenty inches on the Stephenson locomotives), it will fill the upper portion entirely, preventing the displaced air from flowing back. The only source of air would then be from the intake to the firebox, under the boiler, so a powerful draft would be created through it. Moreover, the draft could be regulated by increasing or decreasing the pressure of the steam jet. Gurney drew high-pressure steam for the jet from the boiler itself, not from the cylinders. By patient trial and error, he constructed a ring of jets, each about an inch long and a quarter-inch in diameter, shaped like large hollow needles. This ring projected off a main stem, rather like the branches of a Christmas tree. The jets, by contracting the steam, kept the required pressure up. This "tree" was mounted in the lower part of the chimney, exactly in the middle, so that the cone of steam created by the jets would fill the space evenly and completely.[33]

Gurney first tried the jet on an "improved" carriage in the large work yard behind his Albany Street premises in late 1825 or early 1826. His daughter Anna, then about fourteen years old, was able to watch the action from an overlooking window. She recalled later that when her father got up steam and activated the jet, the draft roaring up the chimney "was something terrific to see or hear." On the first trial run, the carriage leaped into motion with such power that Gurney could not hold it on its course. It knocked down one of the

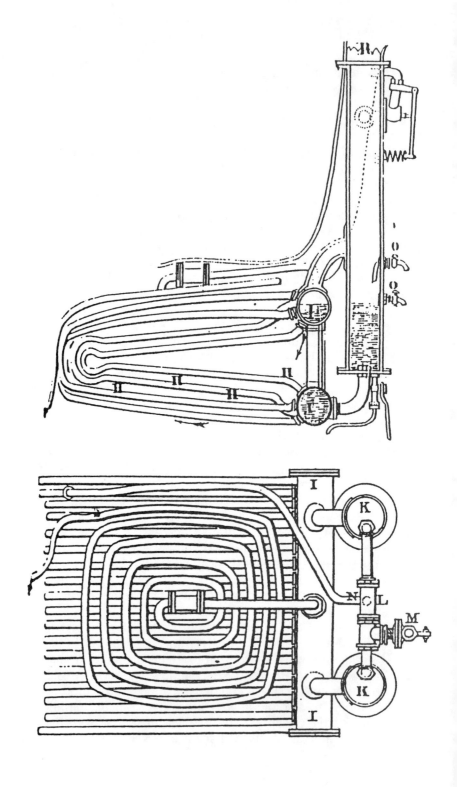

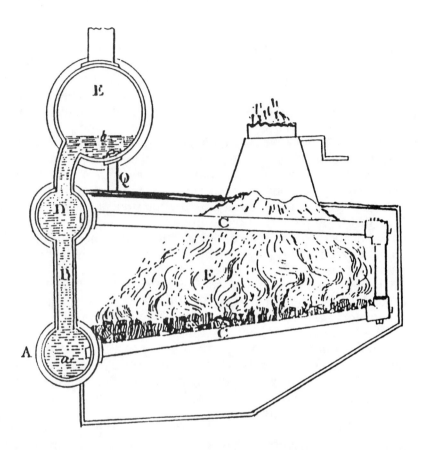

Views of two versions of the Gurney tubular boiler. *Opposite:* side and top views, showing tube arrangement (H), horizontal steam separators (I), and vertical steam separator (K). *Above:* side view showing tubes mounted around firebox. From Alexander Gordon, *A Treatise on Locomotion,* 2d ed. 1836.

pillars of the colonnade before he could shut off the steam and come to a halt. Then, in Anna's words, "he stepped down from the carriage and walked a little distance looking as white as death. This was an awful moment for him, as he felt he had drawn upon some unearthly power over which he had no control."[34] When we remember that the speed of a horse-drawn carriage in those days seldom exceeded ten or twelve miles per hour, averaging closer to four or five, and that physicians warned that faster speeds would endanger human health, we can appreciate Gurney's anxiety. However, he soon recovered. He sent for his younger brother, Samuel, who had been to America, and was at that time working in France. Together they made a number of experiments and modifications to bring the steam jet under better control. The hired workmen soon got used to the power of the jet. As the carriage steamed around the yard, they took to throwing small pieces of brick or metal into the firebox, cheering as the material shot out of the chimney. After dodging some of these hurtling objects, Gurney ordered a halt to the practice. People in the neighborhood naturally came to see what was going on. From time to time, the carriage was driven out of the yard, into Albany Street and down to the nearby Life Guards barracks, usually accompanied by a crowd of spectators. Other steam engineers visited the workshop, some from the Continent and some even from America. Most of the engineers thought the steam jet of little value, especially for travel on the public roads, because it gave off such a loud roar. The Gurney brothers tried to modify it with centrifugal fans, special cylinders, and other devices. It took over a year to reduce the noise, which continued to be criticized by rivals.[35]

The steam jet was also applied to steamboat engines, where the noise was less objectionable. According to Gurney's testimony before Parliament, and his later pamphlet on the subject, a jet was installed on a vessel called the *Alligator* as early as 1824, and then on the *Duchess of Clarence*. Samuel Gurney, after working with his brother for a time, installed a jet in a one of the ubiquitous steam "packets" that plied between London Bridge and Richmond. Another engineer, William Keene, witnessed the experiments in Albany Street, and shortly afterwards added a jet to a steamboat he used on the swift-flowing Garonne River in France. It was later applied to every kind of steam vessel, and by the 1850s it was standard equipment for European naval vessels.[36]

By October 1827, Gurney had made several improvements on his original design. The steam carriage now resembled a common stage-coach on the outside, with the boiler located in the stern luggage rack or boot. To calm passengers, he replaced the noisy steam jet with a horizontal blower fan, adapted from contemporary winnowing machines, to force air into the firebox. He burned coke instead of coal to reduce the volume of smoke from the chimney. The steam generated by the boiler was led by pipes to two eight-inch cylinders fitted with slide valves. A special mechanism shut off the supply of steam when the cylinders were two-thirds full, allowing the steam inside to expand naturally to its limit, a measure which saved fuel. The pipe from the boiler to the cylinders was equipped with a throttle valve, worked by a handle at the right hand of the driver in front, so that the steam pressure, and thus the motion of the vehicle, could be regulated. In a later model, the driver worked the valve with his foot, so that if he was accidently thrown off his seat, the steam supply was shut down.[37] The waste steam from the cylinders was led back to the cold-water tank, where it was condensed and recirculated. The two pistons were connected to the rear axle by horizontal drive shafts, and the axle was formed into two opposing nine-inch cranks. The axle ends had round plates fixed to them, to which the wheels could be bolted for transmitting power; or the wheels could be allowed to turn freely. In this way the engine could be linked to both hind wheels for maximum drive, or released from one to facilitate turning. A second lever, also worked by the driver, reversed the action of the steam in the cylinders, throwing it onto the other end of the pistons, so that the whole mechanism could be stopped quickly or run in reverse. This carriage was still equipped with two auxiliary propellers. It had friction brakes on the hind wheels in case the action of the engine was not sufficient to slow or stop the vehicle going down hills.[38]

The body of the carriage was fifteen feet long. It could hold six passengers inside and, as was the custom with stagecoaches, fifteen outside, plus a fireman on the back. The driver steered by means of a lever attached to a pair of guide wheels that were mounted in front of the carriage. As the guide wheels were turned, a connecting shaft swung the wheels on the front axle in the desired direction. The carriage could turn within a twenty-foot diameter, a much tighter ratio than a coach with a team of horses. Detailed notices in the *Observer* and the *Gentleman's Magazine* for December 1827 said that the carriage, which weighed three thousand pounds and carried a twelve-horsepower engine, could be steered "with a felicity scarcely conceivable." In fact, the writer had seen a child of five or six (probably Gurney's son John) drive the carriage through a twisting obstacle course, set up especially to show how versatile it was. A member of Parliament, Sir John Ross, happened upon one of Gur-

The Gurney steam carriage in 1828. Model and photography by D. W. Inkel, "Four-in-Hand Miniatures," Bourne, Lincolnshire, U.K. Porter collection.

The Gurney steam carriage, undercarriage assembly, showing horizontal cylinders and steering mechanism. Model and photograph by D. W. Inkel, "Four-in-Hand Miniatures," Bourne, Lincolnshire, U.K. Porter collection.

ney's road trials and asked to drive the vehicle. He drove for half an hour after a few minutes' instruction.[39]

During the rest of 1827 and in 1828, Gurney built several versions of his steam carriage and drove them frequently on the public roads around London. He tried out different drive mechanisms and regulating devices, and he improved the steam jet. When the carriages stopped by the roadside for adjustments, fuel, and minor repairs, passersby crowded around to inspect and ask questions. Newspaper reporters considered the carriage an entertaining story, and Gurney did nothing to discourage visitors to his factory. A writer in the *London Courier* for 10 September 1827, for example, reported enthusiastically that "this beautiful invention" could be driven safely at eleven or twelve miles per hour fairly quietly and without vibration. Thus, while other inventors came forward with numerous variations, Gurney's name became most closely associated with the steam carriage in the public mind. One knowledgeable writer on the subject, Dr. Dionysius Lardner, concluded: "To Mr. Gurney is due, and will be paid, the honour of first proving the practicability and advantage of the project; and in the history of the adaptation of the locomotive engine to common roads, his name will stand before all others in point of time, and the success of his attempts will be recorded as the origin of the success of others in the same race."[40]

6

The Steam Carriage as a Commercial Venture

WHILE GURNEY WAS DEVELOPING HIS INVENTION, THE RAILWAYS WERE STILL struggling with the financial uncertainties left over from their speculative failures of 1826–27. The Liverpool and Manchester Railway, the first to use its own steam-powered locomotives for all trains, did not open until 15 September 1830. Thus the opportunity was ripe for commercial exploitation of the steam carriage. But Gurney could not do this by himself. He had grown up in a region where large-scale industrial organization was almost unknown, and where a workshop with a dozen men was considered a substantial factory. He was not familiar enough with the nascent community of mechanical engineers to recruit anyone with the skills, experience, and vision necessary to manage an operation sizable enough to dominate the intended market. Neither did he enjoy the confidence of parliamentary insiders and City bankers, who could support his enterprise with the necessary capital and influence. He was therefore forced to solicit start-up capital from individuals willing to risk considerable funds in return for future gain. He had already, in 1826, granted a license to John Ward, a retired East India Company official, to establish a regular carriage service from London to Liverpool and on to Scotland. Ward paid a fee of £15,000 plus a royalty of three and a half pence per mile. Ward's contract was to be held in abeyance until the workability of the carriage was demonstrated. Once that was done, Gurney entered into patent agreements with several other entrepreneurs to provide them with carriages for proposed turnpike passenger services. In September 1827 he and his brother Thomas Gurney (like Samuel, recently returned from America) signed a fourteen-year lease to supply eight steam carriages to Captain William Dobbyn of Somerset, to run from London to Bristol and, later, to Bath. Dobbyn paid £1,800 in advance for this project.[1] William Hanning, a rich agriculturalist who had already built a stagecoach turnpike between London and Exeter, gave an advance of £700 in November 1827 for steam carriages to run between those cities and on to Plymouth. Hanning would become the chief backer of Gurney's projects, investing between £6,000 and £10,000 over the next few years. Gurney's chief engineer James Stone, Charles Thiselton of the Cockburn Bank, a London physician named Patrick Mackie, and Colonel (later Major General Sir) Charles Viney were the other investors.

As David Beasley carefully explains in his account of the business, the principle of limited liability had not yet been established. All partners in a registered company risked their entire personal assets, regardless of how much they invested in a particular venture. Joint-stock companies, which did offer some protection, required expensive acts of Parliament. Solicitors were therefore assigned to create an agreement by which the patentees could carry out all the activities of a company without actually forming one. Such an agreement helped Gurney raise money, but it gave rise to new problems. He was to discover, like many other inventors before and since, that his business partners had a tendency to interefere with his work, make deals with each other behind the scenes, bicker incessantly, and generally impede his progress. They were often slow in providing promised capital and then threatened to withdraw when lack of funds halted production. Yet he could not go forward without them. His Albany Street premises were leased for £1,000 per year, including taxes. Wages were another £2,500, and something like £12,000 went into buildings, machines, and equipment from 1825 through 1830. Like other manufacturers of the early nineteenth century, Gurney had to put up a good deal of his own capital.[2]

In October 1827 the *Berkshire Chronicle* announced that fifteen coaches had already been built to run between London, Bath, and Bristol. Refueling depots were being set up every six or seven miles along the way, said the *Chronicle,* because the carriage used sixty gallons of water per hour. The writer advised that service would begin about the 10th of November and that the "ingenious and gallant inventor would lead out of London on the first voyage."[3] Unfortunately, the *Chronicle* was completely mistaken. Production was slower than anticipated, and the promoters encountered many obstacles while trying to secure their intended routes. The delay began to check the momentum that had built up during the trial runs. In December both the *Mirror* and the *Gentleman's Magazine* gave detailed, favorable impressions of the carriage, but the *Morning Herald* carried a critical review, evidently based on hearsay evidence. Its writer complained that "guiding the 24 horse power that would be applied to the elbows" of the driver was humanly impossible for any length of time. Even if that problem should be overcome, passengers on the outside of the carriage would be suffocated by the engine smoke and carbon monoxide pouring out of its relatively short chimney. Gurney responded to this criticism by installing a filter of sand mixed with lime in the chimney, which absorbed most of the noxious gases.[4]

The strange new vehicle was a natural subject for satire. In 1827 a newspaper editor wrote: "Oats, straw, and travelling fares, ought to fall in prices, as we shall have steam-carriages, dispensing with cattle, substituting a mop and poker for Jarvey's whip, and a bushel of coals in lieu of an additional pair of horses. In consequence of the success of Mr. Gurney's steam carriage, we presume coach *horses* will become *dog* cheap in a short time!" A broadsheet of 1828 displayed a "Dialogue Between Two Neighbors," which played upon fears of explosions, sulfur fumes, etc., and "A New Song" suggesting that horses, and thus hostlers and corn dealers, would no longer be needed if the carriage was successful.[5]

By this time the carriage had been driven to Edgware, Stanmore, Watford, and Barnet, as well as to Regent's Park. In May 1828, with the steam jet in use, it was taken up Highgate Old Hill, which many had predicted could not be done. The workmen, apparently overexcited by their achievement, forgot to lock the rear wheels onto the drive shaft after turning the carriage for the descent, so Gurney, who was driving, could not slow down by throttling back the steam. He lost control of the speeding vehicle and one of the wheels was torn completely off as it careened down the hill. Fortunately the axle dragged it to a halt, and no one was hurt.[6] The reporter for *Blackwood's Edinburgh Magazine,* who reported this accident, went on to say that the damage had been readily repaired and that "Gurney's carriage is now ready, like a pair of lovers, for a run on the North road."*[7] A broadsheet published that spring, "The New Invented Steam Carriage," displayed side and rear views, identifying the various parts, and giving a fair description of its features. However, it noted a criticism James McAdam had made about its narrow carriage wheels, saying that broader rims would be less likely to tear up the roads. Also, it alluded to future problems by stating that the Marquess of Landsdown might introduce legislation in Parliament imposing tolls on such carriages, if several dozen of them started operating on the roads.[8]

Nevertheless, fears about riding at high speed next to a steam

---

*The allusion is to the early nineteenth-century practice of eloping by journeying north to Gretna Green, a village just across the border in Scotland, where quick marriages could be obtained.

GURNEY'S NEW STEAM CARRIAGE.

"Gurney's New Steam Carriage." Broadsheet, 1827. By permission of the Science & Society Picture Library, London.

A Gurney steam carriage at Highgate Tunnel, ca. 1828. By permission of the Science & Society Picture Library, London.

boiler persisted, even in Gurney's own family. Anna Jane Gurney recalled that her father was often tempted to give up working on the carriage because her mother, Elizabeth, was convinced that it was extremely dangerous. Her natural anxiety at her husband's experiments with high-pressure steam and reckless speeds was no doubt exacerbated by seeing seven-year-old John take the steering rod of the carriage on at least one occasion. Goldsworthy, who had great affection for his wife, felt her distress deeply; but Colonel James Viney, his friend and one of the principle investors, encouraged him to continue, and calmed Elizabeth's fears on several occasions. He promised her a gold chain as a reward for her support when the carriage succeeded.[9]

By July 1828 the weight of the carriage had been further reduced. The cold-water storage tanks were placed underneath the carriage frame to lower the center of gravity. A writer for the *London Weekly Review*, observing the trials near Regent's Park during July and August, said that the carriage carried ten people outside and several inside at the rate of nine miles per hour. The writer was especially impressed by the operation of the tubular boiler. "This beautiful specimen of mechanical invention appears at length to be brought to a state of perfection, beyond which we hardly think it possible to make any essential improvements," he concluded. "To persons not acquainted with the numerous difficulties which present themselves to bringing into full operation such complicated pieces of machinery it would be difficult to convey an adequate opinion of the merits of this invention."[10]

After the initial enthusiasm wore off, however, critics intensified their warnings about accidents, ill heath, and inconvenience. *Blackwood's Edinburgh Magazine*, which had reported on the accident at Highgate Hill the previous May, suggested that the engine and boiler should be removed to a separate locomotive to which carriages could be attached. Gurney saw the wisdom of this change. During the winter of 1828, he secluded himself within the factory walls "night and day," as Harris recounts it, "never leaving them for a moment, nor writing a letter, or even seeing a friend, but giving the whole of the time to his great work." He designed and built a new locomotive about twelve feet long, which could pull either carriages or wagons. It was equipped with a quieter steam jet, double steam separators, and a new version of the tubular boiler. Loaded with enough coke and water to go six to eight miles, it weighed about twenty-two hundred pounds.[11] The old propellers were gone, but a pair of iron "shoe drags" had been added, which could be forced against the road surface by the driver, slowing the carriage during descents, or even raising the rear wheels off the road for emergency stops. By the middle of July, Gurney, Hanning, Mackie, and Thiselton were ready to secure patents on the latest improvements and display them publicly. The patent charges were shared proportionally by the interested parties, but as usual, Gurney's expenses were charged against future proceeds.

By July 1829 the steamer was deemed ready for an extended trial. Preparations began for a trip to Bath. The reasons for choosing that destination are not hard to guess. Bath still enjoyed a reputation as a fashionable spa, so any number of influential people would witness the steamer's arrival. The route was in good condition, having been used for the Royal Mail since 1784, and in fact was to be used by one of Gurney's licensees. Winding through the Kennet and Avon river valleys, it also promised easy access to water for the boiler.

Since the steamer had run so many times around the Life Guards Barracks near Gurney's workshop, the military authorities had become aware of its potential for moving troops and equipment. Sir Charles Dance, Lieutenant Colonel of the Life Guards, was one of the interested officers. He invited Quartermaster General Sir Willoughby Gordon to inspect the steam drag. General Gordon came to the Dance estate at Bushey Heath, Hertfordshire, on 22 July. He reported that the drag "may be directed with greater precision than can any carriage drawn by horses under the direction of a coachman," and could be stopped instantly when necessary. The high-pressure boiler consumed large quantities of water and fuel, which would require resupply every few miles along a turnpike route. But the noise and dust were less than those given off by a coach-and-four, and burning coke instead of coal reduced smoke to a negligible level. General Gordon calculated that if the expense of running the carriage was threepence per mile as claimed, the proprietors could make a clear profit of 500 percent on intercity routes. He predicted mechanical difficulties, accidents, and frightened horses upon the first introduction of steamers in regular service, but concluded that "it will eventually, and at no distant period, force itself into very extensive use."[12]

General Gordon commissioned Colonel Dance to accompany Gurney on the trip to Bath and take careful notes. Dance's report was published and reprinted by Gurney in the pamphlets he wrote to defend his claims. Since both Harris and Beasley have recapitulated the report with additional details, providing excellent accounts,[13] only the highlights of this historic journey will be included here.

Gurney and his chief engineer, James Stone, drove the locomotive to Cransford Bridge Inn on the west side of London on the night of 27

July, with assistant engineer Tom Bailey stoking the fuel. At Cransford Bridge they attached a light barouche carrying Thomas Gurney, the patentees Colonel Viney and Captain Dobbyn, and two other engineers from Gurney's operation. William Hanning, Sir Charles Dance, and two of Dance's rich friends, William Bulnois and a Mr. Davis, led the procession in a two-horse phaeton, although this was soon outdistanced by the steam carriage. A post carriage, filled with coke as contingency fuel, brought up the rear, with David Dady, Gurney's factory manager, and Thomas Martin, an assistant engineer, riding outside.[14]

The locomotive traveled at about fourteen miles per hour to Longford. There, poor visibility on a bridge under repairs caused a run-in with the Bristol mail coach. To avoid an accident, Gurney forced his vehicle into a pile of bricks, which broke one of the drive shafts leading to the rear axle. He drove on with power to only one wheel, and by the time they reached Reading, four hours and ten minutes from Cransford, they had overtaken and passed almost fifty horse-drawn vehicles, and six horses. Nevertheless, Gurney discovered some drawbacks to his arrangements. The clinkers that accumulated in the firebox reduced heat and lowered his speed, so that he had to scrape them out frequently to maintain power. Also, after every six or seven miles, the men had to stop, form a bucket brigade, and haul water from a nearby pond up to the carriage. In a few places, fuel had not been secured ahead of time, or was of poor quality. Obviously, a regular steamer service would need dependable fuel and water depots along the way. Finally, because one drive shaft was broken, the men had to shoulder the carriage over the top of the hill outside the town of Marlborough. But to everyone's surprise, it did not race down the other side. The engine was throttled back and gave sufficient drag to the wheels to coast safely into the town.

They reached Melksham, ten miles short of Bath, at about eight o'clock in the evening, having averaged six miles per hour, including all stops. They found Melksham crowded with laborers attending a local fair, so Gurney drove very slowly through the main street. Unemployment was high in Melksham following the financial crisis of 1826 (the same crisis that delayed work on the new railways), and a group of weavers in the crowd, like Luddites, attacked the newfangled machinery that seemed to symbolize the threat to their livelihood. Gurney and two others were injured, and the carriage was chased out of Melksham in a shower of stones. The damages to machinery and humans were repaired in Bath during a three-day rest. Gurney diverted the spa residents by driving the carriage up and down Pultney Street in the town center. Then, in the middle of

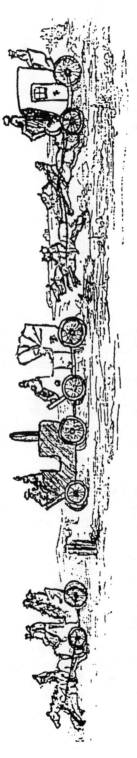

The Gurney steam drag and carriages on the high road to Bath, July 1829. From the *Revue Britannique*, 1835. By permission of the Bude-Stratton Town Museum.

a Sunday night, when the workers were sleeping off their holiday, the steamer was dragged by horses back through Melksham and fired up outside of that danger zone. The second drive shaft having been repaired, power was given to both rear wheels, and the carriage climbed several steep hills at seven to eight miles per hour, to the cheers of spectators. After parading through Reading, led by the Mayor and leading citizens, they arrived back at Cransford in the late afternoon of 31 July.

Sir Charles Dance reported the full particulars of the journey to his superiors, considering it "decisive of success." The *Times* of 5 August covered the achievement in glowing terms, adding that the patentees were immediately undertaking to bring steam carriage service to the public. One week later, at the request of the Duke of Wellington, who was not only prime minister but also commander in chief of the army, Gurney gave a demonstration at Hounslow Barracks Yard, attended by a crowd of military and scientific dignitaries. With his brother Thomas beside him on the steamer, he drew Wellington's barouche around carrying the Duke, Sir Willoughby and Lady Gordon, Sir Charles and Lady Dance, and the Dances' two little boys. Then, he hitched up a wagon loaded with twenty-seven soldiers and drew it through rough sand and gravel at ten miles per hour with only one drive wheel engaged, to show off its maneuverability and practicality. Finally, he gave it full power, barging around the yard seven or eight times at speeds up to seventeen miles per hour. Anna Gurney, who was present at this demonstration, wrote that Colonel Viney then reminded her mother, Elizabeth, that he had promised a reward for her forbearance; he sent her a gold chain shortly thereafter.[15] Next day, the *Times* ran a very favorable report on the demonstration. On 22 August, it printed a long letter from a military engineer, John Herapath, addressed to the Duke of Wellington, "on the utility, advantages, and national importance of Mr. Gurney's Steam Carriage."[16] The trip to Bath and the trials at Hounslow Barracks, said Herapath, "had established the merit of the invention on the only incontrovertable grounds, an experimental basis." He himself had published research on the subject, which had been regarded as so much science fiction. But now the results were completely confirmed, and steamers were certain to become the chief mode of conveyance on public roads. They had been regarded as clumsy and unwieldy vehicles, he continued, but Gurney "had so artfully packed his machinery that one would be apt to ask, on first glance, 'where does the power to propel this ponderous burden reside?'" This letter was subsequently published as a pamphlet. An engraving of the original steam carriage, labeled with all specifica-

Goldsworthy Gurney demonstrates the "steam drag" to the Duke of Wellington at Hounslow Barracks, August 1829. By permission of the Bude-Stratton Town Museum.

tions, was published to commemorate the trip to Bath, although it pictured the wrong vehicle. The journey had been closely followed by the Bath *Chronicle*, and further details of the Hounslow trials were also published in the September issues of the *Annual Register,* the *Atlas*, and the *Mirror.*[17]

Gurney felt that he had demonstrated the efficacy and safety of his invention for all practical purposes. A steam carriage cost about £600 to build, three times the cost of a horse carriage, but it could run faster and farther. Fuel consumption was still on the expensive side but could be shown to be less than the cost of keeping horses. Economies of scale should reduce fuel expense when carriage lines were in full operation. Gurney was therefore ready for commercial operations. Having seen the vehicle tested, Sir Charles Dance eagerly joined the ranks of Gurney's partners. He bought out the shares of Sir James Viney, who had secured exclusive rights to a line from Bristol to Birmingham through Cheltenham and Gloucester, and another from London to Holyhead. Dance decided to start service on those routes. William Hanning renewed his contract for eight carriages to run on the Great West Road, and an agent from Paris obtained a license to operate a carriage in that city.[18] The manufactory was organized to construct the thirty-odd steam carriages that they would eventually need for regular service on the turnpikes.

Into the midst of these preparations came the determined figure of William Crawshay, Jr. (1788–1867). Crawshay owned the Cyfarthfa Ironworks in the Merthyr Tydfil mining region of South Wales. He had virtually grown up at Cyfarthfa, and by February 1830, when he traveled to London, he had built the family firm into the largest ironworks in the world. He was thrice married, father of fourteen children, and master of an incredible castle built, in 1825, over a full acre of ground.[19] Crawshay had read about the run to Melksham and Bath and the successful trials in London. He decided that a Gurney steam locomotive would serve admirably at his coal and iron mines. "With considerable difficulty," he persuaded Gurney to ship a carriage to Cyfarthfa for experiments. Gurney had already turned down similar offers. He thought that his carriage, designed for roads, would not perform as well on rails as locomotives built especially for that purpose, and he did not want to be distracted from his pursuit of efficient turnpike travel, which was difficult enough. Crawshay, however, was adamant, and at length Gurney consented. A locomotive, or drag, was drawn by horses to Cyfarthfa, where it was equipped with cast-iron flanged wheels to run on rails. Crawshay built a short line of railway, similar to that used at his father's works at nearby Hirwain, for experiments. During the test, the drag, weighing three thousand pounds with water and fuel, drew a twenty-five hundred-pound carriage, holding twenty-three tons of pig iron cast especially for the purpose. After repeating this test, Gurney proposed to run the steam drag over to Crawshay's residence along the common road, which had a ten percent incline. To everyone's amazement, the drag—with the flanged railway wheels still on it—not only steamed easily up the road but climbed a sharper rise, covered with broken limestone, to a large yard beside the residence. There, Gurney executed a series of figure eights within an area seventy-six by forty-eight feet, never using more than two-thirds of the space for turning.[20]

The day after this demonstration, the engine was sent up to Hirwain and placed upon Crawshay's father's railway, which was level for three miles. Five carriages of pig iron, and one fitted with seats for almost a hundred people, a total weight of 20.4 tons, were attached to the engine. Crawshay Jr. laid and lit the fire, and five minutes later the engine started off. It covered the three miles in thirty-nine minutes. The engineer then turned the drag around and returned in thirty-two minutes. In later experiments, it was loaded with fuel and water to four thousand pounds and drew nearly thirty-four tons at a speed of two and a half miles per hour. "In all cases," reported Crawshay, "Mr. Gurney's engine has drawn from 15 to 16 ½ times its own weight, upon a level road, and has more than sufficient steam for the purpose."[21] A second engine was secured from London in the autumn of 1830. In November, Crawshay reported that the two engines were drawing thirty to thirty-five times their own weight at three to four miles per hour and, with a load of twenty-five tons, could go as fast as eight miles per hour. During the calendar year 1831, each engine conveyed 42,000 tons of coal, iron ore, and iron, exclusive of the carriages on which they were drawn, in journeys of twenty to thirty tons. They consumed 299 tons of coal, costing £44 17s, and the total operating expense was £112 9s, or less than one-fourth of a penny per ton, per mile. Crawshay was so impressed that he set his mechanics to adapt Gurney's boiler to all his other locomotives. Unfortunately this initiative was not sustained. The Welsh coalfields erupted in strikes and work stoppages in the early 1830s. The Crawshays gave up their operations, and the promising development of a Gurney railway locomotive was neglected.[22]

By February 1831, Gurney had completed three locomotives for turnpike use and laid down the frames for eight more. With the first three, Sir Charles Dance began a regular steam service on the nine-mile road between Gloucester and Cheltenham. If that proved successful, he planned to extend service to Bristol and Birmingham. Sir

Charles first drove a drag and carriage around the streets of Cheltenham for a few days to show its reliability, and distributed public notices promising travel every day except Sunday. Fares were 2s. 6d. inside the attached carriage, 1s. 6d. outside, and 2s. on the steamer itself. A carriage carrying from twelve to thirty people made the run four times a day, "starting punctually from the Commissioners Yard, Cheltenham, at 10 and 2 o'clock and leaving the Spread Eagle, Gloucester at 12 noon and 4." Actually, only one of the drags was in service at any time. The others were used to train the drivers and engineers. The service continued for four months, from 21 February to 22 June, during which time the carriages carried nearly 3,000 passengers, "including many ladies," and traveled nearly 4,000 miles. On several occasions they carried as many as thirty-six passengers each way. They covered the distance in fifty-five minutes on the average. Defective boiler pipes were the principle cause of delays, but there were no accidents or injuries. Sir Charles boasted that steam travel could be achieved at half the cost of horse-drawn coaches, and in fact by May 1831 the competing coach lines had been forced to drop their regular fares from 4s. per head to 1s., to counter the popularity of this new mode of transportation.[23]

A carriage similar to Dance's was shipped to Scotland in March 1831 for John Ward, who had been waiting to exploit the license he had purchased five years earlier. This carriage was equipped with a new braking system devised by Gurney and John Herapath. It made trials between Glasgow, Paisley, and Renfrew, carrying an average of nine passengers per trip at a speed of nine to ten miles per hour. Because it had been damaged during the sea voyage to Scotland, Gurney refused to allow it into active service. He returned to London, instructing his engineer to pack up the machine until he had decided whether to repair it at Glasgow or return it to the manufactory. The engineer, himself leaving for London, removed a number of vital parts to keep others from using the carriage. But Ward and his partners were impatient at the delay. They fashioned replacement parts, repaired the engine without Gurney's knowledge or consent, and took it out to run around the Cavalry Barracks. An explosion resulted. The carriage was destroyed by fire, and two local boys were injured. Adverse publicity was immediate and widespread.[24] A self-styled poet, Thomas Hood, wrote:

> Instead of journeys people now go upon a Gurney
> With steam to do the work by power of attorney
> But with a load it may explode
> And you all may be undone

And find you're going up to heaven
Instead of up to London.[25]

Gurney replied to these reports with a letter to the press, published on 11 June. "I boldly assert," he wrote, "that with a carriage built on my principles and an engineer at all acquainted with it, no such accident as that stated to have happened at Glasgow could possibly occur."[26]

During the summer of 1831, he designed and built a small "one-horse" carriage equipped with a lightweight steam engine. It was intended to carry two or three people or a load of parcels. It looked like a cross between a cart and a cabriolet. It weighed around 500 pounds, and was designed for seven-mile stages, consuming about twenty-five bushels of coke and seventy gallons of water at each stage.[27] If it had been introduced at the end of the century, it would have been recorded as one of the first pioneer automobiles. In 1831, however, it remained a singular curiosity.

Altogether Gurney produced about a dozen complete engines, all designed for passenger use. One or two carriage builders envisaged "trains" of several carriages, running in tandem and carrying goods along the common roads, but few people thought that freight hauling was feasible, and no one tried it in practice.[28] As Gurney's trials at Cyfarthfa showed, steam locomotives could pull much greater loads of freight on rails than on roads. Their advantage over long distances was overwhelming.

The success of the Gurney demonstrations from 1829 through 1831 and the inauguration of Sir Charles Dance's regular steam carriage service appeared to have guaranteed a good future for the new mode of transportation. However, success aroused both opposition and competition. In the next few years, these elements managed to undermine Gurney's whole enterprise and prevent all further development. The competition came from other steam coach builders and from the nascent railway lines. The opposition was mounted by turnpike trustees, operators of stagecoaches, hostlers and grooms, and others with a vested interest in horse-drawn vehicles. Farmers who provided grain for the horse trade and stagecoach inns joined in. The public was also divided about the safety of steam locomotives on common roads. So long as they were in the experimental stage, their detractors could content themselves with ridicule, warnings of danger, or bland assertions of unworkability. But when regular services on turnpike roads were announced in the newspapers, people along the line of travel demanded that their parliamentary representatives take action. At the same time, self-styled engineers with more ambition than mechanical sense caused a number of accidents that brought steam carriages into disrepute. It had taken Gurney seven years to develop his novel boiler and powerful steam jet and combine them into a commercially feasible vehicle. In another seven years, the project was utterly in ruins.

7

Opponents and Rivals

STEAM CARRIAGES DID NOT ENJOY UNQUALIFIED POPULARITY ALONG THE STREETS and roads of Great Britain. The stone-throwing crowds at Melksham, on the trip to Bath, were only the most publicized instance of hostile reaction. Gurney and other steam inventors often encountered stage-coach and omnibus drivers who sideswiped their vehicles, created traffic jams to obstruct their passage, lodged complaints against them with local magistrates, and wrote letters to newspapers, alleging all manner of accidents and damages. These were the outbursts of indi-viduals threatened by economic competition, such as accompany the introduction of any new article of commerce. In time they would have been bypassed and forgotten. But there were other opponents, much better organized, who successfully challenged the use of steam on common roads through parliamentary legislation. These included turnpike trustees, stagecoach proprietors, and agricultural leaders. The House of Commons supported the idea of steam carriages and urged a period of open experimentation, but the House of Lords resisted and subverted that movement, just as it had resisted the call for political reform. By the time the legislative game had been played out, Gurney's venture faced numerous rivals with their own versions of steam locomotion. In the end they were all overcome by the rail-ways, which grew during the years of controversy from a single line to a conglomeration of over 1,500 miles of track, and displayed a scale of organization and finance wholly beyond the vision and ca-pacities of the steam carriage entrepreneurs.

The troubles began at the scene of Gurney's first commercial suc-cess. In the middle of June 1831, Sir Charles Dance's lead engineer, James Stone, had the standard five-foot wheels on one of the steam drags replaced with three-foot wheels for a higher power ratio, and pulled two wagons, containing ten tons of iron bars, at high speed along the level, hard-packed Bristol road out of Gloucester. On the way back, he encouraged twenty-six spectators to climb on for the ride and drove up a long hill with only one wheel engaged to the drive mechanism.[1] This spectacle led a number of local farmers to apply to Dance for licenses, so that they could carry their produce to market cheaply and quickly. However, it infuriated the turnpike trustees, some of whom were connected to the horse coach trade. The gateman at the Cheltenham tollgate warned Stone that the turnpike trustees disliked the new vehicle and would try to obstruct its passage. Failing that, he thought, they "might bring down a tickler from London," which Stone understood to mean an act of Parliament. Sir Charles wrote to the trustees on 20 June, stating his intention to continue the service in spite of their hostility. "I cannot believe," he said, "that the enlightened body of gentlemen who I now have the honour to address will seriously resolve to obstruct such an undertaking, sanctioned as it is by the King and encouraged by the first people in the country." He was sadly mistaken. A few miles out from Cheltenham, there was a slight depression in the road, which the carriage normally traversed with ease. On 21 June, engineer Stone found it overflowing with crushed granite. The rough gravel was commonly used for improving roads, but this was the wrong season for laying it. Moreover, instead of being spread level, it had been piled onto the road fourteen to eighteen inches deep for a considerable distance. Other coaches failed to get through. They were forced to send for fresh or extra horses, and the passengers had to get down and walk past the obstruction. James Stone eased the steam carriage through the granite, went on to Cheltenham, and returned by the same way, undeterred by the obvious attempt at sabotage. The next day more stones were piled up. On 23 June, they took their toll on one of the cranks in the rear axle. The other crank was not broken; the carriage was able to make it back to Gloucester on one cylinder, with a little shoulder help to get over the hilltops.[2] On 25 June, the Gloucester turnpike trustees condemned the steam carriage as "a public nuisance." Their chief surveyor complained to Parliament that the carriage produced "a very great noise" which frightened passing horses, and that hot coals dropped from the ash pit onto the roadway.

Sir Charles was urged to take legal action against the surveyor and trustees of the turnpike but declined, saying he "felt only pity and contempt for those who could resort to such means for preventing a great national undertaking." The axle was quickly repaired (Stone noted that the rest of the carriage and engine assembly appeared in excellent condition, despite four months of service), and Sir Charles fully intended to resume running.[3] Just then he received a note from Gurney, advising him that over fifty bills had been introduced to the House of Commons by the turnpike trusts to place prohibitive tolls on steam locomotives and carriages. Some of these bills had already gone through; others were in progress; and yet others were being prepared by agents. One of them would raise the Cheltenham toll to twelve shillings per round trip, compared to four shillings for horse-drawn coaches.[4]

Gurney had received this information from businessmen in Glasgow who were negotiating with him and John Ward for the patent rights to carriages in Scotland.[5] They were alarmed enough to back out of the negotiations immediately.[6] Why the parliamentary members for Cornwall did not alert him directly is a mystery, since they subsequently gave him strong support. It is true that the new tolls were buried in detailed schedules, attached to each bill, and two or three such bills normally lay on the Speaker's table on any given day. But the sudden arrival of over fifty should have been cause for alarm.

Some turnpikes had always had clauses in their parliamentary grants allowing tolls on vehicles powered by means other than animals, but the occasions for levying such tolls were few and far between. When Gurney began building carriages at the Regent's Park factory, a turnpike gate on the south side was relocated by its owner so as to block his access to the Barracks Yard, where he tested the vehicles, so that a toll could be collected. By 1830, however, the few experimental steam carriages running around London were usually waved through the gates or charged the rate for regular coaches, about one or two shillings. Now some of the trusts were asking six to ten times that much for steam carriages.

Sir Charles Dance's first reaction to Gurney's news was to urge him to prepare as many new licenses as possible, because his farming enthusiasts were still eager to sign up for the right to use the Gurney locomotive. His second reaction was to come to London, where he, Gurney, and William Hanning met with a solicitor and parliamentary agent on 7 July at Cockburn's bank in Whitehall. Over the next few days, they drafted a petition to Parliament, asking that the tolls be repealed, and found a sympathetic M.P. known for progressive economic views, Colonel Robert Torrens, to introduce it. They knew that Parliament would not act without a lengthy investigation, but the petition would legally halt the progress of any bills not yet passed into law. Gurney canvassed other steam carriage inventors, such as Walter Hancock and Nathaniel Ogle, to join him in this action but, in the end, it became "Mr. Gurney's case."[7]

Gurney argued that Parliament, by granting high tariffs on steam carriages, not only deprived him of rightful compensation after he had invested thousands of his own money in the development of his carriage, but deprived the public, as a whole, of the benefits of this revolutionary mode of transportation. The situation was similar to the recent persecution of the first steam packets on the Thames by the London watermen, who had claimed guild privileges and tried to double the rates by measuring the packets in unusual ways. Parliament's intervention had allowed the steamboats to develop into a reliable and popular means of transport, and Gurney petitioned for the same opportunity.[8]

The immediate question was whether the new turnpike tolls were in fact prohibitory. The Commons therefore appointed a select committee "to inquire into the proportion of tolls which ought to be imposed upon coaches and other vehicles propelled by steam or gas, upon turnpike roads, and also to inquire into the rate of toll actually levied upon such coaches and other vehicles under an Act of Parliament now in force." The wider question, whether the new vehicles were practicable, profitable, and safe, led the committee "to inquire generally into the present state and future prospects of land carriage, by means of wheeled vehicles propelled by steam or gas on common roads."

Chaired by Charles Jephson, Esquire, the committee took evidence from the third to the seventeenth of August, adjourned until the following session, and made its report on 12 October 1831. It began by interviewing Gurney about the circumstances of his petition. Sir Charles Dance was traveling on the Continent at this time, but his engineer, James Stone, testified, as did Alexander Gordon, Richard Trevithick, the patent expert John Farey,[9] and several of Gurney's rivals. When the committee realized the magnitude of their assignment, they asked for additional powers and prepared for a long enquiry. Thomas Telford and John Macneill, engineers noted for their experience with road surfaces and draft horses, were asked a series of questions about the effects of heavy locomotives on turnpikes. Colonel Torrens spoke about the economic benefits to be derived from better transportation, and Gurney's old acquaintance, Davies Gilbert, secretary of the Royal Institution and a member of the Commons committee, testified to the advantages of steam over horse power. The committee also reviewed all recent turnpike bills and drew up charts showing equivalencies between horse-drawn and steam-powered vehicles.[10] They looked into the danger of boiler explosions; into reports that the sight of steamers, and the release of steam and smoke, frightened nearby horses; into the reputed noise of Gurney's steam jet; and into the amounts of money invested by Dance and others. Their report, in October, set out the relevant findings:

(1) That carriages can be propelled by steam, on common roads, at an average rate of ten miles per hour.

(2) That, at this rate, they had conveyed upwards of fourteen passengers. [Dance had claimed 36.]

(3) That their weight, including engine, fuel, water, and attendants, may be under three tons.

(4) That they can ascend and descend hills of considerable inclination with felicity and safety.

(5) That they are perfectly safe for passengers.

(6) That they are not (or need not be if properly constructed), nuisances to the public.

(7) That they will become a speedier and cheaper mode of conveyance than carriages drawn by horses.

(8) That, as they admit of greater breadth of tire than other carriages, and as the roads are not acted on so injuriously as by the feet of horses in common draught, such carriages will cause less wear of the roads than coaches drawn by horses.

(9) That the rates of toll have been so imposed on steam carriages, that [they] would prohibit their being used on several lines of road, were the charges permitted to remain.

The report credited Gurney with "the first extensive trial of Steam as an agent in draught on common roads," in 1829. It noted that steam carriages could now maintain speeds of twelve to twenty miles per hour, compared to eight m.p.h. for horse-drawn vehicles, and could run at one-half to two-thirds of the expense. Running on McAdam's new asphalt pavement reduced power needs and fuel expense by another three-fourths, but the operators did not need to wait for paving in order to run successfully. Steam carriage drivers had demonstrated that they could turn sharp corners and control speed coming down hills more effectively than drivers with a team of horses. Both types of vehicles used basic five-foot wheels, but horse-drawn wheels were made as thin as possible to reduce friction, so that they cut into the roadway, as did the horses' hooves. In contrast, steam-driven wheel rims were made from three to six inches wide to increase traction, so they actually packed down the road surface. The committee acknowledged that steam carriages were still expensive and needed further development, and that rivalries among promoters led to unwarranted claims and patent infringements. Some members of the public were, perhaps irrationally, prejudiced against steam, and many others feared the loss of employment connected with horses. But that, they said, was not Parliament's problem to solve. Parliament's problem was that tolls were being levied on at least some steam carriage routes to the detriment of projectors and investors, and this threatened to destroy a potentially revolutionary achievement.[11]

Modern readers may feel nostalgic for the days of horses and carriages, and think the introduction of steam locomotives and automobiles a possible mistake, but the men of 1831 harbored no such sentiments. "The substitution of inanimate for animal power, in draught on common roads, is one of the most important improvements in the means of internal communication ever introduced," they argued. "Its practicability [has] been fully established; its general adoption will take place more or less rapidly, in proportion as the attention of scientific men shall be drawn by public encouragement to further improvement." The committee recommended "that legislative protection should be extended to steam carriages with the least possible delay."[12] A proposed scale of tolls was appended to their report, essentially making steam carriages equal to horse carriages of the same weight and number of wheels, but varying the toll according to the width of the wheels.[13]

The enthusiastic review given steam carriages by the Commons committee in 1831 should be read with some caution. It was standard practice in Parliament that when a case like Gurney's came before either House, the committee it was referred to took evidence on behalf of the petitioners, but did not give opponents much of an audience. The objective was to determine if there was a genuine argument, to gather the evidence, and place it before the House. Members interested in the issue or in the petitioners were appointed to the committee as a matter of course. Members opposed to the petition, or favoring alternative measures, often found a place as well, and played the part of devil's advocate, but the real opposition was expected to emerge in debates on the second reading of a bill. Thus, on 12 October, the select committee on steam power presented an overwhelmingly favorable report to the Commons, and Mr. Jephson immediately brought in a bill to implement the proposed toll regulations.[14] Members whose constituents were connected with the horse trade, as well as grain-growing agriculturalists, who stood to lose a lucrative feed market, spoke out against the bill, warning of economic distress as well as danger to everyone else on the roads. There was indeed a sizable population engaged in business with horses: not just coachmen and innkeepers, but hostlers who provided post horses for short rides, harness and carriage makers, stable boys, grooms, and so on. Gurney estimated that a thousand horses were kept at Hounslow alone for stagecoach and riding use, and another thousand along the five-mile Paddington Road in the metropolis.[15] But the ubiquity of horses for hire did not always translate into political power. Everyone in Parliament was experienced with them and knew that they could be wearisome, inconvenient, and dangerous. The turnpike trusts were also suspect: many of them were scandalously mismanaged, and gatekeepers often insolent, or arbitrary in their charges.[16] Many of the Commons belonged to one or more trusts, but they were not active agents, and usually made little or no profit from the investment. So the opposition that might have been mounted to Gurney's petition did not materialize. The bill passed at the end of October and was sent up to the House of Lords.

Among the Lords, the agricultural interest was much stronger, and the general attitude toward mechanical inventions and commercial novelties far more conservative, than in the Commons.[17] The Lords had also just rejected the second bill for Parliamentary Reform, sent up by a Commons elected almost solely on that issue. Distracted by riots and rumblings across the country and threats from the popular press, the Speaker moved slowly upon the turnpike toll regulation bill, and when it was finally given its first reading, a small group of peers decided that they must have their own select committee investigation. Witnesses were once more called and challenged, objections repeated in the face of clear evidence to the contrary, hypothetical hazards put forward for serious discussion. The select committee met infrequently. By the time it completed its work, "the session was too near its close to allow of the Bill being passed."[18]

Gurney had every hope that a similar bill would be taken up in the following session. But Parliament was now in the full throes of the great Reform Bill crisis. Old seats were being lost (especially in Cornwall, which had more pocket boroughs and fewer voters per constituency than any other county in Britain), new seats added, new candidates arriving at Westminster with radical agendas. Gurney's friend, Sir George Cayley, a Yorkshire Reform liberal, was returned, along with his nephew, Edward Stillingfleet Cayley (1802–1862), and a new supporter from East Cornwall, Sir William Molesworth. But being new to the House, they were unable to be of much help at this time. The Commons had passed its bill; the Lords had declined; and it was up to the latter to revive the issue.

In the meantime Gurney's business fell apart. So many turnpike toll bills had already passed through Commons that Sir Charles Dance decided that further operations were futile until the toll regulation bill sponsored by Charles Jephson could restore a modicum of commercial stability. Despite his promise not to let opponents bully him off the Cheltenham Road, therefore, Dance shut down his daily service. In this there was, as Gurney later acknowledged, a mixture of realism and panic. The initial support shown by the Commons, in its report on Gurney's petition, had cheered investors, who assumed that Jephson's bill would go through quickly, so Gurney had many new requests for licenses at that time. The subsequent delays caused a negative reaction and spread an impression among the public that Parliament, having studied the matter at length, would permit tolls to be imposed everywhere. In fact, there were still many roads open to steam carriages, and many routes where tolls were moderate enough that a well-run operation could generate a profit. Steam carriages were not subject to the statutory regulations imposed on stage-coaches, and the Hackney Coach Act, which applied to the London metropolitan area, specifically exempted steam vehicles from licensing requirements.[19] Key sections of main turnpikes, however, had become prohibitively expensive. Furthermore, the original steam carriage investors were nervous about the length of time it was taking Gurney to produce serviceable vehicles. Sir Charles Dance, the most visible patentee, had never been an easy partner to deal with: "He is no engineer," Gurney said later, "and he is constantly changing his mind."[20] William Hanning, the principle financial backer of the enterprise, had already grown cautious and was refusing requests for new capital advances. Three of his eight carriages were being tested, and drivers trained, on the Finchley Road in London, but he was tired of footing the bill for every experiment and feared that in spite of the legal protection offered by the patent, he would be drawn into an unlimited liability. When the Lords refused to pass the toll regulation bill, Hanning also pulled out.

Another investor, businessman William Bulnois, withdrew soon afterward. Bulnois had contracted for three carriages in 1830, after participating in the ride to Melksham and Bath. He had given a deposit of £600 on condition that his carriages be delivered after Dance's and Hanning's had proved themselves in operation. John Ward had already queered his chances by blowing up the first engine Gurney shipped to Glasgow. The negotiations for selling his Scottish patent now collapsed, and he also gave up an intended route from Birmingham to Edinburgh.[21]

Gurney tried to rally his cause in February 1832 by publishing a pamphlet describing the progress of his steam carriage. He gave details of the successful runs on the Cheltenham Road, accused the trustees of that turnpike of malicious obstruction, and quoted liberally from the 1831 report of the Commons committee. He included a drawing of the steam drag as it appeared at that time—a modest vehicle, shorter than the carriage it drew, with the horizontal cylinders and drive shafts partially obscured by the wheels and frame. It was a startling contrast to the ponderous sixteen-passenger juggernaut depicted on broadsheets in 1828 and 1829. "Having now placed the plain facts connected with the subject before the public, and showing that the great problem of propelling carriages by steam on the common roads has been solved," he concluded, "I shall now retire to other pursuits until the moral and political difficulties previously stated are so far removed as to show that further individual exertion may be useful."[22] Alexander Gordon followed up this pamphlet with a series of lectures on the steam carriage at the Mechanics' Institute in October 1832, which drew huge audiences. He then published the lectures in his *Treatise on Locomotion,* which ran through several editions.

The failure of his commercial contracts left Gurney without resources. As nearly as one can calculate from the scattered evidence of his Albany Street manufactory, he had obtained about £18,000 of investment capital from the five patentees and several licensees since 1825, mostly from Hanning, Dance, and Ward, and he had sold three carriages to Dance for £1,800. His own contribution in the form of materials, factory fittings, wages, rent, and taxes, amounted to something over £18,000. The factory was large, and in the years 1830–31, annual expenses were running to £16,000–17,000, half of which were wages. It was quite obvious that he could not continue without substantial backing.[23] Reluctantly he gave orders to his foreman, David Dady, to close up the shop, disassemble the carriages, and sell off all the engines, parts, and manufacturing equipment at auction. These had cost about £4,800, but sold for only £3,000. A pair of engines on frames, worth at least £60, went for only £11. The patent tubular boilers were purchased for use in stationary engines or for steamboats.[24]

It is hard to calculate what Gurney might have earned from his steam carriages had he been allowed to manufacture and license them on the scale established in 1831. Some of his contracts set royalties according to the capacity of the carriage boiler, others according to mileage. Advance payments, cash premiums, and capital investments were mixed together in his evidence before Parliament, and he produced no account books to verify claims of expenses. Shares in the original five-member patent totalled £30,000, but not all of that was paid in. The carriages were selling for as much as £600 when complete, but many were intended for lease. Each of the eight carriages intended for William Hanning was priced at £200 but was expected to bring in £700 annually. If that amount held for Sir Charles Dance's three carriages and those intended for Bulnois and other lessees, the total would reach about £14,000. John Ward had contracted for carriages and mileage worth £32,000 on the London-

Liverpool-Holyhead route in 1831, and promised another £15,000 for the Scottish patent rights. Gurney himself reckoned that he had lost £6,000 per annum from 1831 through 1836, but Ward estimated that he could have made as much as £27,000 per year from licenses and mileage on existing contracts. David Beasley's tabulation of Gurney's losses also includes £150,000 for "fair expected mileage duty on the remaining great roads" not yet contracted.[25] Setting these figures against an annual wage, rent, and materials expense of £16,000 for the Albany Street factory, one can clearly see that Gurney stood to make a fortune. Of course, during the years he had dedicated to the steam carriage, he had abandoned his medical practice and chemistry lectures, which he claimed had been bringing in £1,400 annually before 1825.

Gurney's retirement from business and active experiments left the field open to a number of rivals, all of whom benefited from his imaginative development of boilers, cylinders, steam jets, horizontal pistons, and control devices. Very few of them ever ran carriages for hire on a regular route, but the official support shown by the House of Commons, and the prospect that Gurney's original patent would run out in 1836, encouraged them to continue their experimental competition and to publicize their successes. Some of them were serious inventors in their own right. Up to this point, I have narrated the progress of Gurney's invention as if he acted virtually alone, and pioneered all the principles and mechanisms associated with later versions of the steam carriage. But like the field of chemistry, steam locomotion was a common enthusiasm in the 1820s, and as suggested previously, skilled workmen and fellow inventors shared any number of projects, ideas, and bits of information. David Gordon had already built and abandoned several steam carriage models by the time Gurney constructed his first. Others were made by W. H. James, Julius Griffith, and John Seaward. As they emulated Gurney by testing each new development on the public roads, in full view of visiting mechanics and newspaper reporters, the number of enthusiasts mounted quickly. A steam carriage, after all, was basically a combination of existing machines. Carriages were commonplace, the hardware and mechanics for adapting them to steam power were readily available, and long sections of specially built railway were not required in order to run experiments. Only the boilers were new enough to patent. A lightweight boiler that could withstand the jolts of roadway travel took a good deal of work to design, but the basic principles had been established, and the materials and techniques of construction were not hard to come by. Gurney alleged in 1831 that twenty to forty other vehicles were being built by various individuals as a direct result of his famous trip to Bath. This may have been an exaggeration at the time, but Alexander Gordon described eight or nine partnerships in the second (1836) edition of his *Treatise on Locomotion* and said that about twenty other inventors, "some hopeful, others hopeless," were building steam vehicles.

Inventors, though often secretive by necessity and idiosyncratic by nature, can seldom develop their ideas in isolation. By the very specialty of their interests, the steam enthusiasts were bound to utilize the same, or related, iron foundries, mechanics, and patent draftsmen, and talk to the same journalists. They had little theory to guide them. Trial, error, and adaptation were their only means of development. Like the community of science lecturers Gurney had joined upon his arrival in London, the inventors borrowed, stole, adapted, and improved each others' ideas and equipment. Gurney was no exception. He shared his chief mechanic, James Stone, with his friend and co-inventor, Sir George Cayley, and borrowed liberally from Cayley's designs for hot-air engines. The "pilot" steering wheel assembly on his first carriage and the idea for his horizontal cylinders and crank axle may have been appropriated from a contemporary named Andrews.[26] Gurney was also familiar with men who were developing engines for steamboats. He installed experimental versions of his steam jet in local river craft as early as 1824, and around 1826 his brother Samuel Gurney put one on a steam packet carrying passengers on the Thames River between London Bridge and Richmond. Another acquaintance, William Keene, adapted it for a steamboat that plied the strong currents of the Garonne in France. During the same period, the brothers John and Samuel Seaward, who ran an ironworks at Millwall, began building marine engines, introducing a number of features Gurney had invented or adapted for his carriages: tubular boilers, horizontal direct-action drive mechanisms, a double-acting cylinder, and a steam jet. They also used crank drives that could be detached from the side paddle wheels when the boat was under sail or needed to be turned, much as Gurney had done with his early carriage models. It is impossible, and perhaps unnecessary, to show how closely the Seawards were associated with Gurney. Their tubular boiler could have been one of those salvaged from Gurney's factory after it shut down, but they could equally well have built their own. John Seaward had studied chemistry and mechanical engineering with Trevithick in Wales as a young man, and his brother Samuel had apprenticed with Maudslay and Field, one of the premier ironworks in London, who fashioned special parts for experimental carriages.[27] Obviously the possibilities for exchanging ideas and skills among railway, steam carriage, and steamboat engineers around London were plentiful.

The closest rival in terms of inventive genius and commercial success was Walter Hancock (1799–1852), a shy but persistent watchmaker, who turned to steam carriage design in 1824 after reading about Julius Griffith's vehicle. With the assistance of his brother, an experienced toolmaker, he patented in 1827 a unique boiler incorporating vertical water chambers. The design and construction of this boiler obviated some of the problems Gurney had faced. Because it used rectangular chambers instead of tubes, the welds were less likely to burst, and the interior dimensions were such as to allow steam to generate without an admixture of water. Used steam from the cylinders was pumped back into the firebox rather than up the chimney, thus saving water and reducing noise to a whisper (Hancock admired the power and economy of the steam jet but considered it too noisy for city use). John Farey, who did the drawings and specifications for both Gurney and Hancock, considered Hancock's boiler better than any other proposed or tried.[28] On the other hand, Dionysius Lardner, another expert on mechanical inventions, said that Hancock's boiler had less power than Gurney's and burnt through the grating bars after two or three trips.

Hancock built nine practical vehicles between 1829 and 1836. His first was a small three-wheeled vehicle, which traveled many miles about London. He then produced a series of four-wheeled carriages carrying eleven to fourteen passengers each. Like Gurney, he used a two-cylinder engine, placed the boiler and drive mechanism in the rear, and equipped the carriage with five-foot ironclad wheels. But unlike Gurney, he built the steamer as a single unit rather than as a separate drag. Alexander Gordon considered it "a composite of all the best ideas," and his son Lewis Gordon, who frequently rode on it, recalled that Hancock "exhibited perfect control over his engine, in guiding, turning, stopping, and backing."[29] Hancock began regular passenger service between Stratford and London in February 1831, thus anticipating Dance's service by a few days, and attained speeds of up to fifteen miles per hour for extended periods. In fact, he drove a steam carriage to Parliament to present his petition against turnpike tolls in July 1831. Larger, omnibus-type carriages followed in 1832 and 1833. These failed to compete successfully with the new horse-drawn omnibuses on London's main streets, but Hancock operated a more elegant coach between the Bank of England and Paddington, along the City Road, from August to November 1834, carrying 4,000 passengers. He then drove a large, rough-riding, noisy charabanc, or autobus, with seats for twenty-two passengers, for twenty weeks along the same route in 1836, and kept it in service elsewhere for another four years. Like Gurney, Hancock was abused and harassed by horse coach drivers and forced off the City Road by magistrates, who refused him the necessary licenses to operate legally. He also found his relations with business partners "rather disagreeably chequered." The manager of the ironworks where he built his carriages damaged one of them intentionally so that he could keep it "under repair" while constructing his own version. Moreover, Hancock designed a very light, two-seater steam phaeton for his own use, just as Gurney had. It was the most successful of his steamers, and the two inventors might have popularized this kind of small, private vehicle had not the continued imposition of heavy tolls, and the falling off of financial support, forced them to give up building steam vehicles. Hancock devoted fifteen years and £12,000 of his own money to the cause, but finally quit.[30]

W. H. James of Holborn, "a gentleman of superior mechanical talents," had built a tubular boiler in 1823 and his first carriage in 1824. After running out of money, he found a wealthy partner, Sir James Anderson of Ireland, "the Steam Knight of Buttevant Castle," to help him build several carriages with boilers and other design features similar to Gurney's. The two experimented with twin steam chambers, chain steering, and a primitive clutch for changing gears. They built a tractor with four-wheel drive and a universal coupling on the drive shaft. Their carriages of 1828 and 1832 embodied many excellent ideas, but they spent all their money experimenting and never got the basic boilers and pipes to work reliably. W. H. James went off to America in hopes of introducing steam carriages to the New World. Anderson tried again in 1838–40 and was still experimenting with carriages twenty years later.[31]

The Heaton brothers of Birmingham built several complicated but efficient steam carriages between 1830 and 1833. John Farey, their consultant on patent drawings and specifications, said that the Heatons' boiler was one of the best in the business, but they failed to attain the average speed of ten miles per hour stipulated by their financial backer.[32] A more successful trial was made by John Scott Russell, professor of mechanical philosophy at Edinburgh, who patented boilers and engines for carriages in 1833, and in the following year put six of them into service on the seven-mile road between Glasgow and Paisley. Russell's carriages were designed as single units, like Gurney's earlier types, with the boiler and engine at the rear. They ran for many months, becoming very popular with travelers, but faced the inevitable opposition from horse coach proprietors. Heaps of stones were piled on the road, as at Cheltenham; a wheel broke going over them, and the boiler burst in the ensuing crash, killing five passengers. The carriages were then forbidden to travel in Scotland, although two of them subsequently made runs around London.[33]

Another prominent inventor was Nathaniel Ogle, a Royal Navy captain with a penchant for speed. With his foreman, William A. Summers, he built a three-wheeled, three-ton carriage, whose boiler was a cross between Gurney's and Hancock's. Ogle claimed to have gone thirty-five miles per hour on a trip from London to Southhampton and twenty-four m.p.h. loaded with "whole families of ladies" at other times. Summers corroborated this testimony and added that the engines had worked ten hours a day, four days a week, for the past twelve months. When Ogle was interviewed by the Select Committee of Commons in August 1831, he was setting up a factory in Whitechapel to produce a four-wheeled version and said that he had many orders for carriages in hand. He dismissed the problem of turnpike tolls, stating that most turnpike operators did not charge him, while to others he just tossed a few coins as he passed the gate.[34] In 1834 he formed a company with 4,000 shares of stock, but only one subscriber ever paid his money. Ogle was left with £3,800 in expenses from that venture and claimed to have spent £47,000 in all before he gave up.[35]

Credit for the most picturesque vehicle should be given to Dr. Church of Birmingham, who patented novel designs for carriage frames, tubular boilers, and wheels with elastic shock-absorbing rims between 1832 and 1835. In the latter year, he formed a steam carriage company with a sizable capital and produced a large, elaborately decorated vehicle that looked like the Brighton Pavilion on wheels. In a carefully staged public trial, Dr. Church carried forty passengers, but he was unable to maintain a speed of fifteen to twenty miles per hour without breaking down, and finally abandoned the enterprise.[36]

The competitors most discouraging to Gurney were men who, having worked in his Regent's Park factory, incorporated many of his ideas into carriages of their own manufacture after he was forced out of business. Francis Maceroni, John Squire, and Sir Charles Dance were three of these. Colonel Francis Maceroni (b. 1788), the son of an Italian merchant, had served the King of Naples during the Napoleonic wars and fought with the Spanish insurgents in 1822–23, but was living in Manchester when he became interested in Gurney's work in 1825. An opportunist with vague sources of income, he attached himself to Gurney's Regent's Park workshop on the recommendation of Sir Anthony Carlisle, ostensibly to work on his own inventions. He stayed for six months and became involved enough in Gurney's work—he signed one of the early carriage contracts as witness—that he persuaded several friends to invest in the enterprise. "At last I found that the system of tubular boilers was totally errone-ous," he later testified, "and after I left Mr. Gurney, we had some little difference." After a sojourn in Constantinople, helping the Turks fight the Russians, he returned to London in the late summer of 1831 to join forces with Gurney's former carpenter, John Squire. By 1833 the partners had developed a new version of the tubular boiler and lo-cated it at the rear of the carriage, with horizontal pistons mounted underneath, very much like Gurney's.[37] It was a simple, compact vehicle that carried twelve to fourteen passengers, developed thirty horsepower at fourteen miles per hour without a steam jet, and climbed hills easily. Maceroni was a great publicist. He invited jour-nalists to visit his workshop, and in October 1833, he took a group of them for a ride. Then, he advertised in the newspapers that anyone who showed up at 3 P.M. daily could take passage with him and receive dinner into the bargain. The carriage ran for hire for some weeks between Paddington and Edgware without serious mechanical troubles. Maceroni claimed that he never had difficulty with turnpike tolls and thought the charges levied on the Cheltenham Road were "a perfect fiction of Mr. Gurney and his friends." In 1834, buoyed by a new toll relief bill passed by the Commons, he built a new, larger carriage. But failure in the House of Lords was followed by failure of the partnership, and he fell into financial difficulties. To fulfill the terms of Belgian and French patents he had negotiated earlier, he shipped his two remaining carriages to Brussels and Paris in the care of a fellow Italian speculator named Colonel d'Asda. D'Asda drove the carriages around, to great publicity, for several months, but then sold them and disappeared with the money. Maceroni pub-lished a book on road steam power in 1835 and tried raising new capital, but another railway investment panic in 1837 doomed his chances. In 1841 the disclosure of serious business mismanagement ended with the seizure of all his assets.[38]

Sir Charles Dance, after pulling his carriages off the Cheltenham turnpike, took them to be repaired and refitted at the London iron-works of Maudslay and Field, where his chief engineer and driver, Thomas Bailey, had found employment.[39] The firm "improved" the boiler in several respects, and Dance obtained a patent on it in February 1833. In September a rebuilt drag with the new boiler, pull-ing an omnibus, made a much-publicized run from London to Brigh-ton and back with fifteen passengers. Dance then drove daily, for two weeks, from Wellington Street to Greenwich to demonstrate the locomotive's safety and utility, but did not set up a regular service.[40]

It was bad enough that some men borrowed Gurney's patented designs without credit or compensation, but it was worse when they incorporated them into inferior vehicles. "It is much to be regretted," wrote Alexander Gordon in 1836, "that there are many builders engaged in constructing steam-carriages who have disregarded the experience furnished by Mr. Gurney. We could adduce many instances wherein excellent engine-builders have altogether failed in making a steam-carriage; and other instances wherein, after a great expenditure of money and time, they could not compete with that gentleman."[41] Unfortunately for the reputation of steam carriages, the number of failures and accidents mounted as quickly as the number of inventors and promoters. One of Walter Hancock's engineers burst his carriage's boiler while trying to gain speed and died, not of burns, but of a paralytic stroke. Colonel Maceroni's carriage tore the corner off a house in London. A society lady's coach was upset by another steamer. Two people were killed by a boiler explosion in Manchester. Russell's carriage blew up in Scotland, killing four. A boy died, and two men were injured, at the first trial of a new carriage in London. A twelve-ton amphibious steam locomotive, built by a naval officer at Hammersmith, exploded in the street. And so on. Gurney was appalled. "A great number of caricatures of steam carriages have certainly taken place," he admitted in 1836; "a great many undigested experiments have been made on the public roads, which have tended much to prejudice the public mind against the subject." The worst of it was that since his name had been so widely associated with steam locomotion in the mind of the public, "I, unfortunately, have the credit of the evil arising from many of the carriages which now appear."[42]

Gurney, like Walter Hancock, had suffered the fate of countless inventors whose mechanical ingenuity surpassed their commercial skills. Being first in the field, they had to invest much of their own capital, search for reliable partners, contend with archaic patent laws and irregular legal restrictions, and fight off competitors. They discovered the principle that the most vulnerable period for a small business is in the first wave of success. That is when expansion demands more capital than anticipated; when the customized, experimental methods of building a prototype must give way to regular production by hired workmen; and when investors and customers expect the results optimistically projected at the start of the venture. Having built the steam carriages and driven them in so many situations, Gurney was too adept at operating them, too responsive to their every whim, to appreciate how unreliable they remained for everyday scheduled service in the hands of the average trained mechanic.

As a science lecturer, Gurney had assumed that a public demonstration of the principle of steam locomotion would attract practical engineers to the project. When that did not happen, he assumed that the building and operation of a reliable vehicle would convince everyone of the advantages of steam travel, regardless of its challenge to the prevailing customs and commercial economy associated with horse-drawn carriages. Thus he disregarded his own warning, issued in his lectures, about the difficulties of giving up a practice, such as fireplace heating, with which everyone was associated in some way, and for which many had deep-rooted sentiments. Preoccupied with the mechanical perfection of his invention, he could not think creatively about the social, political, commercial, and technological contexts in which it would have to operate.

8

Mr. Gurney's Case

Dᴇsᴘɪᴛᴇ ᴛʜᴇ ꜰᴀɪʟᴜʀᴇ ᴏꜰ ʜɪs ᴍᴀɴᴜꜰᴀᴄᴛᴜʀɪɴɢ ᴠᴇɴᴛᴜʀᴇ ᴀɴᴅ ᴛʜᴇ ᴘʀᴏʟɪꜰᴇʀᴀᴛɪᴏɴ of competitors, Gurney was soon encouraged to renew his petition to Parliament for repealing the tolls levied on steam carriages. His friend and supporter Alexander Gordon had organized, in April 1833, a "Society for Promoting the Application of Steam to General Transport and Agricultural Purposes," which enrolled twenty-eight members of Parliament and a dozen other distinguished gentlemen. The society aimed to encourage steam tractors and farm machinery as well as carriages, making it more acceptable to the agricultural interests.[1] A kindred organization, called the National Institution of Locomotion, financed through the London banking firm of Coutts & Co., formed chapters throughout England, Scotland, and Wales to promote the mechanization of agriculture.[2] Also in 1833, a group of experienced road engineers, headed by the seventy-eight-year-old Thomas Telford, president of the Institution of Civil Engineers, and John Rickman, Commissioner for Highland Roads and Bridges, set up a professional trial to determine whether a steam carriage could maintain speed on a long run. On 1 November 1833, the group drove one of Sir Charles Dance's carriages along the mail-coach route from London to Holyhead by way of Birmingham and Liverpool, a distance of 216 miles. As often happened, one of the boiler tubes burst, and it became evident that Dance's engine was too small for the job. Nevertheless, it averaged seven miles per hour. The engineers concluded that "with a well-constructed engine of greater power, a steam-carriage conveyance between London and Birmingham, at a velocity *unattainable by horses,* and limited only by safety, might be maintained."[3] Telford, Sir Henry Parnell, and Mr. A. M. Robertson of Her Majesty's Commissioners of Woods and Forests then attempted to form a company, capitalized at £350,000, to radically improve the road surface, allowing increased speeds with less fuel consumption, and to construct the necessary system of fuel and water depots. Telford and Robertson both died, but the remaining engineers recruited new investors to try again.[4] By 1835 the firm of Maudslay and Field had produced three new steam vehicles for them.[5]

Despite the presence of these new organizations and the dozen or so competitors whose success also depended upon parliamentary action, Gurney found no one willing to assist his appeal to government except his friends in the House of Commons. There, he was supported by his fellow inventor, Sir George Cayley, and by the new member from East Cornwall, Sir William Molesworth.[6] Sir William, making his maiden speech at the age of twenty-four, introduced Gurney's petition on 29 April 1834. The document rehearsed the efforts he had made to bring the steam carriage to perfection and the difficulty and expense of extensive experiments and road trials. It then stated that the prohibitory turnpike toll acts passed by Parliament during and since 1831 had compelled him to retire "without being able to obtain any personal compensation or even remuneration from his patent, after having expended on it the whole of his property and the best years of his life." Since the term of his original patent was now nearly expired, Gurney prayed that the House take his hardship into consideration, and as recommended by the Select Committee of 1831, repeal the legislation granting such high tolls upon steam vehicles.

Sir William supported the petition by pointing out that Gurney had been obliged to take out patents before making any trials of his inventions, because they would have to be displayed on the public streets from the beginning and would thus be open to the observation of one and all. He had calculated that four or five years would be spent in developing a reliable machine, and this had in fact been the case; but no sooner did his steam carriage start performing regularly on the roads than Parliament allowed prohibitory tolls to be enacted. Thus the public stood to reap the benefits of his industry and genius, while Gurney himself would be left a ruined man. Sir William compared Gurney to James Watt and Edmund Cartwright, each of whom had been given an extension of his patent and a reward by Parliament. The agricultural interests believed, he said, that they could prevent the loss of their market for horse feed by placing obstacles in the way of steamers, but "one may confidently predict that steam-carriages will run upon the roads of this kingdom when the names of those individuals will entirely be forgotten, whose ignorance and whose petty interests have induced them to oppose this important application of elementary power."

Sir George Cayley also spoke to the agricultural opponents. Though a million horses may no longer be needed (and good riddance!), he said, it would take time to replace them with steam. In the meantime, population growth was such that the grain would soon be consumed by eight million people, who would otherwise go hungry. Another member, Charles Buller, argued for national pride: "It has been too often charged against us as a national stigma that we suffer men of talent and science, whatever service they may have rendered to the community by their inventions and discoveries, to lie neglected and indigent; and that, in too many instances, we have failed to discover, or at least acknowledge, a man's worth till he is dead. . . . We are a 'reformed' Parliament; and I trust the House will, in the case of Mr. Gurney, evince that they are really a reformed House. . . ." Buller noted that the petition did not ask for compensation, though Gurney was well entitled to it. "His modest and reasonable request is simply that the restrictions thus placed upon his honest and beneficial industry be removed. When he has fully persuaded the public of the peculiar and all-important advantages of his invention, then it will be for this House to consider, whether they are not, in justice, bound to give a suitable reward to the man who has done and sacrificed so much in his prosecution of a great national object."[7] After others spoke on Gurney's behalf, his petition was laid upon the table to await investigation by a select committee.

The parliamentary session of 1833–34 was the first full session after the elections decreed by the Reform Act of 1832. One hundred forty-two borough seats had been redistributed, and new members elected from all over England and Wales. Although the Whigs, a majority for the first time in decades, could be counted upon to support industry and innovation, most members were ignorant of the evidence and arguments that had been given on behalf of steam carriages in 1831. They had also to contend with new legislation for factory regulation, the abolition of slavery in the West Indies, and Edwin Chadwick's proposed revision of the Poor Law. The Select Committee on "Mr. Gurney's Case" did not, therefore, act quickly. When it finally convened, with Sir William Molesworth in the chair and other friends in attendance,[8] it took evidence not only from Gurney but from all the inventors and projectors who had entered the field since Gurney's retirement. Because his patent rights and lost earnings were now at issue, they also looked into all of his contracts and interviewed those who had invested in his carriages. Gurney had to describe, once again, the whole development of his steam carriage, and calculate from the various contracts how much he might have gained had he stayed in business. He spent half a morning explaining the difference between "horse-power" as applied to the variable and uncertain power of a horse, and "horse-power" as applied to tireless steam engines. Asked about numerous reports of accidents and failures, he wearily reminded the committee that he had been out of business since 1831 and could not be held responsible for other men's mistakes. The safety and reliability of steam locomotion had been demonstrated many times, he said. It could be ensured simply by regulating the size and construction of boilers and by requiring periodic pressure tests.[9]

The Select Committee ran out of time before finishing its work. On 17 July they reported the evidence taken so far and recommended resuming the enquiry early next session. This was done, and despite two changes of ministry in the ensuing months, the committee issued a final report on 10 July 1835. They urged the immediate repeal of exorbitant turnpike tolls on steam vehicles (150 new bills had passed since 1831) and the adoption of a new scale, based on the weight of steamers and the width of their wheels. Boilers would be tested and carriages licensed according to the regulations Gurney had suggested. The committee recognized Gurney's claim to the first successful application of steam on common roads. In view of the delays imposed by Parliament, they recommended granting a fourteen-year extension of his patent on the original boiler and engine arrangements constructed in 1825. However, they added, considering the great national importance and value of the steam carriage, the conditions of company law, and the interests of competitors who expected the end of the patent, it would be more in the public interest for the government to buy out Gurney's patent rights. They therefore recommended that the Treasury compensate him for three years' lost revenue, which was calculated at a minimum of £16,000.[10]

A bill to regulate the turnpike tolls was duly introduced in the autumn of 1835 and passed by the House of Commons.[11] Investors immediately began applying for licenses, and a new rush of enthusiasm for steam carriages ensued. Gurney actually contracted to build carriages for a company to run omnibuses between Devonport, Plymouth, and Exeter, the venture being reported in the *West Briton* newspaper in February and April.[12]

But again the House of Lords refused to cooperate. At first the peers seemed favorable, or at least indifferent, to the bill. The populist Whig, Earl Radnor, known for his "active support of all measures bearing on social amelioration,"[13] persuaded his peers to reduce the quorum for the Select Committee so that it could expedite its report. But in the committee sessions, the railway interests' most prominent supporter, Lord Wharncliffe, managed to focus the inquiry almost entirely on explosions, damages to passing carriages or nearby structures, fires from chimney sparks and ash pans, the noise of the steam jet, and traffic accidents attributable to steam vehicles.[14] Three well-known railway engineers—William Cubitt, Robert Stephenson, and John Braithwaite—were encouraged to ventilate their animosity towards road steamers. Cubitt had joined the company of engineers seeking to capitalize a long-distance route, after Thomas Telford's abortive attempt of 1833, but after careful reckoning, he had concluded that the cost of establishing fuel and water stations over a long-distance route was prohibitive. Moreover, he said, the carriages had to be built very tight and strong to withstand the wear and tear of road travel. A fully capitalized company would need upwards of one hundred carriages to maintain service, and they required experienced, highly skilled driver-mechanics. So Cubitt concluded that steam carriage lines were, at that stage of development, uneconomical.[15] Robert Stephenson, of course, could be counted upon to disparage any alternative to his railway locomotives, but his testimony revealed a shocking ignorance of how steam carriages really worked. Despite being refuted by Gurney and his associates, the engineers' warnings and critics' complaints were all reported to the House, with a recommendation to deny the bill. The Lords' committee said that steam carriages remained unduly expensive to operate and terrifying to horses and other road traffic. Excessive turnpike tolls were probably not the best way to legislate on the subject, they added, but to rescind them now "would only give rise to wild speculations, ruinous to those engaging in them, and to experiments dangerous to the public."[16] Lord Radnor and other radical peers who favored steam carriages could not prevail against the railway-landowner alliance represented by Lord Wharncliffe, and the bill was lost.

By the time the House of Lords finally quashed their hopes for a financial recovery, Gurney and the other steam-carriage proprietors had lost the head start they had enjoyed over their chief competition, the railways. The opening of the Liverpool and Manchester Railway in September 1830 is generally considered the inaugural event of the great railway age that dominated Queen Victoria's early reign. But as with other circumstances in Gurney's career, the context and timing of that event were more significant than its public celebration. In the first place, the Liverpool and Manchester engineers could not have carried goods and passengers in sufficient volume to make the railway pay without improvements to their steam engines drawn directly and indirectly from Gurney's innovations. In the second place, the railway was an entirely new concept in business organization, operating on a scale of planning, capital, and labor far beyond the capacity and vision of those who built steam carriages for road travel. And because it was so new, there were fewer legislative restrictions that competitors could employ against it. The irony was that the two modes of transport developed quite independently. Almost no one realized that they could function in a complementary way until it was too late.

Gurney may be said to have contributed three important ideas to steam locomotion: the steam jet, or "blast," which produced such a tremendous draft through the firebox and chimney; the tubular boiler, which was light enough, safe, and effective for use on road vehicles; and horizontal cylinders, with drive rods mounted within or under the framework. The steam jet, patented in 1825 after secret development in his workshop, quickly became known to other engineers. Although Gurney did not use it on some of his early carriages because of its noise, he did employ it on later steam drags and, of course, on vehicles tested in the Regent Street neighborhood. Railway engineers, including George and Robert Stephenson and Timothy Hackworth, inspected the jet and understood its principle, because it was basically an improvement on Trevithick's steam exhaust arrangement.[17] George Stephenson thought it irrelevant to his needs at first, and ignored it.[18] Hackworth, chief engineer of the Stockton and Darlington railway, did not. He built one version of the steam jet into his engine, *Royal George,* in October 1827, and another into the *Sanspareil* in 1829. During the first round of trials at the famous Rainhill competition on 6 October 1829 (a publicity stunt to counter the enthusiasm generated by Gurney's trip to Bath in July), the *Sanspareil* actually outperformed Robert Stephenson's *Rocket.* Hackworth later wrote that Stephenson visited his workshop that evening to inspect the *Sanspareil,* and that at the trials next day, the *Rocket* was equipped with a steam jet of its own. It doubled its previous speed. Gurney's partisans later claimed that the steam jet increased locomotive power by fifty percent, but the most recent account gives a figure of fifteen to twenty percent. At any rate, there is no doubt that the jet was a critical development in early rail technology.[19] It was subsequently used on almost all steam locomotives, just as it was used on every steamship commissioned by the British Navy. In his evidence before Parliament in 1831, patent engineer John Farey confirmed that the steam jet had originated with Gurney. Many years later, in 1857, Samuel Smiles attributed the invention of the steam jet to his hero, George Stephenson. Gurney wrote a detailed rebuttal, citing not only his patent of 1825 and the early parliamentary evidence but the testimony of William Keene, given to a select committee in 1849, that he had observed the steam jet in operation at Gurney's workshop as early as 1826.[20] Smiles modified his claim in later editions of his biography of Stephenson.

Between Trevithick and Vivian's first locomotive of 1802 and Stephenson's *Planet* of 1830, almost all steam railway engines had vertical or inclined cylinders, whose rods connected to the drive wheels either by cogwheel arrangments or by "grasshopper" levers. Some of the early steam road carriages used similar devices, but they were awkward and took up too much space on vehicles designed to carry both engine and passengers together. Gurney's solution was elegant and effective. He mounted the two cylinders horizontally, just below and within the carriage frame, with drive rods running directly to the rear axle. This arrangment removed a dangerous and unsightly mechanism from the vicinity of passengers and crew, making it almost invisible within the frame and springs.

It is sometimes claimed that Robert Stephenson also derived the principle of the tubular boiler from Gurney, but this is not true. Tubular boilers had been known for years before Gurney showed how to make them relatively safe and effective, and although the first railway locomotives were built with barrel boilers, the transition to tubular arrangements was almost inevitable. However, in the boilers developed by Hackworth and Stephenson from an original design by Marc Seguin, the tubes were actually flues, transmitting heat from the firebox through a tank of water, whereas Gurney's tubes generated steam and carried it around the firebox. There was no need for railway engineers to adopt a light tubular boiler because the weight of the engine only improved traction on the rails. When Gurney and Sir Charles Dance did try to introduce a larger, heavier version of their boiler in the early 1830s, they discovered that Stephenson, backed by the railway magnates, had gained a monopoly on such designs.[21]

Gurney's other principle innovation, the steam separator, was also ignored by railway engineers. The separator, sometimes called a "blowing box," was that horizontal chamber, wrapped around the top of the boiler tubes, which separated the steam from the water that often blew out of the steam pipes under pressure. It also received exhaust steam from the cylinders before releasing it up the chimney. The separator was crucial to the success of Gurney's tubular boiler (as Joshua Field and Sir Charles Dance discovered when they tried to eliminate it). It not only kept water out of the cylinders, but eliminated the startling blasts of steam, released from the cylinders at each cycle, which otherwise exploded from the chimney in great clouds, throwing soot and cinders into the air. The separator could have been of considerable benefit on the much larger and noisier railway locomotives. But railway owners and engineers accepted the noise and steam blasts as a necessary evil, since they operated for the most part in open country. Besides, according to Alexander Gordon, they were ignorant of the steam separator's existence. After the success of the *Rocket* and the opening of the Liverpool and Manchester line, railway engineers and steam carriage promoters tended to ignore each other's work, each group confident that the other was on the wrong track. The two modes of transport developed independently, to their mutual disadvantage.[22]

The first railways had been built for industrial uses (like the Crawshay track at Cyfarthfa, where Gurney's engine was tried), and during the early stages of locomotive development, the prospect of riding as a passenger anywhere near the steam-blasting, fire-breathing, spark-throwing engines was frightening. The Stockton and Darlington line, sometimes labeled the first true railroad, carried passengers only in horse-drawn carriages with flanged wheels. When the Liverpool and Manchester Railway opened in 1830, it was expected to generate most of its revenue hauling freight. Although road steam drags could also pull freight wagons, they really could not compete with the railways on that score. James Stone's trial in June 1831, with which this chapter opened, was perhaps the best trial on common roads: it carried ten tons along a level, hard-packed road for about five miles, and a bit more up a hill. Four months earlier, Stephenson had pulled fifty tons up an incline at Rainhill, and in April, Joseph Locke's *Samson* engine had drawn a gross weight of 151 tons, loaded in thirty wagons, the entire length of the Liverpool and Manchester railway.[23]

It was logical, therefore, for steam carriage proprietors to concentrate on passenger service, leaving freight to the railways. But to the amazement of the directors of the L & M, the passenger coaches, provided merely for publicity value at the opening of the line, proved so popular that they immediately overtook freight as the principal source of revenue. With Parliament already proving as nervous about trains as they were about steam carriages, the engineers were forced to design safer, more comfortable engines, passenger coaches, and trackside amenities. By 1835 trains were carrying as many as 3,500 passengers per week along the main routes, where horse coaches had carried 400, and they were doing it at lower fares.[24] The long-distance road steam carriages, which were designed essentially to replace horse coaches, simply could not compete in this market. For that matter, neither could the horses.

In an ironic twist, Gurney, Hancock, and other steam inventors were approached in 1839 by stagecoach proprietors and turnpike trustees, all of whom were going bankrupt from railway competition, and asked to consider providing steam carriages for short-haul feeder service between villages and railway stations. This apparently proved commercially unfeasible.[25] Neither did the steam inventors develop small, two-or three-passenger steam "runabouts" for the personal market. A few were made by and for wealthy individuals, and Gurney and Hancock each made one for himself, but the techniques and facilities for the mass production of cheap vehicles were not yet available. This was a great missed opportunity, for as Michael Robbins has written, "The augmented volume and the cheapness of passenger conveyance that the railways provided was one of their most important distinguishing features in relation to the world they lived in; it was something that was not paralleled until the arrival of the internal-combustion engine and its application to transport on the road."[26]

David Beasley has made a case for believing that railway interests encouraged the turnpike trusts' opposition to steam carriages, warned their own shareholders against investing in them, and brought their considerable financial influence to bear on the legislative battle in Parliament.[27] The railways enjoyed a tremendous advantage because of the integrated nature and sheer scale of their operations. The proprietors secured legislation (the Newcastle and Carlisle Act of 1829) that designated the tracks as private property, so that independent contractors could not run on them as Gurney was trying to do on the turnpikes. This quickly left the railway proprietors' steam engines as the sole means of power. The construction of new railways engaged thousands of laborers, foremen, engineers, surveyors, and attorneys. It drew such vast sums of capital from the savings of a speculative public that in 1836–37 there was another "railway boom," followed by the inevitable bust, that diverted investment capital away from road steam projects. Grain-growing farmers joined with turnpike trustees and horse-coach operators to fight the railways, just as they fought the steam carriages. But large landowners like Lord Wharncliffe, who wielded great political power, were given premiums and railway stock for rights-of-way, and were promised cheap, rapid transport for their produce. Turnpike trusts had no power to levy prohibitive tolls on railways, as they had on steam carriages. Town councils quickly realized that the location of a railway junction, or even a station, in their community meant increased trade, new buildings, and higher tax revenues. In short, the railways represented a hitherto unimagined scale of enterprise and public participation, which dwarfed the resources and aspirations of their rivals. By the end of the 1830s, they had become so much a part of people's experience and expectations of "progress" that road steam carriages, if thought of at all, were considered simply an auxiliary mode of conveyance.

The railway engineers, such as George and Robert Stephenson

and I. K. Brunel, were men of outstanding energy, confidence, and organization. They were not only technically inventive but also unusually skilled at project management, a form of enterprise developed only in the nineteenth century. They had grown up in the rough-and-tumble of industrial workshops and understood the gritty reality of contract work. They were also used to dealing with large capital investors and bankers. In contrast, the men who built steam carriages for road travel were usually gentlemen or military officers with little industrial or business experience. Gurney's testimony in parliamentary committees indicates that his enthusiasm for invention made him careless of expenditures, accounts, and contract documents, and overly trusting about the financial reliability of investors. Tom Wadeson, one of Gurney's longtime mechanics, stressed these qualities in a letter to Gurney's friend, Sir George Cayley, in the late 1830s. "I wish I could place complete confidence in any of his experiments," he wrote. "I should be extremely sorry to lessen in any way the friendship existing between yourself and Mr. Gurney, but common honesty becomes all men. I consider Mr. G. a clever man as a philosopher. At the same time, to be candid, I think (I may be mistaken) he has done more injury to the cause of steam coaching than any other individual, for he has caused a lavish expenditure of capital without producing a carriage half so simple as what you patented thirty years before."[28] "It ought to be borne in mind," wrote Alexander Gordon in 1839, "that hitherto the attempts to introduce locomotion on turnpike roads have been made by a few individuals, in many cases poor men, and without any large capital to back them. In some cases where capital has been spent, the money has been entrusted solely to the inventor of the carriage, and I believe even the inventors themselves admit they are not the best economisers of money."[29]

Historians of technology have not been kind to Gurney and his fellow inventors. Francis Evans, surveying books written about steamers, horse carriages, railways, and canals since 1833, concluded that steam carriages were technically deficient in steering, suspension, transmission, boilers, and drive mechanisms. They were too heavy for reliable operation, used too much water, vibrated so much that their frames disintegrated, and generated odors, heat, and noise too close to the passengers. Fundamentally, said Evans, inventors could not graft the dynamics of steam locomotion onto the principles of a road carriage, because the former required a strong downward thrust of power upon the roadway, whereas the latter required lightness and a minimum of traction. They had reached, unfortunately, "the limit of contemporary technology."[30]

Such is the judgment of hindsight. At the time, of course, the mechanics' magazines and encyclopedias worried just as much about the technological limits of horse-drawn carriages and canal transport, as Evans demonstrates. Railway locomotives were also problematical, largely because British engineers had little scientific training. In the early 1820s, no principle of physics could be adduced to prove that high-pressure engines were more efficient than low-pressure engines. Even when the Liverpool and Manchester railway was nearing completion in 1828, a majority of consulting engineers favored pulling trains with rope winches, powered by stationary engines. Neither Timothy Hackworth nor Robert Stephenson had mastered the technical requirements for a really effective steam locomotive by the time Gurney's carriage made its successful run to Bath in the summer of 1829. Stephenson's *Rocket* won the Rainhill trials later that year on the basis of reliability, but engine breakages and failures continued to be the main concern of railway proprietors for a decade afterward.[31] Railway locomotives proved far noisier than steam carriages; they sent blasts of steam in every direction; and they showered nearby streets, fields, and people with sparks and hot ashes. As late as 1836, a parliamentary committee reported that they could not be made safe for operation in towns without impeding their performance.[32] There is no doubt that they achieved technical supremacy over steam carriages, but not necessarily as simple mechanical inventions; they did so as part of an innovative transportation system combining engineering design with large-scale finance and management. Had the railway promoters used their resources to gain control over the turnpikes and develop a national network of road transport, steam carriages might have enjoyed a similar success.

In September 1839, Colonel Maceroni, ever the publicist, issued a challenge to Sir James Anderson and Walter Hancock for a public competition. However, only Hancock showed up for the trial run at the appointed time, and he suffered defeat owing to a broken axle and boiler when his carriage ran out of control into a ditch.[33] That same year Tom Wadeson, who must have regarded himself as a virtual partner in the enterprise by this time, began tinkering with one of Gurney's steam carriages on his own, took it out on the road to Hounslow without informing anyone, and suffered a fatal accident. Soon afterward Walter Hancock carried the local Stratford cricket team to their match in his steamer, drove it home, and put it into storage. James Walker, in his presidential address to the Institution of Civil Engineers in 1840, reviewed the efforts to perfect steam carriages for common roads, and concluded: "The system is inferior to that of railway traveling, and it is now generally given up as hopeless."[34]

9

Steamboats, Lighthouses, Castles, and Hot Air

WHILE DEVOTING ENORMOUS AMOUNTS OF TIME AND ENERGY TO DEVELOPING the steam carriage and arguing his case in Parliament, Gurney still managed to pursue other lines of inquiry and produce other inventions. Research undertaken for his chemistry lectures was still bearing fruit, and his communications with other scientists, both amateur and professional, provoked new ideas. The sheer variety of the subjects he investigated, and the connections he saw among them, help to extend our understanding of his approach to science and technology, which was more typical of his times than his adventures with steam carriages suggest.

Much of his research was pursued in the northern Cornish port of Bude Haven, where he established a second home in the spring of 1830. The town, serving an area settled in Roman times, was built on the slopes of downs overlooking the estuary of the River Neet where it emptied into a rock-edged bay, one of the few good harbors along that coast. The northern slope held a few shops and a thin scattering of cottages occupied by fishermen, while a thirteenth-century manor house, owned by the local patron, Sir Thomas Acland, anchored the south side. Bude had neither the bustle of Padstow nor the relative sophistication of Truro. However, it was only a few miles from the farm at Launcells where Elizabeth Gurney had grown up, and a canal had been dug inland from the harbor in 1823, promising economic growth. Goldsworthy was optimistic that steam carriage patent royalties would yield a steady income, so he designed an entirely new residence for his family.

The house that Gurney built was a remarkable edifice. It was patterned after a gigantic "medieval" mansion erected in 1825 by William Crawshay near his ironworks at Merthyr Tydfil, where Gurney had recently delivered and tested a steam locomotive. The great stone walls and crenellated castle towers of Crawshay's mansion so impressed the ambitious inventor that he decided to replicate them on a reduced scale, suitable to his relatively modest income and smaller family. He leased a two-acre site among the sand dunes from the local landowner and parliamentary leader, Sir Thomas Acland.[1] His neighbors, who lived along the ridges above the tidal plain, thought the location entirely unsuited to building. But Gurney had been reading in the technical journals about new formulas and applications for concrete. The engineer John Smeaton had experimented with hydraulic cement in the mid-eighteenth century, and in 1796, James Parker had patented "Roman cement," manufactured from Kentish beach gravel, low in lime but high in aluminium and ferric oxide, which made it set quickly under water and resist hydraulic pressure. Although Parker failed to exploit it commercially, Thomas Telford recognized its value and used it for building aqueducts and harbor works. He may even have used Roman cement for the canal he constructed inland from Bude harbor, which ran just beside Gurney's new building site.[2] So there was plenty of opportunity for an inquisitive inventor to learn about this new material. When Gurney was warned that his house would quickly collapse, he replied, "Wait and see!" Scouring out the landward side of the dunes, he packed down the sand and poured concrete into a slab for the foundation. On this he erected a homely little two-story stone "castle," containing about a dozen rooms leading off a central corridor, and looking out over a small garden. During the next few years, he devised new types of heating and lighting for this residence, and many of his letters to journals or friends were written in its rooms. Sitting down by the harbor, away from most other houses, the Castle quickly became a local landmark. Although Gurney lived in it less than a decade, it remained in private hands well into the twentieth century. Today, much altered by various tenants, it houses the offices of the Bude-Stratton Town Council, which dedicated its chamber to Gurney's memory in 1993 to commemorate the 200th anniversary of his birth.[3]

Despite his investment in the coastal community and his oft-expressed delight at living again in Cornwall, Gurney was constantly required to travel up to Bristol, Exeter, and London to attend to his other concerns. Since the steam carriage lines never succeeded, and the railway did not reach Bude until the 1860s, he traveled back and forth to the capital either by coastal packet or by stagecoach. The latter meant a journey of some forty hours each way, interrupted frequently by changes of horses and costing about 8 or 9 pounds. One would like to think that his amiable temperament and enthusiasm for new ideas made him an interesting companion on the long, jolting rides. Horse-drawn coaches, however, could only remind him of the frustrations he was experiencing in Parliament.

It is evident from his later correspondence and public testimony

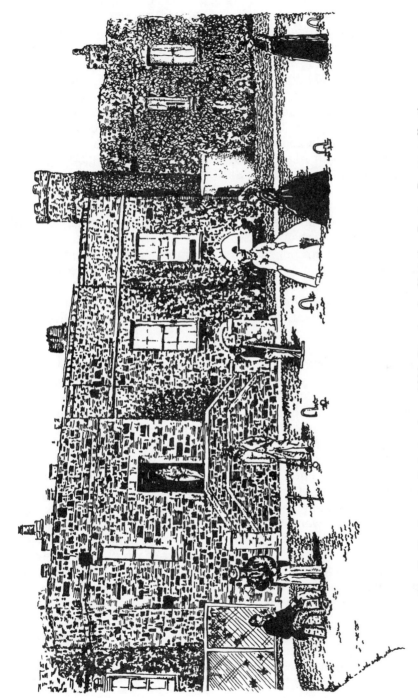

The Castle, from a photograph ca. 1890. Drawing by Christine Porter. Porter collection.

that he developed a wide range of acquaintances and working associates in London, who not only benefited from his ideas and expertise but helped him in return. Such cooperation was to be expected, especially among the class of gentlemen scientists with which he identified. However, we have seen that other sorts of men exploited such exchanges of information. Inventors like Gurney naturally relied on mechanics, metalworkers, equipment suppliers, and assistants of all sorts, who communicated in turn with other men working in the same fields. As is true today, workmen with special skills and knowledge of particular inventions might be drawn away to a different employer with related interests, one who would gladly pay for inside information on successful developments. It has been suggested that the steam jet, in fact, found its way into the Stephenson locomotive works in this way. Certainly other features of Gurney's locomotives were adopted by his employees and associates after he was forced out of business. Steamboat builders like William Keene and the Seaward brothers adapted locomotive improvements to their own vessels, and in fact perpetuated many of Gurney's ideas long after they vanished from land transport.

But the steam engine community was not the only one open to Gurney. We have seen that he associated with scientists at the Royal Institution, the Society of Arts, Manufactures, and Commerce, and other centers of patronage and research. In the early 1820s, he and Michael Faraday exchanged notes and attended each other's public lectures. They both wrestled unsuccessfully with atomic theory, and they shared the conviction that chemical reactions were related in some way to electricity. Faraday, older by two years and more closely associated with Humphry Davy, had developed his own style of investigation and lecturing. Gurney was the more flamboyant of the two, more enthusiastic in the lecture hall and less disciplined in his research. Faraday, although of fiery temperament and strong convictions, cultivated the persona of the objective, detached expert, who let Nature present herself through his brilliant experimental discoveries. His lectures were often difficult for amateurs to follow, but "he exercised a magic on his hearers which often sent them away persuaded that they knew all about a subject of which they knew but little."[4] He avoided Davy's moralizing and theological opinions, and sought ways to move beyond his tutor's obsession with the voltaic pile. In 1823 he and Davy conducted the first experiments to show the relation of gases to liquids, and between 1831 and 1835, he discovered and explained the basic principles of electromagnetic induction, for which he won lasting fame. Largely indifferent to the commercial ventures which seemed to fascinate Gurney, he lived modestly on an income from the Royal Institution until 1836, when he accepted a small pension from the government.[5] In the same year, he was made scientific advisor to Trinity House, an ancient mariners' guild that oversaw most of the lighthouses along the English coast. In that capacity he rekindled his association with Gurney.

Trinity House was interested in Faraday, not just for his general scientific knowledge, but for a series of experiments he conducted in the 1820s to develop superior reflecting optical glasses, of great importance to lighthouses. The experiments were not particularly successful, but they gave Faraday a good working knowledge of lighthouse apparatus. Meanwhile, Gurney's research on the oxyhydrogen blowpipe was proving useful for long-distance lighting. It may be recalled that the blowpipe, when directed at a piece of pure lime, produced an intensely bright flare, which illuminated the whole lecture hall and cast stark shadows. Gurney called the effect "limelight." Explained in the lectures he published in 1823, it was quickly noticed by scientific and technical men searching for new types of lighting. One of these men, Lieutenant Thomas Drummond of the Royal Engineers, replicated many of Gurney's experiments, taking his cue, as Gurney did, from the work of the great eighteenth-century Swedish chemist, Berzelius. In 1826, Drummond was assigned to conduct a topographical survey of Ireland. The survey required long-distance trigonometry: he had to establish a set of triangular measurements along a rough and often fogbound coast. To penetrate the fog and carry a signal across bodies of water, Drummond built his own version of the oxyhydrogen limelight. He found that it produced a beam clearly visible for ninety-five miles (from Ben Lomond, Scotland, to Long Nazel, Ireland), whereas the usual Argand oil lamp beam projected only twelve miles.[6] After Drummond described his experiments in the 1826 *Philosophical Transactions,* the limelight became known as the "Drummond light."

The first Drummond light consisted of three-eighths-inch lime pellets, or rings, positioned on a rod in front of a twenty-one-inch, silver-plated parabolic reflector. Since the apparatus was designed on the principle of a lighthouse light, applying it to that purpose seemed an obvious step. In 1829, Drummond was hired by Trinity House to undertake further development. He managed to make versions that were 264 times brighter than the Argand oil lamp. But there were problems. Replacing spent lime pellets required two men of moderate skill, such as most lighthouses did not have. The lime tended to shrink rapidly as it burned, and it could fuse and crack or explode, exposing the delicate reflector to the direct force of the blowpipe flame. Keeping the gas mixture properly regulated was difficult.

Drummond thought that he could remedy these defects, but before he could test his newest design, he was appointed Lieutenant Governor of the Royal Military Academy, Woolwich.[7]

Although Drummond's work was reported once again in the *Philosophical Transactions* (1831), most men engaged in lighthouse development ignored it, repeating the earlier experiments in a futile quest for a practical device. When Drummond appeared before a parliamentary committee in July 1834, he criticized this waste of time and money, but also conceded that his own invention should not be installed in lighthouses until it was properly improved. The commissioners for Trinity House and for Scottish lighthouses agreed.

The 1834 parliamentary committee, chaired by an industrious Radical MP named Joseph Hume,[8] had been set up to reform Britain's archaic, dangerous system of lighthouses. Hume's inquiries exposed curiously overlapping jurisdictions of medieval origin, charitable bequests mixed in with ships' fees, whole sections of shoreline unaccounted for. The committee recommended government regulation and a central board to oversee all facilities. The proceedings were widely reported, and Gurney, who was busy defending his steam carriage against prohibitive toll bills, was close at hand. He wrote to the lighthouse committee, calling its attention to his description of the oxyhydrogen blowpipe in 1823 and to his remarks made then about the future application of the limelight to lighthouses. The committee recommended in very emphatic terms that the new central board hire him to perfect the Drummond light.[9]

Thus, when Michael Faraday arrived at Trinity House early in 1836, he found Gurney already engaged in experiments.[10] The two men worked well together, and the venture did yield some new applications—but not to lighthouses. Gurney finally had to concede that the design was fundamentally impractical for its original purpose. However, during his many experiments with blowpipes, he had tried directing a stream of oxygen into the flame of a standard Argand oil lamp* and found that this multiplied its brightness. He had already demonstrated in his 1822 lectures that such an infusion of air or oxygen improved combustion, reducing carbon ash and other impu-

---

*François Argand had invented in 1783 an oil lamp with three distinctive features. It had a hollow wick that provided an internal as well as an external air supply, a glass chimney to increase the draft while reducing flickers, and a device for raising and lowering the wick to regulate brightness and fuel consumption. The Argand lamp was to the nineteenth-century household what the electric light is to the twentieth. Cf. Wolfgang Schivelbusch, *Disenchanted Night: The Industrialization of Light in the Nineteenth Century,* (Berkeley and Los Angeles: University of California Press, 1988): 9–13.

rities. Multiplying the number of concentric burner rings, so that three or four cones of flame burned within each other, increased the effect dramatically, up to 140 times the power of the Argand lamp commonly used for lighthouses. The new device was similar enough to the Argand to make Gurney's improvements easy to implement and sufficient for most purposes.

Because most of the experiments to perfect the new lamp were actually performed while Gurney was sojourning at his new Castle in Bude Haven, he named it the Bude Light.[11] Although it operated on a different principle from the original Drummond light, it was often confused with that invention in public notices, and Lieutenant Drummond himself did nothing to clarify the matter when he testified before Hume's committee on lighthouses in 1834. Harris's memoir claims that Drummond acknowledged his debt to Gurney's original research in a separate letter to Hume. This letter does not appear in the parliamentary archives, but a later parliamentary committee stated that "Mr. Gurney is now acknowledged, both at home and abroad, to have been the inventor of what is called the Drummond Light," and it identified the Bude light as a new, distinctive apparatus.[12]

It happened that Gurney was also, at this time, giving evidence before a parliamentary committee investigating coal mine explosions. In his enthusiasm for his new invention, he suggested that a Bude light be used to illuminate the mine shafts, replacing the uncertain candle-powered Davy lamps carried by miners. A bank of Bude lamps could be set up outside the main shaft, the flames safely distant from the explosive mine gases. Their light could then be concentrated into a powerful six–inch beam, directed down into the mine, reflected into the separate tunnels by parabolic mirrors (similar to those used for lighthouses), and even directed to the coal face by "personal reflectors," the size of a half-crown, carried by each man. "The light at the distance of a mile would enable you to read the smallest print," he declared. Although Gurney's claim was expressed with typical hyperbole, the degree of intensity he described was probably obtainable. Another witness, who had seen Gurney's experiments at Trinity House, said that the beam of light was so strong that colored glass lenses were used to cut the glare. And since colored light was found to penetrate fog more effectively, it would no doubt work better in the dust and smoke of mines.[13]

Michael Faraday was also indirectly responsible for Gurney's eventual membership in the British Association for the Advancement of Science. The connection was not personal, and it would hardly be worth mention, except that it illustrates an important change in the scientific community that sustained Gurney's investigative energy. It has already been noted that the Royal Society, like the Royal College of Physicians, grew increasingly exclusive during the early years of the century, so much so that other scientific and medical organizations initiated their own programs of research and instruction. Humphry Davy, elected president of the Royal Society in 1820, tried to restore ties to the renegades but continued to act like his predecessor, Joseph Banks, a "benevolent monarch" presiding over scientists and their rich, high-ranking patrons. The Society's council was a coterie of friends, selected by the president. Financial accounts were closed except to him and the treasurer (the equally conservative Davies Gilbert). Papers were read infrequently, and only by the president's permission; publication was slow.[14] Many researchers, contrasting the disorganization and amateurism of British science with the state-sponsored institutions of France and Germany, believed that reforms were crucial to future progress. In 1830, after Davy had died and Davies Gilbert had succeeded him, a group of younger Fellows led by Faraday and the famous astronomer, Sir John Herschel, demanded the election of a new president and other organizational changes.[15] Their challenge coincided with parliamentary reform agitation by workers and the provincial middle classes, the election of the first Reform ministry of Lord Grey, and the July Revolution in France. All the revolts were linked together in the minds of Gilbert and his council. When they won reelection by a narrow and disputed margin, they purged the leading dissidents. Herschel left the country to continue his work abroad, while Faraday withdrew to a small government pension and his post at Trinity House. The other reformers, most of them Gurney's age or younger, joined the new British Association for the Advancement of Science. The BAAS, initiated in the north of England, was a broad-based, practical organization that sought to promote research activity in local provincial societies, then coordinate it nationally by means of periodic reports and peripatetic meetings. It gave many men a chance at membership whose social pretensions were not appreciated by the Royal Society, and soon provided most of the science news printed by provincial and London newspapers.[16]

It is not clear just when Gurney joined the BAAS, but at its annual meeting held at Plymouth in July 1841, he read a paper to the Chemical section, describing a series of experiments on explosions in hot-water heaters and boilers. Like most of the chemistry papers offered at this session, it was reported to be fairly tedious. However, it illuminates a line of research that runs through the background of Gurney's whole career. During the late 1830s, he and other men[17] had devised steam heating systems for houses and other buildings, running long pipes from an external boiler through the walls to primitive radiators in the interior rooms. He had proposed such a system in his lectures of 1822, commenting at the time on the changes it might make in domestic life. Within a decade he would recommend one for the new Houses of Parliament. But his long experience with boilers of all kinds revealed a hidden danger: if the supply of water was stopped for any reason and the boiler ran dry, the engine would keep running for a while on the residual pressure, blowing hot air and combustible gases through the pipes until they overheated. At that point their insulation would catch on fire, weak joints would burst, and fire or explosions might occur within the building. In his paper Gurney proposed a simple solution to this problem. The joints where the steam pipe left the boiler and where it returned could be made of a softer metal, such as lead, that melted at temperatures above 400 degrees. If the boiler ran dry and overheated, these joints would fail, release the steam, and isolate the pipes leading into the building.[18]

Gurney had already described a similar remedy for boiler explosions that occurred around mines, especially in Cornwall, where steam engines were used to ventilate the deeper shafts. Appearing before a committee on mine accidents in 1835, he explained that barrel boilers burst when their water ran low and the exposed sides developed "hot spots," which created instant pockets of high pressure when hit by rising steam bubbles. He recommended putting a lead seam along the boiler at the minimum water level, so that if the water supply fell below it, the lead would melt and release the steam pressure.[19]

To make sure that boilers did not run out of water in the first place, he had also invented a self-acting water feeder, called the "lock" because it acted somewhat like the lock in a canal. The lock was a cold-water tank, fed by hose from a pond or reservoir. It was connected by separate valves on both the top and the bottom of the boiler, which were opened and closed by an internal float. When the water level of the boiler ran low, the float opened the valves, allowing cold water to flow in from the lock. At the same time, it released steam through the top valve back into the lock. When the water rose to the desired height, the float shut off the valves. The steam blown into the top of the cold-water lock condensed, forming a vacuum, which pulled fresh water through the hose from the pond. This ingenious device was based on the principle of the old Newcomen steam engines, where the piston was drawn by a vacuum of condensing steam in the cylinder rather than pushed by high pressure. There is no evidence that the "lock" was adopted by Cornish or English mine owners, but similar self-acting valves were in use at sugar refineries both in England and on the Continent. John Seaward, who shared so many of Gurney's improvements, developed a self-acting feeder for his steamship engines not long after Gurney's invention.[20]

During the years in which Gurney was working on steam locomotives and lighting apparatus, he made the acquaintance of Sir George Cayley (1773–1857), a rich Yorkshire landowner twenty years his senior.[21] The two men were natural allies: they were both sons of provincial gentry who had been educated in scientific and technical subjects. Both had a natural mechanical aptitude and liked to work with their hands. Cayley was a Yorkshire liberal, Gurney a Cornish one. Both conducted agricultural experiments at home, although Cayley's was the larger and more permanent estate. The major difference between them was that Cayley was a shy man of few political ambitions, who felt most comfortable tinkering at his workshop on the family estate near Brompton, whereas his gregarious friend presided over county organizations and tried all his life to make a mark in London.

Cayley, like Gurney, pursued a great variety of projects during his lifetime, most of which generated more controversy than success. He is best known for his work on hot-air engines and their potential for powering airplanes. By the 1840s he was building and testing airframes, powered balloons, and gliders, which his biographer claims can be recognized as practical even today. To help them land, he invented a light "tension" wheel, mounted on the undercarriage, that anticipated the later spoked bicycle wheel.[22] Cayley's first paper on hot-air engines* appeared in *Nicholson's Journal* in 1807, and Gurney, a devoted reader, would have been familiar with his work. In the 1820s when he began experimenting with boilers and engines, Gurney hired a mechanic named Tom Wadeson who also worked for Cayley. It is likely that the two inventors became acquainted through Wadeson and tried adapting the hot-air engine to roadway carriages or locomotives. Gurney also tried to apply Cayley's design for tractor treads, called the "Universal Railway," to his early steam carriages to overcome the assumed lack of friction. As a strong advocate of parliamentary reform in a county known for its radicalism, Cayley was induced to stand for election in 1832, after the passage of the Reform Act. He and his nephew, Edward Stillingfleet Cayley (1802–1862), easily won seats in the new House of Commons. He was thus

---

*Hot-air engines worked on the same principles of expansion and condensation as steam engines. The hot air activated a cylinder connected to drive rods.

able to give timely support in the legislative battle to regulate excessive turnpike tolls on steam carriages. Politics, however, was not his element. He disliked the hustle and bustle of the capital, and when the reform Whigs left office in December 1834, he was only too glad to return to Yorkshire. Gurney wrote to him the following February: "Your letter, wherein you say you had no wish to be again in Parliament except on my account, affected me very much, so that the impression will last all my life. Much as I am indebted to you and much as I could wish for your valuable services in the House next session, still, under all consideration, and knowing the natural and powerful bent of your mind to other subjects, I am glad you are not returned again to sit within the walls of St. Stephen."[23]

Cayley and Gurney continued to work closely together in the following years. In 1835, Gurney credited his friend with the idea of using reflected light to illuminate mine shafts. A decade later, when Gurney was using a version of his steam jet to ventilate a colliery in Wales, he wrote to Cayley for technical advice: "What is the amount of air consumed by one pound of charcoal compared to one pound of coal?" "What is the difference in the weight of a 300-foot long column of air [i.e., the mine shaft] heated to 200 degrees, and another of the same length at 60 degrees?" He explained his attempts to generate a sufficient draft through the mine and asked, "What shall I do?" Cayley's reply is not recorded, but he sent over an anemometer, constructed by his instrument maker, with which to measure the air currents in the mine shaft. A week later, Gurney reported that "the experiment has been singularly successful!" He then gave specifications for making another anemometer, sensitive enough to register the slower air movements in the mine: "The whole must not weigh more than an ounce."[24]

Advice also flowed in the opposite direction. In 1837, Cayley signed an agreement to share profits with Gurney in consideration of "his valuable cooperation in bringing my invention of the expanded air engine (now only exhibiting its powers in an experimental engine) to the most efficient and convenient form." There is a charming drawing of the two men, along with Cayley's nephew Edward, Tom Wadeson, and another mechanic, working on the engine at Brompton Hall, the Cayley family estate.[25] Gurney, who was then engaged in experiments for lighting the House of Commons, wrote often from London to keep Cayley informed of competing engine designs by Ericsson, Stirling, and others.[26] He was confident that the practical difficulties of the hot-air engine would someday be surmounted, and it would become "a useful and economical power."[27] Whenever it was the subject of a talk or a paper at one of the scientific

Cayley's engine, set up in the Brew House at Brompton, showing mechanics Wadeson and Vick, Sir George Cayley and Edward Cayley (in hats), and Goldsworthy Gurney. From J. Lawrence Pritchard, *Sir George Cayley: The Inventor of the Aeroplane* (London: Max Parrish, 1961), plate xii.

and technical societies in London, he appeared in the audience to defend Cayley's interests. In 1850 and again in 1853, he spoke at length in debates at the Institution of Civil Engineers. On the latter occasion (it was February, and Gurney was investigating heating and ventilation at the new Houses of Parliament), Cayley was sick and had sent in a written description of his work. In a long letter, Gurney reported to his friend that a rival's paper, read on the first night—"a very stupid and absurd one"—gave major credit for the engine to Stirling. "Such stuff as this was painful to listen to." Gurney did not listen long. Called upon to comment, he launched into a recital of Cayley's contributions, together with a rebuttal of the other claims, that consumed the rest of the evening and required the group to meet a second time. As a kind of apology for his "long-winded story," he said that he considered that the question would become of national importance, and credit would be given to the man who originated the engine, "and therefore that you were the only true inventor and that I was your prophet and such ought to go down to posterity." Gurney was still agitated about the meeting when he wrote to Cayley, and at the end of his rambling, disconnected account, he exclaimed, "God Save the Queen!" Cayley's biographer wryly comments, "Gurney was indeed a voluble friend."[28]

A bare recital of Gurney's varied topics of investigation would give an impression of random curiosity and impulsive enthusiasm. He seemed to throw himself into whatever venture presented itself on any given day, responding to requests from friends or to articles discovered in science journals. Except for his lengthy, strenuous engagement in steam carriage building, he seldom pursued any particular invention long enough to develop it into an artifact for widespread use or public consumption. Even when he did, as in the case of the oxyhydrogen blowpipe, he typically resisted opportunities for commercial exploitation, preferring to work out the details of application to a particular situation and leave the market to other men.

To some extent these traits are consistent with the image he cultivated for himself as a gentleman scientist and inventor. His family background, the exemplars of his Enlightenment-influenced education, and the social aspirations of his medical and scientific colleagues all encouraged his persona of amateur expert, one skilled beyond dilettantism but not requiring the accoutrements of a salaried position to support or justify his contributions to society. Jeanne Peterson has written that in nineteenth-century British society, the important social division was not between aristocracy and the middle and working classes, nor even between men and women, but between those whose social status was won through educational and career achievements and those born and raised in "gentle" families, whose social confidence encouraged, but did not derive from, learning and strenuous activities.[29] Goldsworthy Gurney belonged to an intermediate group of people. In Cornwall, among his family connections, he could play the roles of gentleman surgeon, local magistrate, and experimental farmer, while appearing to amuse himself with eccentric projects like his Castle and the Bude light. In London he sought fame and fortune through scientific and technical achievements, but he preferred to do so through patronage, public notices, and privately financed ventures rather than as institutional scientist, like Davy and Faraday, or industrial entrepreneur, like George Stephenson. His petitions and testimony in Parliament regarding tolls on steam carriages reflect this ambivalence. He was at pains to detail the years of effort and personal expense jeopardized by legislative obstruction, and the "lucrative profession" as a surgeon and science lecturer which he had given up along the way, but he insisted that his petition sought only the removal of barriers to progress in the public interest rather than any personal compensation. In later years he would tell parliamentary committees, "Money does not tempt me—I have independent means," and yet complain bitterly to government officials when denied remuneration for services.

Social self-image, however, does not entirely account for the apparently eclectic character of his interests and activities. Two other explanations may be suggested. First, what may appear in the documentary records as discontinuous and unrelated investigations actually represents several lines of experimental inquiry, opened up during the intensive preparations for his lectures in 1822 (or even before that, in Wadebridge), which cross-fertilized one another over several decades. The question of overheated boilers examined in his BAAS paper in 1841 is intimately connected to the question of corrosive explosions that led him to develop the tubular boiler for his steam carriage. The practical application of steam radiator heating for buildings, acknowledged in the same paper, was forecast in his lecture on "caloric" at the Surrey Institution. Experiments with the oxyhydrogen blowpipe led to the invention of the limelight and then the Bude lamp. Later chapters will show these same devices and scientific principles at work in yet other applications.

Disregarding the many mechanical devices he either built or designed, from glass-tube pianos to lighthouse signals, one can discern in Gurney's four decades of work a general focus on the nature and applications of expansive and combustible gases. These included chlorine, oxygen, and hydrogen at first, then steam and the coal gas used in lamps. In the 1830s and 1840s, he turned to hot air, with Cayley, and methane in coal mines. In the 1850s he perfected two types of radiant heating and took up the problem of sewer gas. The composition and combustion of gases was related naturally to his background in chemistry, explored through scientific journals, lectures, and society conferences. The light and mechanical forces generated by gases excited his interest in engines, furnaces, and lamps. His lifetime of investigation, therefore, is more unified than a strict chronology of the available records would suggest.

A second explanation for Gurney's apparent eclecticism stems from his characteristic way of thinking, as far as it can be inferred from his activities. The history of technology, like the history of science, has been overburdened with stereotypes of inventors, the most misleading being that of the isolated genius. Among the thousands of individuals credited with technical developments since 1800, one can discern some significant differences in the ways in which they approach innovation. In almost all cases, of course, conceptualization, empirical investigation, manipulation of apparatus, and application of results occurs, or is imagined, together—not all at the same time, but not in any particular order, either. The differences lie in a tendency or a preference for one type of thinking over others. Some inventors doggedly pursue work on one or two principles, processes, or mechanisms for long periods of time, compelled by obsessive curiosity, by the security of exclusive expertise, or by the belief that the object of study holds the key to nature's mystery. The frame of their thought tends to link the invention to some superhuman dimension of value, without necessarily considering how human beings might respond to it. More famous inventors, like George Stephenson, I. K. Brunel, Thomas Edison, and Henry Ford, move quickly from experimenting with particular items to conceptualizing an entire system in which those items might function. For them a steam engine becomes immediately part of a railway, a light bulb one element in an electrical power grid. Their personal ambition is cast in the dimension of social organization.[30] Gurney belonged to a third type, which tended to think by analogy and by practical application on the human scale of individuals and small groups. As I have argued above, each of his varied investigations contributed some concept, skill, or information to the others. He was a genius at cross-fertilization, at seeing the utility of an idea or a mechanism in a new situation. We might say that he was most effective at lateral thinking in the realm of everyday affairs. Applying a scientific concept to a concrete problem was always easier for him than abstracting the appropriate concept from experimental results, and he lacked the true engineer's sense of how a particular invention might function within a fully developed system.

The advantage of Gurney's analogical, instrumental thinking is that every idea or experiment, successful or not, contributes to others in a steadily accumulating fund of knowledge, insight, and skills. Thus his oddball attempts to modify the workings of pianos led to the use of piano wire to construct a plaster flame damper for the oxyhydrogen blowpipe, which in turn derived from experiments with the Davy lamp; and his practical knowledge of the limitations of the Davy lamp would later inform his attempts to ventilate mine shafts. To be most effective, such thinking must be exercised in constant trial-and-error experimentation, stimulated by frequent personal contact with other scientists and inventors. Such an approach suited Gurney's gregarious disposition.[31] However, this type of thinking has its disadvantages. One is the lack of long-range, systematic development in particular areas, in favor of the shifting, episodic application of partially-worked-out ideas to a variety of problems. Gurney's solution to the overheating boilers, for example, was to insert lead seams that melted at a high temperature. This solution undoubtedly worked, but it also left the boiler in need of refitting. His improvements to the oxyhydrogen blowpipe made it safe enough to use, but one suspects that the reason Gurney did not seek patent protection for it was that it needed redesigning by a trained engineer to make it sturdy and efficient enough for commercial use. Another disadvantage is the tendency to work so closely with the physical apparatus or artifact, getting it to perform through constant fiddling and intuitive adjustments, that fundamental design flaws are ignored or disguised. This problem was most evident in the case of the steam carriage's tubular boiler, which continued to suffer frequent, though minor, ruptures through the period of its development and required highly trained mechanics to keep it going. Because of his personal, hands-on involvement, Gurney also tended to underestimate the true cost of operating his vehicles. He argued that the boiler tube ruptures were a negligible nuisance compared to the danger of explosion from larger boilers, and calculated expenses without regard to his own considerable investment of time and effort. But professional engineers, such as William Cubitt, were bound to assess the machine and its logistical support requirements by less personal criteria.

Gurney's personality, social background, provincial education, and mechanical genius combined in an extraordinarily well-informed, fertile, and productive approach to scientific and technological concerns. They also limited his ability to recognize and cope with the political and economic forces organized by critics and competitors. The legislative defeat of the steam carriage trade through prohibitive turnpike tolls was, as we shall see, only the first of several such setbacks.

10

Mine Ventilation

P<small>ADSTOW LIES NORTH OF THE PRINCIPAL MINING AREAS OF CORNWALL, BUT GUR-</small>
ney could not have grown up in the county nor practiced medicine
there without being aware of mining operations. Copper, tin, lead,
iron, and zinc had been extracted from the region for centuries.
Originally dredged from shallow pits, the ores had been pursued
continuously for so long that shafts and galleries of great depth,
length, and complexity were now common. The same was true of
the semi-anthracite coalfields of the Merthyr Valley in Wales and the
anthracite in Lancashire. New coal fields opened south and southwest of Durham in the 1830s; shafts into the Hetton seam sank as
far as 1,600 feet, with the galleries that spread out from each shaft
over a mile in length. Coal fed the new iron trade associated with
early blast furnaces and steam engines, but demand multiplied rapidly with the coming of the railways. After Parliament ended duties on
coal and lowered export tariffs in 1831, mining became big business.
Britain's output of coal grew from thirteen million tons, in 1815, to
forty-four million in 1845, to 100 million in 1855—sixty percent of
the world's total production. Estate owners sold their mining rights
to the new capitalists or joined forces with them to exploit the earth.
Small operators, constantly short of capital, were also plentiful. Until
the 1850s there was little regulation, or even inspection, of the mines
by government.[1]

The normal method of deep mining was to sink one or more vertical shafts, which were used to haul men, equipment, and coal up
and down and to ventilate the mine. Galleries were then driven sideways from the central shafts to the boundaries of the coal field,
following the seams but running slightly uphill. When a gallery
reached the end of the seam, the miners turned around and began
digging their way back. Thus the coal could be transported downhill
to the lifts, while the waste was left behind to fill in the empty seam.

The first problem with sinking deeper shafts was water seepage.
The earliest Newcomen engines, working with low-pressure vacuum

cylinders, were developed to pump water out of Cornish mines. This is the main reason why Cornwall became practically synonymous with steam engineering for half a century, and why men like Richard Trevithick trained a whole generation of apprentices. The high-pressure engines of Boulton and Watt enabled coal mine operators to pump out ever deeper shafts, and by 1800 up to a thousand engines of various types were in operation around the kingdom.[2]

The second problem with deep mining was adequate ventilation. Various minerals in the soil gave off flammable gases, more so when the ore was exposed to air, broken up, and pushed back into porous waste pockets. The mines were illuminated with wax candles, which generated their own effluvia. Men and horses perspired freely in the underground passages, which reached temperatures of 80–100 degrees Fahrenheit. The results could mix into a choking, combustible fog pervading the whole pit.

Each of the metallic ores produced its own special gases, but coal was perhaps worse than any of them. Both the coal itself and the processes of mining it gave off explosive and poisonous fumes. The most familiar was carbureted hydrogen, known since the eighteenth century as "fire damp," and to modern chemists as methane. With half the specific gravity of air, it collected in the upper parts of the galleries. Its volatility rose as it mixed with air, up to about one in seven parts, then gradually decreased with greater ventilation. It was hard to get rid of, because it percolated through the layers of earth between seams. Sometimes a mine would catch fire and burn for years on end, smoldering even when flooded with water.

The Davy lamp was invented (1815) as a way of protecting the miners from explosion by fire damp. Its fine-wire-mesh cover was supposed to prevent the flame of the miner's candle from igniting the gases around him, while it consumed whatever fire damp leaked inside the lamp chamber. As we have seen, Gurney made a number of experiments on the Davy lamp and showed that it did not guarantee safety. Frequently, coal or metallic dust collected on the outside of the wire mesh and became hot enough to ignite the gases. Small gusts of air could draw the candle flame through the mesh as well. Gurney's findings were supported by tragic experience in the mines during the 1820s and 1830s. Despite the appearance of many improved safety lamps, miners continued to die.

Investigators discovered that there was another, heavier type of carbureted hydrogen, called "olefiant" gas, which exploded at a lower temperature and hung in the air just below layers of fire damp. It tended to explode on contact with the red-hot iron mesh of the safety lamp. So did a related gas, sulfureted hydrogen, released by iron pyrites in the mines. Sulfureted hydrogen, along with carbonic acid gas released by old workings and explosions, also caused instant death by inhalation. Carbonic acid gas (NCO_2) was called "choke damp," or "black damp." It was heavier than air, so it occupied the lower parts of working galleries, and the only warnings it gave were a cloudy effect seen only in clear air, a particular odor, and the guttering or extinction of the miner's lamp. Finally, following an explosion, either deliberate or accidental, the miners encountered a lethal compound containing carbon monoxide, called "after damp."[3]

The Davy lamp's overblown reputation for safety encouraged miners and mine owners to dig into much more dangerous areas than they would otherwise have dared. The lamp was cumbersome, its mesh cover reduced visibility, and it required constant cleaning to prevent buildup of flammable coal dust on the screen. Miners, fatalistic by training and not well educated, often used the lamps improperly or not at all, preferring to judge conditions by slight variations of their candle flames. Before going down, they could check the upcast shaft to see if the return air coming out of the mine was "muddy" or "thick" (which meant contaminated), "heavy" (dangerous), or "fiery" (explosive). In some of the older mines, fire damp was detected by a "fireman" swathed in wet rags, who crawled along the low galleries, carrying a candle mounted on a long pole. When the flame reached a pocket of gas, it exploded, the man ducked low to let the blast blow over him, and the space was then deemed safe to work in. Inadequate ventilation was almost worse than no ventilation at all, since in the latter case, no miner would venture into a shaft, whereas in the former, fire damp reached its most volatile combination with air. Between 1810 and 1835, as mines were sunk ever deeper, at least 2,070 miners were burned to ashes or blown to bits. For those who survived, the average life expectancy was about fifty years. "The miner," advised a parliamentary panel, "is proverbially short-lived."[4]

The solution to this problem was ventilation. Most mines had a downcast shaft, which drew cool surface air down into the mine, and an upcast shaft, through which hotter air was exhausted. The difference in temperature between the two shafts set up a natural air flow, normally 2,000–3,000 cubic feet per minute, which was then directed through the mine by a complicated set of partitions called "brattices" or "courses." There were a number of defects in this traditional method. The main problem was to keep the downcast flow of fresh air from leaking into the upcast current before it had coursed throughout the mine. The miles of partitions snaking in and out of chambers simply could not be kept tight enough. Small boys, called "trappers," were employed to open and shut sets of trap doors that allowed coal trucks to run through the partitions without letting air escape. Other boys turned the cranks on small mechanical fans to create air currents in the far galleries. These wretched creatures, squatting in damp pockets, in pitch darkness, for ten or twelve hours a day, were notoriously unreliable. As one mine expert lamented, "Attention is not a very common quality of boyhood, nor great discrimination."

The main brattices were built of stone or brick, but those in the newer tunnels were only half-inch planks, made for easy repositioning, and liable to be dislodged. Sometimes miners would dig out side pockets of coal as they drove the galleries out from the main shaft, and these would fill with gas. The air flow could be reduced by a rise in temperature or barometric pressure above ground, and it could be deflected or stopped by piles of waste, by equipment and horses, and by the movement of the corfs, or coal bins, up and down the shafts. The collapse of a roof in the "goaves," or worked-out seam ends, created conditions in which gas percolated up through the jumbled rock and through cracks in the roofs and floors of the galleries. Finally, any explosion could blow away half the brattice work, impeding the ventilation and exposing the surviving miners to deadly after damp.[5] People tend to think of mines as static tunnels dug through hard rock, but as Gurney was to learn over the years, they are actually variable systems of flowing or percolating water, gases, and air. The pressure and direction of currents changed almost minute by minute throughout the mine area, challenging the ingenuity of those in charge of ventilation.

There were several primitive methods of increasing the air flow through the mines. Since the seventeenth century, fires had been lit at the bottom of the upcast shaft, heating or "rarifying" the air to increase the difference in temperature with the downcast or intake shaft. One danger of furnaces, of course, was their proximity to the workings and therefore to fire damp. Another was the owners' practice of "banking" the furnace fires overnight to save fuel, so that gases built up in the workings. By 1830 some owners found that they could heat the upcast shaft with the steam engines they used to haul coal to the surface. An alternative was to cool the downcast shaft by creating a waterfall, although that meant pumping the water back out. Mechanical exhaust fans were not applied to the upcast shaft until after 1835, when William Fourness of Leeds invented a practical version, but few men trusted ventilating machines, because a breakdown would cause immediate danger to everyone in the mine. In any case, as Gurney and others were to learn, the temperature differential and the pressure of air currents in the shafts were extremely difficult to measure and control.

Due to such complications, the expansion of British mining in the 1820s and 1830s led to an alarming increase in accidents and deaths. The scandals finally forced the reformed Parliament to investigate. In June 1835, after 101 men and boys were killed at Wallsend Colliery, Newcastle-on-Tyne, the House of Commons convened a select committee to investigate coal mine safety. The committee took testimony from miners, mine owners, scientific men, engineers, and geologists. The committee confessed that they were unable to solve the problem of mine accidents, but hoped, by publishing the evidence, to rouse and educate the public. To their credit, they were not so much concerned with the production delays and disability expenses that worried the mine owners as with the sheer inhumanity of a system that killed or maimed so many British workingmen. They finally recognized the inadequacy of the Davy lamp and the need for effective systems of ventilation. However, the great variety of geologic formations and methods of mining in Britain made legislation difficult, and they specifically avoided advocating the kind of government inspection system being set up, at that time, by Edwin Chadwick for the Poor Law guardians.[6]

Goldsworthy Gurney, already attending the House in support of the bill to regulate turnpike tolls on steam carriages, was examined by the committee on mines on 17 June 1835. He acknowledged that he was more familiar with Cornish mines than with those in the North, where fire damp was more common, but he said that he had made extensive experiments with explosive gases in 1822.[7] He explained how fire damp became more volatile as it mixed with certain proportions of air, and why the Davy lamp could be rendered unsafe by gusts of air or by coatings of coal dust. He had written a letter to the *Times* about the problem in the summer of 1824, he said; it led to some discussion in scientific institutions, but there had been no reply from Davy himself.

As mentioned in the previous chapter, Gurney suggested replacing the Davy lamp with light from an Argand lamp, or from his new Bude lamp, installed at the surface (where it could burn safely) and reflected by mirrors down the mine shafts and along the galleries. This proposal was apparently too novel for the committee. It was not mentioned in their report, and there is no evidence that it was ever tried by mine owners. By 1839, Gurney himself admitted that it was impractical. However, his testimony on the Davy lamp was supported by other witnesses. It led the committee to conclude that adequate ventilation of the whole mine was the only method of improving safety. Gurney, in fact, was challenged by one of the members to come up with a solution of his own.

At this time he was primarily concerned with his petition on steam carriages, which was stalled in the House of Lords. But his mind typically seized upon the analogy between locomotive chimneys and mine shafts, and he realized that the steam jet could provide the same powerful draft for mine ventilation that it gave to steam boilers. He arranged, therefore, to return to the Select Committee on Mines on 20 July.[8] After showing the dangers of using furnaces, fans, waterfalls, and other methods, he explained how the steam jet worked. By constructing an hour-glass-shaped bottleneck in the upcast shaft and mounting a ring of high-pressure steam jets directly underneath it, one could literally drive the warm air up and out of the shaft, creating a tremendous vacuum, which would draw the atmosphere through a mine at the rate of 350,000 cubic feet per hour, venting ten miles of mine shafts every fifteen minutes. A few bushels of coke would generate the sixty pounds of pressure needed, yet the steam actually used would be minimal. Furthermore, the boiler for the jet could be located at the surface of the mine, safe from fire damp, with the steam pumped down to the jet apparatus through a long pipe. Committee members found the concept and the power of the steam jet hard to imagine (few of them had followed the evidence on steam carriages that closely), but after a good deal of questioning, they concluded that Gurney's invention was certainly worth recommending to mine owners.[9]

The evidence collected by the Select Committee of 1835 at least gave ammunition to Lord Ashley, who campaigned as diligently for the miners as he did for factory workers.[10] In 1840, Ashley secured the appointment of a royal commission, which compiled a three-volume, illustrated indictment of foul air, explosions, wretched hours, and the exploitation of women and children. The Mines Act of 1842, supported by both parties, stiffened safety regulations and got females and younger boys out of the pits. The House of Lords, however, all but eliminated the government inspectors proposed by the Commons, and the number of accidents to men and boys continued to climb.

While Parliament debated, an independent group of community leaders near the South Shields minefield conducted its own investigation of mine safety. The South Shields Committee was formed after a colliery explosion in August 1839 claimed fifty-three lives. Members, none of whom were miners or mine owners, gathered testimony from experts, paid unannounced visits to mines, and supported experiments over three years before issuing a scathing denunciation of traditional procedures and working conditions. Honorary Secretary James Mather, an erstwhile medical student turned wine merchant, published the evidence in 1843, and thereafter campaigned personally for improvements. The South Shields Committee corresponded with Gurney and considered his information so important that they published the letters verbatim.[11] His first, dated 27 September 1839, outlined the general principles of the steam jet and offered to apply it to any available mine for testing.[12] The committee sent him the layout and dimensions of a particular colliery, and by the end of October, he had calculated the size of the boiler and steam jet necessary to ventilate it. In February 1840 drawings and specifications were exchanged, with several modifications suggested by the committee, which tested the jet locally, as it had done with equipment proposed by other experts. In December 1841, Gurney sent the committee data on the power of the jet and its costs, compared to the benefits to be derived.

In its final report of 1843, the South Shields Committee praised the steam jet in the highest possible terms. "Viewing this question in all its bearings, its power, its safety and economy, facility of execution and command, the Committee cannot hesitate to recommend ventilation by high pressure steam, as peculiarly fitted for the present condition of mines, and adapted for them in every stage of their operations." The more the committee examined the jet, the more valuable it grew in their estimation, so that "they now feel assured it is fully adequate to every condition of the mine, and will produce with more certainty and safety an increased rate of ventilation than can be effected by any other means."[13]

The Mines Act of 1842 and the South Shields report in 1843 inspired a flurry of activity among conscientious mine owners and inventors to devise more effective brattice systems, better safety lamps, and new ventilating equipment. Several proprietors of small, shallow mines wrote to Gurney, asking about the steam jet. He sent drawings that showed how to run a high-pressure pipe down the upcast shaft from a surface-mounted boiler, and details of the jet apparatus. He also suggested mounting the jet in a special shaft slanting out from the upcast, leaving the latter free for raising coal baskets. Converting theory into practice was as difficult as ever, however, and many enthusiasts had grasped only the rudiments of the theory to begin with. As James Mather later reported, some owners ran high-pressure steam pipes down their upcast shafts, turned up the ends, and thought they were making "steam jets" like Gurney's. Others adopted his needle-like "tree" of jets but ran their pumps at low pressure, producing a totally ineffective pulsating blast. One competitor, Dr. Brunton, produced a horizontal windmill to extract air from the top of the upcast shaft; another, Struvé, built a pair of eight-foot-diameter low-pressure pumping cylinders on Newcomen's principles.[14] The *Mining Journal* ran dozens of letters, reports, and drawings of novel equipment and methods.

In the winter of 1845–46, Gurney gave a public lecture on the steam jet at the Regent Street Polytechnic Institute, founded by Sir George Cayley in 1839, near the site of Gurney's old steam carriage factory. In the audience was Thomas E. Forster, owner or manager of many large mines around Newcastle-on-Tyne. Forster decided to try a steam jet in one of his more congested mines, Seaton Delaval, comprising more than seven million cubic feet spread over 400 acres. He reviewed his copy of the South Shields Mine Committee report, found Gurney's description of the apparatus, and constructed one of his own. It was basically a set of three-sixteenth-inch jets, arranged in a circle like a chandelier, blowing steam at fifty pounds' pressure up a shaft that had a sectional area of forty feet. The upcast shaft already had a furnace with a boiler at the bottom; Forster merely bent the boiler exhaust pipe into the desired shape, attached the jets, and by trial and error, centered them so as to fill the shaft with the desired cone of steam.[15]

The draft through the mine increased from 53,000 to 79,500 cubic feet per minute. Air circulation improved over a mile away from the upcast shaft, and all the lingering fire damp disappeared. The expense, including the intial investment of £217, was less than with the conventional furnace previously used, which was eventually shut down. All this Forster reported to the *Gateshead Observer* in December 1848, adding: "I claim no credit to myself, except in making the first trial; for it is Mr. Gurney's invention, and to him alone is due the credit."[16]

Since Gurney had been unaware of the experiment, Forster wrote to apprise him of this unexpected success. The letter alone would have satisfied many men, but Gurney knew that the equipment would need continual adjustment to keep working effectively, and he was naturally eager to see his design realized in practice. In April 1846 he travelled to Seaton Delaval at his own expense and spent days helping arrange the jets, and conducting experiments of his own, in a second shaft. As mentioned previously, he obtained help with calculations and instruments from Sir George Cayley. Forster was impressed by his generosity. He later told a committee of the Lords, "I think the country at large are very much indebted to Mr. Gurney for the trouble and pains he has taken."[17]

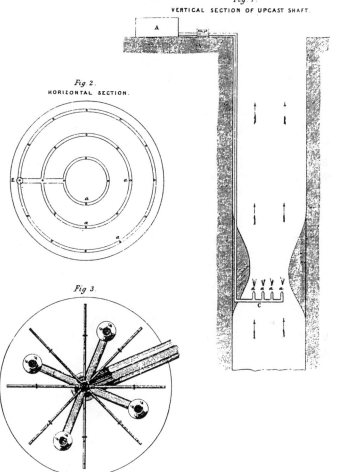

PLAN Nº I.

DIAGRAMS of GOLDSWORTHY GURNEY'S APPARATUS for VENTILATING MINES.
[*Referred to in the Evidence of Goldsworthy Gurney, Esq⁺ of 22ⁿᵈ June, 1849; T.E. Forster, Esq⁺ 5ᵗʰ July, 1849 and G.Elliot, Esq⁺ 6ᵗʰ July, 1849. Pages 63, 51, 264, & 286*]

Fig. 1.

VERTICAL SECTION OF UPCAST SHAFT.

A

Fig. 2.
HORIZONTAL SECTION.

E

a
a
a
a

Fig 3.

Diagrams of Gurney's apparatus for ventilating mines. House of Lords *Sessional Papers* 1849 (613) VII, Report of the Lords Committee on Accidents in Mines, Appendix 1.

The steam jet ventilating system was also applied to chemical processing plants, particularly alkali factories, which emitted sulfur chloride and hydrogen chloride gas. Typically the toxic effluvia spread out over the countryside, combining with atmospheric moisture to form sulfuric and hydrochloric acids. The damage to nearby crops was considerable, leading to heavy fines from landowning magistrates. The only known remedy was to build extremely tall chimneys, trusting the winds to carry the fumes away. Even this did not suffice: the Don alkali works, for example, had paid £300 in damages to local farmers, despite utilizing a 200-foot chimney. The owner of the Don works, like Forster, read about the steam jet and adapted it to his own needs. He constructed a long, enclosed drain, slanting down into the ground and half filled with water. The jet was installed just over the top of the drain and below a cone that made the steam blast more efficient. Toxic gases, smoke, and dust were directed into the bottom end of the drain, to be drawn by the high-powered jet through the water, cooling and condensing them into liquid form, and thence out the top of the drain into a sewer, where they were disposed of. A single ten-horsepower steam engine provided the forty pounds of pressure needed for the jets. Another manufacturer, Swinburne and Company, used three engines to power six steam jets and added coke or charcoal to the water in the drain to help neutralize the gases. Swinburne's representative claimed that "the head may be held over the steam issuing from the drain without any inconvenience to respiration." Today's readers may not think that pouring acids down a sewer into the local groundwater supply was much of an improvement over toxic chimney emissions, but in 1849 it seemed like real progress. In fact, one of Mather's informants suggested that the steam jet method of condensing toxic gases could be used to recover enough sulfur from copper smelting operations to end Britain's dependence on imports.[18]

In April 1849, Gurney received his second request for help from a mine owner, John Darlington of Astley Collieries near Manchester. Like Thomas Forster, Darlington had read about the utility of the steam jet. When the Astley mine caught fire on 2 April, he wrote to Gurney by way of a London newspaperman he knew. The mine had been closed off, he said, but the fire was still burning slowly, creating fire damp as in a huge retort, and toxic gases were escaping from crevices at the surface. Ventilating the mine through the upcast shaft was out of the question because it would simply draw more oxygen down the other shafts, rekindling the blaze. Flooding the mine with water from a nearby canal was the alternative, but that would ruin its commercial value. What was he to do?

At this time Gurney had returned to Bude and was active as a magistrate for both Devon and Cornwall. He left for Manchester as soon as he could arrange his affairs. Edward Cayley met him there, and the two men conceived a novel solution. They knew that steam engines had been used to produce compressed air, which was forced into downcast mine shafts to promote ventilation. Also, from his experiments with Sir George Cayley's hot air engine, Gurney had discovered that forcing a current of air through a deep bed of burning coals could remove the oxygen, releasing nitrogen and carbonic acid—precisely the "choke damp" that suffocated miners. Why not, they reasoned, force choke damp (which was heavier than air or fire damp) into the downcast shaft and let it fill up the mine, while simultaneously drawing the fire damp out through the upcast shaft? When Gurney told Darlington of his plan, the latter was highly skeptical. Where would they get enough choke damp to fill three miles of mine shafts? "Get it from the winds of heaven," Gurney exclaimed, "and from the waste coal you have lying about."[19] Having convinced Darlington of the scientific merit of this approach, Gurney built a large furnace with an eighteen-inch-deep bed of coal and limestone to produce the choke damp. He sent to Wigan for gas tubes that could be used as vent pipes, and ran them through a water trough to cool the damp before it was pumped into the downcast shaft. The shaft, four hundred feet deep, registered 460 to 480 degrees Fahrenheit, a column of extremely buoyant hot air that required a great deal of pressure to drive down through the mine. On 29 April, after this apparatus began working, Gurney started up a small exhaust furnace, equipped with a second steam jet, at the upcast shaft. Within two hours observers could see and smell clouds of choke damp emerging from the shaft. Soon there was enough to extinguish a safety lamp held in its way. The choke damp was pumped through the mine for over five hours, and spread over the surrounding countryside as it emerged from the upcast shaft. Then, Gurney shut off the choke damp inflow and drew fresh air through the mine, clearing it in two hours and twenty minutes. Darlington and a couple of foremen ventured down the shaft and reported it free of fire damp. The workmen, enthusiastic over the quick recovery, tried to return to the galleries for work, but Gurney, determined to be absolutely sure of their safety, warned them off and left the exhaust running through the night. The next morning the men explored the whole mine and found the fire and fumes gone. On 30 April, Darlington reported the remarkable episode to the *Times*.[20]

Just over a month later, in June 1849, the House of Lords, finally responding to reports of increased mine accidents, convened another select committee. Their ostensible purpose was to evaluate the need for government inspectors and find out whether the mine owners would tolerate them. However, the chairman, Baron Wharncliffe, seemed chiefly concerned to reassemble all the information published by the Commons in 1835 and by the South Shields Committee in 1843. Lord Wharncliffe was the son of the Yorkshire peer who had been Gurney's nemesis in the matter of steam carriages in 1836. He was less obstreperous than his father, and this time Gurney had much stronger support for his cause. Called to testify on 22 June, he brought a working model of the steam jet to the committee room, explained how it worked, and described the methods used to measure its performance in mines. "We can produce a hurricane simply by turning the handle of a stop-cock!" he exclaimed.[21] He referred to the recommendations of the South Shields Committee and recounted his successes at the Seaton Delaval and Astley collieries. John Darlington came down on the 25th to verify his claims, testifying that the equipment used had cost a mere ten pounds. "The steam jet is now used to ventilate the mine; the galleries are perfectly clear; and the men are working with naked candles." Furthermore, Darlington had smothered a second fire that erupted on 5 June in another location by using a furnace at the bottom of the downcast shaft to produce choke damp, according to instructions Gurney had given before he left. Darlington was followed by James Mather, who reviewed the report of his South Shields Committee. He had paid a surprise visit to the Seaton Delaval colliery on 3 July and cited precise data that he had collected on the performance of the jet, compared to conventional furnaces. Thomas Forster also testified at length about Seaton Delaval and other mines, reading his commendatory letter to the *Gateshead Observer* into the official record.[22]

Some members of the select committee assumed that Gurney had a patent on the steam jet and was testifying to his own advantage, a common practice in parliamentary hearings. They were somewhat incredulous when he denied it, saying, "The only interest I have is the common interest of all—to save life, mixed with some feeling of personal merit." Nor was he overconfident about the methods used by Darlington and Forster. Driving choke damp into the downcast shaft had worked this time, he said, but it was an uncertain method, because the long columns of air were quite elastic, responding erratically to the force used against them. Similarly, he was not sure that steam jets located in the bottom of the upcast shaft could successfully be fed through long pipes from boilers at the top except in smaller, shallow mines. With the boiler down in the shaft, however, the jet was bound to improve draft throughout the works.[23]

As we have seen, Gurney was familiar with the instruments used to measure air pressure, temperature, and velocity, and had studied mine ventilation as a question of fluid mechanics. He was therefore able to explain a common fallacy associated with the use of simple furnaces to move the air. The fallacy was in the reading of the pressure gauge, usually a long, U-shaped water pipe connected to the upcast and downcast shafts. Engine mechanics thought that when the gauge showed a high pressure, air was being forced through the mine at high speed. Not so, said Gurney. The mine shafts are like the arteries in a human body. High pressure is a measure of resistance and inertia, not movement.

This "furnace paradox" was related to two other phenomena identified by Gurney. First, the moving air was subject to friction against the irregular sides of the mine shafts and galleries, which produced eddies and increased resistance. This he labelled the "vena contracta," a medical term for arteries clogged by fatty tissues, today called atherosclerosis, which he would have seen fairly often in autopsies. Gurney was credited with the first mention of its effect in mines, in 1849, and would later observe it in the currents of the Thames River.[24]

The resistance of air in the mine shafts increased as the square of its velocity, so there was a limit to the draft obtainable by heating the upcast with a simple furnace. When this limit was reached, the air in the upcast shaft simply became hotter and thinner without increasing the movement of the air behind it. This created a type of reverse vacuum, pulling air from the external atmosphere down the sides of the upcast shaft, while hot air escaped up the center. The result was what Gurney called a "natural brattice" in the shaft, which diminished the draft through the mine. Natural brattices were a problem for the steam jet, too, but only when it was installed off-center, so that the cone of steam did not fill the whole area of the shaft. Otherwise the steam jet, being an essentially mechanical force, was not subject to the limits experienced with furnaces.[25]

Much of Gurney's testimony was condensed and published in the committee's report to the House of Lords on 1 August 1849. A diagram of the steam jet and its placement in a mine shaft was appended, and the jet itself was warmly recommended, as it had been in 1843. The report led, among other things, to the adoption of legislation bringing government inspectors into the mines, as they were already operating in factories, poorhouses, and boards of health. But it did not reduce the number of accidents. Miners continued to die from fire, explosion, and collapsed walls at the rate of a thousand a year. Most mine owners continued to use traditional methods, but a few experimented with the new ventilating fans, pumps, and jets. John Darlington applied the steam jet to a coal pit in North Wales, where explosions and fires had caused the previous owners to abandon the works. Purchasing the estate at a low price, he cleared out the fire damp in a matter of hours and soon had men working at the coal face. Another proprietor, having only one shaft for both intake and exhaust, devised a makeshift steam jet on top of his boiler and directed it through a square vent pipe up the middle of the shaft. Unfortunately, some of these self-designed and self-built systems failed through ignorance of basic principles, and because they were based on Gurney's ideas, he suffered some adverse publicity, just as he had with the steam carriage. But there were also successes. In the summer of 1850, Gurney, Edward Cayley, and James Mather used the choke damp process at Lord Mansfield's South Sauchie colliery near Stirling in Scotland, where fires had raged for almost thirty years, making it "scarcely penetrable." Cayley contrived a water spray, or "Scotch mist," which blended with the damp, cooling it before it was pumped into the downcast shaft. Driven at 7,900 cubic feet per minute, some twelve million cubic feet of the mixture filled the mine over a period of twenty hours, and the apparatus was left running for several days to ensure that all fires were extinguished. Then the jet was reversed and the mine cleared. Lord Mansfield declared himself satisfied that the mine was now safe to work, and upon his recommendation, the apparatus was applied to several other collieries in Scotland.[26]

Mine ventilation was now becoming a highly competitive enterprise, and Gurney's steam jet was not without its rivals and critics. William Struvé, inventor of a large mechanical ventilating fan, presented a paper on the merits of his machine to the Institution of Civil Engineers on 19 November 1850. He was seconded by Frank Forster, the experienced chief engineer of London's Metropolitan Commission of Sewers, and by several mine owners. But James Darlington, who had come down for the meeting, interjected an account of Gurney's success at his own mine, and Alexander Gordon, Gurney's advocate from his steam carriage days, rehearsed the successes of the steam jet and praised its inventor for his public generosity. As the secretary noted, "Mr. Gurney then referred to, and examined at great length, the evidence given before the Committees of the Lords in 1849, and the Commons in 1835, and that before the South Shields Committee in 1843." In fact, the argument carried over into the following week, taking up the whole of the meeting. Struvé challenged the conclusions that Gurney drew from his experiments, and detailed negative results from steam jet installations that Gurney had not personally supervised. Presaging future attacks, he quoted evidence from inquiries by Nicholas Wood, an important colliery agent and former critic of Gurney's steam locomotives.[27]

In November 1851, Gurney was summoned to the Great Lever Colliery at Burden, near Bolton, after an explosion of fire damp. The *Mining Journal* at first reported complete success, but later admitted that the fire had returned and was burning as fiercely as ever. An observer who detailed the operations at Burden wrote: "Mr. Gurney's application of choke damp is universally admitted to be right in theory. The immediate practical success of it depends upon it being under certain conditions."[28] The editor of the *Mining Journal* wrote:

> We have more than once spoken of a certain gentleman's scientific services to mines and . . . the devoted attention to the great subject of their ventilation paid by Mr. Gurney. His evident anxiety to the utmost of his power to prevent those appalling catastrophes that are so terrible to miners and distressing to humanity, his labours undeterred by expense or personal exertion—all mark him as a man to whom the miners are indebted [and] upon whom the Government of our Country should bestow some mark of distinction. We trust this hint will not be lost on the present Government. A man like this belongs to no Government, or rather belongs to all.[29]

Following a terrible colliery disaster early in 1852, Edward Cayley used his influence in the House of Commons to assemble another select committee on mine safety, through which he hoped to publicize Gurney's work. Noting the lateness of the session and the thorough research done by the South Shields Committee (in 1843) and Lord Wharncliffe's committee (in 1849), this group concentrated on practical applications of ventilating machinery. At issue was the efficacy of mechanical fans or pumps, compared to traditional furnaces and steam jets. As usual the proceedings were tilted in favor of one view. Cayley, as chair of the committee, fed Gurney many leading questions and arranged for the committee and witnesses to visit the Regent's Park Polytechnic Institution for a round of demonstrations and experiments. He also subtly disparaged the champion of traditional furnace ventilation, Nicholas Wood. In his report, dated 1 August 1852, Cayley maintained that mechanical means of ventilation were still liable to fail unexpectedly, unlike furnaces and steam jets. Furnaces were sufficient for many situations, especially in deep mines, where they could be insulated from the working galleries, but their susceptibility to the "furnace limit," the "furnace paradox," and the problem of "natural brattices" was pointed out. "To the powers of the steam jet, on the other hand, there appears to be no practical limit." The committee was unanimous in stating that the jet was the most dynamic and least expensive method of ventilating mines. In fiery mines, especially, where fire damp and afterdamp were most troublesome, it was advisable to have a steam jet installed at the downcast shaft to force choke damp down the mine when needed, even if a conventional furnace was used most of the time.[30]

Gurney, meanwhile, took measures outside of Parliament to arouse interest in mine safety. He wrote to the *Times* that the normal reaction of the public to frequent catastrophes and appalling losses of life was to exclaim, "Something must be done!" and then forget all about it. Therefore, after giving his credentials in the field of mining ventilation, he called for the formation of a Society for Preventing Loss of Life in Collieries, on the same principle used by other societies for fire prevention, shipwrecks, etc., to collect and distribute information about fires and explosions. By combining the talents and knowledge of a variety of people, such a society could effect much improvement. This suggestion was reprinted by the *Mining Journal* with praise for Gurney's "spirit of philanthropy which always induced him to exertions for bettering the conditions of the working collier."[31]

It is possible that Gurney himself wished to lead the society he proposed and hoped to use it to advance research on applications of the steam jet. However, others gained the initiative. On 3 July 1852 a large group of owners, managers, inspectors, and others interested in collieries met at Newcastle to form the North of England Institute of Mining and Mechanical Engineers. It was inaugurated 3 September with Nicholas Wood as its president. In many respects, the North of England Institute was merely the first of a dozen related mining engineering societies set up in imitation of earlier metropolitan institutions. Mechanical engineers had formed their own institution in Birmingham in 1847, breaking away from the Institution of Civil Engineers (ICE) in London. Like those precursors, and like the British Association for the Advancement of Science, the new institutes held regular meetings to present papers and discuss technical topics, publishing the proceedings in trade journals. However, even if the North of England Institute had more general objectives, the timing of its inauguration suggests that its immediate purpose was to control the debate over mine ventilation. Gurney, not a trained engineer, was elected an honorary member, following the practice of the ICE. He could hardly have been pleased that such recognition came at the hands of one of his most determined opponents.[32]

Nicholas Wood (1795–1865) had prospered as a locomotive engineer for several railways before turning to mining in 1844 and becoming manager or proprietor of the largest group of collieries in the North of England. He was widely regarded as an expert on all aspects of mining, a researcher as well as practical engineer. Back in 1831, however, he had published *A Practical Treatise on Railroads*, which ran to three editions by 1838, and significantly for Gurney's career, promoted railways at the expense of road steam carriages.[33] Wood was thus very familiar with the steam jet, and despite its contribution to the success of railway locomotives, he was not favorably disposed toward Gurney. When Cayley's select committee discounted his testimony on furnace ventilation in favor of Gurney's and Forster's evidence, and even mentioned in their report that one of his furnaces had recently exploded, Wood sought revenge. He proposed to Cayley that the North of England Institute should conduct a series of experiments directly comparing furnaces, steam jets, and mechanical exhaust fans or pumps. Although Wood himself would arrange the experiments, Gurney, Forster, and other experts would be invited to observe, and the data would be submitted to Parliament at the end of the 1852–53 session for evaluation. Because no direct comparisons had ever been made under objective test conditions, this offer could hardly be refused.[34]

Wood and his associates set to work immediately, and by July 1853 had compiled a massive table of comparative data. This was presented to a reorganized select committee, for which Edward J. Hutchins replaced Edward Cayley as chair and to which Robert Stephenson and Joseph Locke, well-known railway engineers who had opposed Gurney's steam carriage in 1834, were added. Wood had already published his findings as a pair of lectures to the North of England Institute and now reviewed them in detail, denigrating the steam jet at every turn. Gurney's advocate, T. E. Forster, challenged Wood but could only repeat the evidence he had given the previous year. Gurney himself made a bad impression by complaining that his "invitation" to attend Wood's experiments had arrived in the form of a lithographed notice sent in the name of a stranger, and that the experiments were conducted in Durham, 400 miles from his home. "I did not see the use of attending to witness experiments, after they had been got up by another person, on which I had not been consulted," he said. As for Wood's data, "there is not a single table in which you cannot find discrepancies." Wood had neither narrowed the neck of the mine shafts nor installed the steam jet at dead center, so natural brattices developed, as Gurney had predicted in 1843. The same error was made in 1849, he said, and Mr. Wood was shown it and acknowledged it, but made it yet again. Since Wood's steam jets were too small and the exhaust chambers too large, "the experiments were altogether incapable of producing any power."[35]

The two sides clashed again in the spring of 1854, Darlington and Mather testifying on behalf of the steam jet, while a mine owner and agent named George Elliott supported Wood's calculations with data from his own experiments. Gurney was not called to testify. In its fourth and final report, issued at the end of June, the committee concluded that the controversy over the merits of steam jets, furnaces, and mechanical blowers had been beneficial, leading to a general improvement in mine ventilation. For that reason they declined to legislate a specific choice, merely recommending that every colliery be required to have some backup ventilating apparatus in place. Having compared the several devices, however, they stated that "the preponderance of evidence is decidely in favor of the [traditional] furnace." They allowed that the Lords, in 1849, and the Commons, in 1852, had championed the steam jet, but "Mr. Wood's extensive investigations" had proved that for deeper mines the furnace was cheaper and more effective. Gurney's concepts of the "furnace limit" and the "natural brattice" were "theoretical views," not practically relevant to the furnace. His steam jets might be helpful in shallow mines or as auxiliaries to regular furnaces, but could not be recommended as the sole means of ventilation.[36]

Once again Gurney's achievements had been denigrated and suppressed by hostile competitors and old enemies. Whether the steam jet could have been applied successfully to most mines will never be known. Miners in general tended to regard novelty with suspicion, and despite Parliament's earlier advocacy of the new methods of ventilation, some miners openly criticized the "scientific men" from Westminster for poking their noses into matters of which they had no practical experience.[37] Those who accepted the need for change could not agree on the preferred apparatus. The problem for Gurney, as for other inventors of his type, was that his steam jets required a good deal of tinkering and constant supervision to work effectively. Mine conditions changed quickly and erratically depending on the weather, the movement of the coal trams through the shafts, the condition of bratticework, the miners' shift changes, and a dozen other variables. None of the ventilating systems had reached a stage of development at which they could operate without constant attention. Where Gurney or an experienced mining engineer was present, the steam jet apparently performed admirably. But Gurney was obviously unable to superintend every such installation or to train a corps of mechanics for it. Unless an organization, such as the North of England Institute of Mining Engineers, adopted the steam jet as an industry standard, it could not succeed. And the Institute had been captured by a dedicated opponent. A quarter-century later, the Institute published the results of extended comparisons of mine ventilating systems, concluding that the steam jet was relatively ineffective and inefficient. In the meantime an innovative mechanical fan had proved successful and was installed at about two hundred mines.[38]

Gurney might have been crushed by this turn of events, so reminiscent of his earlier ventures, had he not become involved in more rewarding pursuits. In a supreme bit of irony, the publication of the Commons select committee's report on mine ventilation in late July 1854 coincided with Gurney's appointment as superintendent of heating, lighting, and ventilation for the very building in which the committee sat, the New Palace at Westminster.

11

Parliament

On 11 OCTOBER 1834, A DISASTROUS FIRE BROKE OUT IN THE OLD HOUSES OF Parliament and destroyed most of the edifice, leaving only ancient Westminster Hall and Henry III's little Jewel Tower intact. The Commons had to be accommodated in the old Lords' chamber, and the Lords moved to the cramped, stuffy Painted Chamber. After a much-publicized competition, the government selected Charles Barry's romantic medieval design for a "New Palace," as it was called for the next quarter-century. Construction commenced with the usual delays, confusion, arguments, and charges of mismanagement and incompetence that attend all great public works. The New Palace was larger and more complex than any previous building, and there was the added difficulty of accommodating the whims and crotchets of several hundred Lords and members of Commons. Barry had constant difficulties with his overseers at Her Majesty's Office of Woods and Forests. This agency, created by Charles II with Christopher Wren as its first commissioner, was in charge of all royal lands as well as the buildings upon them, and it had just been merged with its twin, the Office of Works, which supervised the building and repair of utilitarian edifices like river walls, sewers, and bridges. The First Commissioner of Woods and Forests was usually a minor aristocrat, politically useful to the government of the day, who was not considered formidable enough for high cabinet office. Through most of the 1830s, the Commissioner was John William Ponsonby, Lord Duncannon, (1781–1847), a reform Whig known for his high principles, easy manners, good business sense, industry, and accuracy.[1] He was responsible to the Treasury and was assisted by two junior commissioners, a solicitor, and an office clerk, who carried on day-to-day business. The technical staff was miniscule: the office contracted with independent architects, surveyors, or engineers for each of its projects, sometimes incorporating itself as a special commission for the purpose. Projects around London and Westminster usually involved liaison with local authorities and their engineers or inspectors. The result of these ad hoc procedures was a good deal of confusion about lines of authority and methods of payment.[2]

By 1839, Barry was so overwhelmed by design changes, shifting timetables, and cost restrictions that he asked Lord Duncannon to appoint two special assistants, one to install a system of lighting in place of the huge chandeliers in the remnant of the Old Palace being used as a temporary House of Commons, the other to design a ventilating system for the New Palace. Gurney was not invited to present his views on ventilation at this time, although he would later become Parliament's chief officer for that purpose. However, he was asked to conduct experiments to determine the best mode of lighting. This opportunity grew out of his previous research on the Drummond light at Trinity House, reported to the Commons committee on lighthouses in 1834. As mentioned previously, Gurney had developed a new version of the common Argand lamp, called the Bude lamp, which featured four concentric rings of gas flame enhanced by oxygen fed through a blowpipe. Having tested it successfully, he reported the results to Michael Faraday in October 1838. Faraday confirmed the superiority of the Bude light by his own tests and recommended it to the trustees of Trinity House for all their lighthouses. He then showed it to the chairman of the Commons lighthouse committee, Joseph Hume, who, like every other member of Parliament, was involved with improvements to the New Palace and impatient with arrangements in the temporary House of Commons.[3] Hume got permission from Charles Barry and from the Chancellor of the Exchequer, Thomas Spring-Rice, to let Gurney test his new light in the "old" Commons. He convened a select committee in the spring of 1839 to oversee the experiments. Included were Spring-Rice, Robert Peel, and Cornish MPs Sir William Molesworth, Sir Charles Lemon, and Sir Thomas Acland, the last of whom held the lease on Gurney's Castle at Bude, where the light had been developed.[4]

The temporary chamber occupied by Commons was in the shape of a double cube, forty feet wide by eighty feet long. It had thirty-foot walls supporting a peaked roof. An interior ceiling of glazed glass panels spanned the room about twenty-nine feet from the floor, and a double row of chandeliers, bearing "a forest" of fifteen-inch candles, hung below the ceiling on chains. Since the great fire of 1834, members were nervous about the old fixtures. The mass of candles generated heat and smoke, and the illumination was neither so steady nor so bright as the newer oil lamps. Backbenchers, seated under the visitors' galleries, peered out through deep shadows, while members directly under the chandeliers were occasionally spattered with dripping wax. Both Argand oil lamps and gas lamps had been installed on a trial basis with disappointing results.[5]

Gurney met with the committee on 30 May 1839 to explain the workings of the Bude lamp. A single lamp with quarter-inch burners could give light equal to two Argands with seven-eighth-inch burners, or to ten wax candles.[6] The Bude cost as much as the Argand to build but used only one-fourth as much oil. In answer to the committee's questions, Gurney claimed that the Bude light was safe to use, could be maintained by ordinary workmen with a minimum of training, and could be vented to carry off the heat of burning. If oxygen was used, it could be easily produced from manganese mined in Cornwall and Devonshire. It could be supplied to the lamps by flexible tubing, so that they could be raised or lowered to trim their wicks or clean the flues. Otherwise a supply of pure air would produce nearly the same effect.[7]

Gurney's testimony was supported by Faraday, who said that the Bude lamp burned longer between trimmings and had a steadier flame. Sir David Brewster claimed that he had recommended the lamp years ago to the Northern (Scotland) Lighthouse commissioners and had described it in an article for the *Edinburgh Review*. Dr. Andrew Ure, a leading author of works on science and technology who had just completed an extensive comparative study of all types of lighting, supported Faraday's recommendation. Dr. Dionysius Lardner, who had celebrated Gurney's steam carriages, and Sir George Cayley also testified on Gurney's behalf. Chancellor Spring-Rice finally agreed to go ahead with the experiment, grudgingly allowing £100 for expenses with no remuneration for Gurney himself.

Gurney hired an experienced brass-lamp manufacturer, Frederick Rixon, to assist him. During June and July 1839, between sittings of the House, they tried a variety of arrangements. Dr. Ure and another lighting expert, Dr. Neil Arnott, usually attended to give advice and witness the results. It was soon evident that a single Bude lamp produced sufficient light for the whole chamber. The phenomenon was so clearly unique that a clutch of newspaper reporters began covering the tests. But there were problems. The first lamp was equipped with a cut-glass shade like a lighthouse reflector, which threw glaring prisms of light over the walls and cast deep shadows under the galleries. Gurney then experimented with different types of globes and reflectors, tried two or three lamps in various patterns, and moved the lamps above the ceiling. He even stretched white calico cloth across the glass to soften the glare. At the end of July, he settled on a set of seven single-burner lights, hung in two rows from each side of the roof, above the glass ceiling, with frosted reflectors that helped illuminate the space below the galleries. This arrangement proved expensive to run, and the House quickly directed Hume to get rid of it. Gurney and his associates then decided to hang the lamps below the ceiling, with ground-glass clock faces mounted horizonally below each one to soften and reflect the light. Most members expressed satisfaction with the results, but Sir Frederick Trench, a well-connected veteran of London improvement schemes who had designed the original chandeliers, launched a violent attack on the whole project. Hume had to withdraw the committee's recommendation to make the installation permanent and instead agree that Gurney should continue his experiments during the upcoming recess, under the supervision of the First Commissioner of Works. As before, the Treasury agreed to cover his expenses, but "his own time and personal services should be paid for by a Vote of the House, it being a matter immediately for their comfort and consideration."[8]

By this time Gurney had made so many minor changes in the Bude light that he felt justified in obtaining a patent on it (8 June, no. 8098, with Rixon). Faraday raised no objections on the part of Trinity House. Further important modifications occurred during the late summer and autumn of 1839. The oxygen supply tubing attached to the lamps in the House of Commons had made it difficult to get at them, to trim the oil wicks, without interrupting debates. Furthermore, the supply of manganese for producing the oxygen turned out to be more expensive and uncertain than Gurney thought. He already knew that air might serve almost as well as oxygen; now he tried substituting purified coal gas for oil. The gas was first drawn from charcoal and then impregnated with vapors of naphtha, turpentine, and India rubber. This procedure, based on experiments he had made in 1822, not only made the gas less smoky when burned, but lowered its combustion temperature by thirty percent. Gurney refashioned the lamps in the House of Commons on the new principles, using a set of gas pipes which had been installed for a previous (unsuccessful) lighting system by Dr. David Reid. The new "atmospheric" Bude lamp proved highly successful. It was much easier and cheaper to supply than the oxygen type and needed less maintenance. In fact, Gurney left supervision of the lamps to his workmen and only inspected them weekly, on principle. He was careful to tell the House, of course, that such inspections were absolutely necessary and should only be carried out by a "scientific man." The new lighting was soon extended to the parliamentary libraries, the lobbies, and one of the committee rooms. Additional lamps were installed in the Clapham Church where a single, eleven-inch burner

The Bude lamp, one of four mounted near Trafalgar Square, 1842. By permission of the Bude-Stratton Town Museum.

lit the whole building; in St. Mary's Church at Spitalfields; and in Rolls Church, Chancery Lane. On 10 January 1842, he placed a large lamp at Waterloo Place, just up the steps from Pall Mall, and some time later installed four more in Trafalgar Square.[9] This was an effective advertisement for his skills, as the locations were crossed by political and financial men daily and were also accessible to curious sightseers. Gurney obtained patents on this atmospheric Bude lamp in March 1841 (no. 8902), and in August 1842 (no. 9451).[10]

Getting paid by government was another matter. Gurney's agreement with the Treasury was reconfirmed by the Office of Woods and Forests in February 1840. The expenses (£777) of testing, installing, and maintaining the new lighting system were paid, but no action was taken to compensate him for his services.[11] A year later the House of Commons sergeant at arms asked him to give an estimate for continuing his services for the period from April 1841 to April 1842. Although reluctant to continue, as he was busy on other projects, Gurney agreed but inserted a condition, that his compensation be finally determined and paid by the Office of Woods or by the House itself. In May 1842 a new select committee, with many of the same members as in 1839, interviewed Gurney, Dr. Ure, and other scientific witnesses, and polled members of the House. Everyone agreed that the Bude light gave forty to fifty percent more light, for the same amount of fuel, than any previous device. Whereas the House had spent £935 for candles and oil lamps in 1838–39, they had spent only £531 for Gurney's system in 1841–42. "In conclusion," they reported, "Mr. Gurney has been employed three years, has effected considerable savings, and has put the House in possession of a cheap, beautiful, and effective system of Lighting, which may be applied to the future Houses of Parliament." They recommended that he receive £1,600 for the four years ending in April 1843. Gurney apparently asked for royalties on his patent as well, but although the committee recognized the originality of his invention, they claimed that their agreement with him referred only to services.[12]

In March 1843, as his contract was drawing to a close, Gurney received a note from the sergeant at arms of the House, William Gossett, asking whether he was willing to continue to supervise the lighting another year. Gurney replied in the affirmative, requesting the same rate of compensation, £400 per annum. Gossett said that he knew nothing about such rates, which could come only from the Office of Woods and Forests. Gurney applied there, but received no answer. He feared what would happen if government officials allowed untrained crews to operate the lighting for minimum wages. In the evening of 31 March, he wrote to Gossett, "We are driven into a corner. I have no answer and it is now past eleven. There is no provision for lighting the House and, unless I contract tonight, great inconvenience will, I fear, arise. I feel morally bound to those who have supported me in this matter, that no discredit should unfairly fall on the system or myself. I have, therefore, signed and enclose a contract to go on as before. No doubt the House will see me paid."[13]

The contract Gurney submitted provided for the cost of men and materials used in maintaining and perfecting the system he had already installed, but left remuneration for service to a future vote of the House. Having learned to his grief in the 1830s what could happen if one of his inventions was left for others to develop, he supervised his lighting system at his own expense from 1843 to 1847. The lights were fitted with self-acting regulators to keep their brightness steady. They were enclosed in airtight glass chambers, and the heat and fumes drawn off through eduction tubes so that they did not interfere with the ventilation, an arrangement worked out previously by Michael Faraday's brother Robert, and nephew James, who ran a gas lighting business.[14] Eventually the whole set of sixty burners was controlled by one of the building's own carpenters, after two days' training.

In his agreement with the sergeant at arms, Gurney had reserved the right to supply the House with his manufactured lights and to collect royalties on the patent. Immediately after this he set up a company to market the Bude light. The company offered shares to the public through an advertisement in the *Mining Journal* on 1 April 1843 which rehearsed the advantages of the light, noted its use in Parliament, and speculated that churches, public buildings, private residences, and shops would all make use of it. The advertisement claimed that the patent owners had consented to transfer their rights to the company in return for shares, convincing proof of their confidence in the venture. It did not mention that the patentees themselves had formed the company in the first place.[15]

Notwithstanding his patent, his company, and his agreement with the sergeant at arms, Gurney's arrangements for the House of Commons were not protected against the frequent changes of personnel and policy at the Office of Woods and Forests. Lord Lincoln, the industrious but headstrong First Commissioner in the early 1840s, alienated his junior commissioners, Alexander Milne and Charles Gore, who together sabotaged his programs.[16] Milne, in charge of public works, refused to continue the annual subvention for Gurney's experiments after 1843, so Gurney had to do the work at his own risk and expense. He was urged by friends to apply again through other channels, but he insisted that he would be vindicated when his system was installed in the new Houses of Parliament. This was a reasonable expectation, given the success he had had so far. But his technical genius had been accommodated and displayed through the influence of political friends, and such influence has a way of shifting at the most inopportune moments. In July 1846, when the Whigs returned to office under Lord John Russell, Lord Morpeth took Lincoln's place. Eldest son and heir of the Earl of Carlisle, Lord Morpeth was kindhearted, fluent in debate, cultivated in the arts, but "without commanding abilities or great strength of will."[17] He readily deferred to Milne and Gore, who controlled day-to-day business at Woods and Forests as they had done under Lord Lincoln. They were now joined by Edwin Chadwick, the aggressive Benthamite reformer, whose campaigns for a centralized board of health and a metropolitan sewer commission were at their peak. Chadwick was determined to bring all activities under unified direction. As usually happens with a change of administration, there were also investigations into irregularities with the building of the new Houses of Parliament, and demands by W. E. Gladstone and his fellow budget-cutters for a thorough review of government spending.

While these political intrigues were going on, Gurney was called upon to give his advice on lighting the New Palace. His system was now familiar to members, but as a result of developing it in public, as it were, its principles were also known to his rivals. Dr. David Reid, already involved in the ventilation of the buildings, proposed a complicated arrangement of Argand lamps suspended, like Gurney's, from receptacles in the ceiling. He also testified that the heat given off by Gurney's lighting would upset his ventilating arrangements. Sir Charles Barry offered a design, incorporating Robert Faraday's eduction principle as Gurney had done, which carried the burned gases back through the middle of the gas supply pipes. Gurney soon found himself squeezed between two aggressive opponents. Reid and Barry were at loggerheads on every issue, and their rivalry was threatening to bring construction to a halt. Parliament, with the wisdom of Solomon, decided to split the New Palace down the middle, giving half to each man for a period of experiment. Barry took the House of Lords, Reid the Commons. Gurney was shut out.

These convulsions also led the Office of Woods and Forests to take over Gurney's experimental lighting in the temporary House of Commons at the end of March 1847. The men he had trained to assist him were retained by the Office to continue the work. This meant a double blow: he lost control of a system still associated with his name, and he lost the use of trained workmen he could have used on other projects. To add injury to insult, the Office of Works refused to recognize his right as exclusive agent for the manufacturer; they purchased new burners directly, without paying him the five-guinea fee, and declined to consider payment of the royalties he had earned in the previous years.[18]

Gurney petitioned Joseph Hume for relief, but in the next session of Parliament, the Whig leaders appointed select committees to probe every aspect of Treasury spending, particularly the scandalous tradition of staff incompetence and muddled finances at the Office of Woods and Forests. As Hume had led the cry for reform for many years, it was a particularly bad time for him to argue that Gurney deserved special treatment and compensation for work that the Office had, in fact, never legally sanctioned. He was nevertheless moved to speak when he learned in 1849 that Barry was to have the contract for lighting the New Palace that Gurney had expected. He rehearsed the series of experiments Gurney had made in the previous decade, the annual expenses paid by the Treasury to 1843, and Parliament's delayed compensation. Giving the development of the House lighting to men less competent and ignoring Gurney's rights as agent for the manufacturer were acts of injustice to "a most able and most liberal man," who had given "long and continuous service in the public behalf." He was, said Hume, the only man in England capable of carrying out the intentions of the original committees. He argued strenuously that Gurney should light the new Houses of Parliament, but he was too late to influence that decision.[19]

Within five years, however, Gurney was vindicated. Barry's Faraday lamps produced too much heat for the ventilating system to deal with, and were removed in April 1852. Dr. Reid then installed his gas lights, both in the ceilings and outside the chamber windows, but these were also found unsatisfactory.[20] In the meantime, the parliamentary committees investigating Woods and Forests had decided to separate it from the Office of Works and put it under a cabinet-level first commissioner. Woods and Forests returned to its former concern with Crown lands, with the durable Charles Gore as commissioner. Sir John Manners became First Commissioner of Works under the Tory government of 1852, but when it fell in December, he was replaced by Sir William Molesworth, the East Cornwall Whig who had introduced Gurney's petition on turnpike tolls in 1834.[21] Sir William saw to it that Gurney's lighting system was selected to replace Reid's on a trial basis. It was installed by 30 June 1853, and within a year had proved its effectiveness to the satisfaction of both Lords and Commons.[22] Gurney was then asked to study the heating and ventilation of the New Palace with a view to integrating them with the lighting. In August 1854 he was appointed sole officer for all three systems.

To understand this remarkable turn of events, and to understand what changes Gurney made after his appointment, it is necessary to go back to 1834 and pick up a different thread in the history of the New Palace, namely the course of experiments for heating and ventilating its rooms. The challenge was enormous. There were to be a bewildering number and variety of rooms, and the number of members, guests, officers, and servants inside at any time could change from a few to over 500 in a relatively short time, depending on whether Parliament was in session and what question was being debated. Scientific knowledge about ventilation, in the early nineteenth century, was highly uncertain. Venting and heating of private homes, theaters, hospitals, and prisons had attained some systematic rules through trial and error, but public buildings were too idiosyncratic, and their uses too unpredictable, to be standardized. There was a difference of opinion about the volume of air needed in such buildings: some said four cubic feet per minute, per person, per room, whereas others considered eight to ten cubic feet per person appropriate. There were also competing methods of creating the draft of air. In the old House of Commons, drafts had been created by a hand-driven fan and bellows. Fans could also be worked by water wheels or steam engines. A thermal method, using a furnace and chimney as was done in mine shafts, was increasingly common in the early nineteenth century. In each case the engineer would have to consider the effect of the draft on people's feet and heads, currents and countercurrents set up by doorways, windows and staircases, and possible contamination by smoke or odors from the committee room fireplaces and the outside environment.[23]

After the fire of 1834, when the House of Commons was sitting in the former House of Lords chamber, a series of select committees heard testimony from ventilation experts, among whom was Dr. David Boswell Reid (1805–63), introduced above. Reid had earned his medical degree at the University of Edinburgh in 1830, but then supported himself by offering lectures and practical courses in chemistry and physiology to as many as a dozen organizations, many of them simultaneously, in addition to his own extramural classes at the university. At the Edinburgh meeting of the Association for the Advancement of Science in the summer of 1834, he invited participants to observe his classroom and laboratory, where they could see his experimental heating, ventilating, and acoustical equipment at work.[24] Since several members of Parliament had attended the scientific meeting, they thought of Dr. Reid when the Old Palace burned just a few months later.

While other witnesses were appropriately cautious and noncommittal regarding the best means of ventilating the New Palace, Dr. Reid appeared confident, technically impressive, and ready to put his ideas into practice in the temporary Commons chamber. He proposed to admit air through vents below the floor, heat or cool it with water pipes, and draw it by furnace action through the chamber and up a 120-foot chimney. Small doors near the furnace would regulate the velocity of the draft, and they could be adjusted by footmen, guided by simple thermometers in the chamber. The Commons were impressed by his drawings and agreed to try out the system. Under Reid's supervision it worked with fair success for five years, although it burned a good deal of coke, in common with most thermal systems, and the *Times* criticized its drafts, which were said to cause rheumatism among the members.[25]

We have already noted that in 1839 a frustrated and overwhelmed Charles Barry asked for assistance in designing the ventilation system of the New Palace. Reid was the natural choice. His thermal draft system could be adapted to the larger edifice, but he had to face the difficulty of drawing in fresh air from the smoky neighborhood of Westminster. For that purpose he proposed to place his air intakes at the top of the Victoria Tower and the Clock Tower, opening whichever one afforded the least polluted air as the wind shifted. To draw off the smoke from dozens of fireplaces needed to heat the smaller rooms—a common problem in Victorian buildings—he would connect all the flues to a giant uptake shaft in the center of the Palace, with a tall chimney tower rising above the roofline. The Commons were unsure about this arrangement, but did authorize the central uptake tower, and extra vaulting in the basement of the New Palace to accomodate the vent pipes.[26]

Within months of Reid's appointment, it was evident that his arrogance and irritability made relations with Barry very difficult. Each had his own theories about ventilation, and while Barry was no engineer, he would not stand for Reid's demands that the architecture of the building be changed to suit his particular needs. He also discovered that Reid could not fathom architectural drawings, locating his vents and pipes by guesswork. After a series of angry exchanges, Barry refused to communicate with Reid except through the mediation of the First Commissioner of Works. The result was a long delay in installing the equipment. After Parliament intervened in 1846, a great wall was erected in the basement between the two parts of the New Palace, and each man set about constructing his own ventilating system.[27]

Barry drew air for the House of Lords from the top of the Victoria Tower at the southwest end of the Palace and passed it through water to purify it. Fans forced the air into an intricate system of vertical pipes, with vents at various heights, blowing it downward into the chamber and then back up through the center of the ceiling. The air could be cooled or warmed as it passed through a basement air channel, and the movement of air within the chamber would be strong enough to prevent drafts arising from opened doors.[28]

Reid's arrangement for the Commons was more complex. The

Clock Tower was his main source of fresh air, which he heated with steam or cooled with water as needed. He then moved it by a combination of furnace drafts and steam-driven fans. The floor of the House was fitted with hot-water heating plates, perforated with holes to allow the air to enter and be pulled upwards through openings in the suspended ceiling. From there it was drawn off through the great central tower, which Barry disguised, for aesthetic reasons, with an outer cone and an inner domed ceiling.

Reid and Barry worked on their arrangements for over five years but could not, under the circumstances, make adequate tests of their effects on human subjects. When the Commons finally moved into their new chamber early in 1852, members complained about dust and soot rising from the floor vents, and they also began to report feverish headaches, dizziness, and symptoms of apoplexy. The *Times* concluded that Reid was a quack and called him "an aerial Guy Fawkes," likely to blow up Parliament, while *Punch* lampooned him. By this time he had alienated not only Barry but Lord John Manners at the Office of Works, and was dismissed from his post.[29]

For the next two years, the ventilation was managed by Barry's chief engineer, Alfred Meeson. Basically, Meeson plugged up many of the floor perforations, opened new air vents around the walls and entrances of the chamber, and kept the system thoroughly cleaned and mechanically fit. But he was hampered by Reid's ignorance of basic architectural principles. He found flues, vents, and pipes heading every which way, and it was hard to tell which ones were connected, or to what.[30]

We know that in the late 1830s, Gurney had conducted experiments on steam heating systems for buildings, and that in the decade before 1852, he had gained a good deal of experience ventilating mine shafts. He had had plenty of time to apply his knowledge to the problems of the New Palace. He gave evidence to parliamentary committees in 1851 and 1852 and in the latter year produced three reports on warming and ventilation in the House of Commons. Among other points, he criticized Reid's central upcast shaft for producing too little draft,* and now believed that his own steam-jet furnace, used at several mines, could rectify that problem. The Lords, still under Barry's direction, were reluctant to participate in more experiments, but in 1854 they, too, agreed to test Gurney's approach. As a committee commented that year, "It appeared unnecessary to

---

*However, when asked whether his lighting system would not overheat the House, he replied that the upcast shaft, with a forty-square-foot firebox, was "sufficient to ventilate a large colliery" and would hardly be affected by a set of lamps.

call evidence to prove the unsatisfactory nature of the present system
. . . it seemed to have been condemned by common consent." Parliament was now convinced that the whole regime of the New Palace
ought to be placed under a single manager. Several experts, whose
systems appeared to work in other public buildings, were interviewed, but Gurney was clearly the front runner. He finally had the
opportunity to investigate every part of the building and made his
report, on 31 March, to a committee chaired by his friend Edward
Cayley.[31]

To study the air currents in the building, Gurney drew a draft
from the Victoria Tower through a large subterranean air tunnel, with
branches leading to the committee rooms, libraries, passages, and
the Lords' and Commons' chambers. He set off gunpowder flashes
in the main ducts to produce dark smoke, then observed and measured the smoke as it appeared in different areas, noting the time it
took to come in and go out. He also suspended feathers from threads
to check the direction and thrust of the drafts. He measured the
various rooms of the building thoroughly, noting the action of fireplaces, windows, and doorways. With Meeson he explored the
underground labryinth of pipes and vents bequeathed by Reid, as
well as the cockeyed tangle of chimney pipes leading from
committee-room fireplaces to one or the other of the ventilating
shafts. He asked the Office of Works for drawings of the sewers that
ran underneath the building, as well as section plans of the chambers
(to help him design the lighting), but "the difficulty I had in getting
this was such, that I am sick and tired of asking; therefore I trust to
inspection mostly, to local and verbal information."[32]

As a result of his investigations, he felt confident that he could
"remove all the material evils that at present exist, at a very trifling
expense." The whole air flow system for ventilation was to be reversed, letting air in from ground level, around the foundation of the
building, and out through the Victoria Tower or the Clock Tower, by
means of his furnace. This approach soon proved a disaster, as
common sense might have predicted: it drew in the horrible smells
of the polluted Thames River, the various workshops and wharves
south of the Palace, and horse droppings and cigar smoke from the
pavements nearby. Gurney deodorized the incoming air with chloride
of lime, a bleaching powder obtained as a by-product of London's
coal gas refineries, but this remedy only worked intermittently. Members continued to complain about the smells and about cold air
being vented from below, which (they said) gave them chilled feet
while their heads were feverish.[33] Gurney soon decided to utilize
Reid's central tower as an intake shaft, drawing air from higher alti-

tudes, but even that was often mixed with smoke from nearby chimneys.[34] However, he did close Reid's floor vents and allow the air to
enter the chambers naturally, being drawn out through the ceilings,
so that the earlier dust and drafts were almost eliminated. For the
committee rooms, he advised installing transoms in the doorways
"on the Venetian principle," opening the windows, and restoring
charcoal fires to the fireplaces.

Gurney's system of Bude lighting for the House of Commons was
to be extended throughout the New Palace, but in the meantime, he
recommended fitting all existing lamps with insulating smoke flues
to help reduce the heat they emitted. In the committee rooms, the
gas mains tended to leak, so he advised closing them during the day
and substituting oil lighting fixtures for gas.

For heating, Reid had installed a complicated arrangement of horizontal iron steam pipes along the walls of every chamber. To prevent
members from burning themselves, the pipes were covered with
insulation, which reduced their effectiveness. They also produced
an offensive smell, which Gurney attributed to the burning and decomposition of organic matter deposited on the pipes from the atmosphere. Rip them all out! he urged; the sale of scrap iron alone would
pay for most of the new improvements. "You can have no idea of
the quantities of iron, of complexity, unless you were to go down
and see it," he testified. "There are tons of iron, and steam and water
pipes, of all kinds and sizes, working one against the other."[35]

In place of Reid's apparatus, Gurney suggested using a "warming
battery" made of zinc plates attached at right angles to galvanized
iron or copper tubes. The tubes carried hot water from a central
boiler and the plates provided one hundred square feet of exposed
heating surface for every cubic foot of stove. A stopcock enabled the
heat to be turned on and off quickly as rooms filled with people and
then emptied. The same device could be used for cooling by running
ice water through the tubes (Gurney had described this in a previous
report). This warming battery, which we would call a primitive radiator, was based on a common principle, but as usual Gurney had
experimented with it, and through trial and error, he had arrived at
the most efficient combination of pipes and plates. He installed one
in a popular amusement arcade, the Panopticon, in Leicester Square,
where it had worked during the winter of 1853–54, and another in
the Court of Exchequer in Westminster Hall. Perhaps because it was
"simple and inexpensive" to make, he did not seek a patent on the
pipe-and-plate device, nor did he form a company to manufacture
more.[36] But an earlier stove, shaped like a giant barrel with twenty-
four vertical fins, and fitted out for a coke fire instead of steam, was

produced at about this time by "The London Heating and Ventilating (Gurney's Patent) Company."[37] Five feet high and three feet in diameter, it was intended as a stand-alone stove for large public buildings. Apparently dozens were purchased by churches and cathedrals. There are still five working Gurney stoves, now fitted with gas burners, operating in Ely Cathedral; another at Durham Cathedral; and a few more in other churches around England. This author can personally testify to the generous warmth they produce on a cold day.

Cayley's committee recommended that Gurney's unified approach be tested immediately, but in such a way that the old system, or another system, could still be substituted. They asked the Office of Works to assist him to make as many of the necessary changes as he could during the upcoming Easter recess, and they pressed him to supervise the work personally. This he was reluctant to do. He had several commercial engagements (even then, people were trying to interest him in new steam carriage ventures), and he was actively involved in coal mine ventilation. In Cornwall, near Launceston, he had purchased a four-hundred-acre farm, Hornacott Manor, where he was conducting agricultural experiments. He was a practicing (not merely honorary) magistrate for Devon and Cornwall and president of the regional agricultural society. Now over sixty years old, he found the air of London bad for his health. Nevertheless, he was so intrigued by the intricate scientific and technical problems of the project that he could not bring himself to walk away from it. Asked if there were no "inducements" that could make him accept the appointment, he replied thoughtfully, "It is a subject I have not much considered. It is said, 'Every man has his price' in some way or other. Money would not be my price; I am happy to say I do not want it; I have independent means. I have a *feeling* upon the subject which will influence me more. The system of lighting was a child of my own, and I thought it right to see him go [ahead]. This is another, and I should like to see him fairly set agoing. I firmly believe I could succeed, and this would be a great inducement." A little later he added, "I would do so, because most of the authorities and members of the House have always treated me with kindness."[38]

He proceeded to alter the ventilating system during the recess, and in May 1854 both the Lords and Commons committees interviewed colleagues about the results. One member, previously opposed to the change, said that the cold drafts had been eliminated quite successfully and the air, even when warmed, was very fresh and pleasant. The temperature could be raised or lowered easily when desired. In fact, the new arrangments "answered as completely as any artificial system of ventilation could do." The committees, agreeing that

Gurney's warming radiator in the Panopticon, 1853–54. From Walter
Thornbury, *Old and New London* (London: Cassell, Petter, Galpin & Co.,
1901), 169.

The Gurney stove, one of five working stoves in Ely Cathedral. Drawing by Christine Porter. Porter collection.

the atmosphere was "sensibly sweeter and purer than before," offered Gurney £1,000 per annum to complete and superintend his integrated system under contract to the Office of Works. After another period of agonizing indecision, he finally agreed. The *Illustrated London News* for 5 August 1854 reported the appointment, describing the improvements he had made in glowing terms. He was provided with an office and residential rooms on the premises. His address in the London Post Office Directory was henceforth "Inspector of Ventilation, Houses of Parliament, Old Palace Yard, S.W."[39]

Gurney's characterization of the heating and ventilating systems as "another child of my own," whom he would like to "fairly set agoing," is curiously suggestive, given the changes that were occurring in his personal life. At this distance in time, and with limited evidence, psychological interpretations are bound to be guesswork. But consider that Gurney had lost his son, Goldsworthy John, in 1847, at the age of twenty-five, only three years after John's graduation from Cambridge. He had already lost his wife, Elizabeth. His only heir was now his unmarried daughter, Anna Jane, who lived with him at Reeds, in the village of Poughhill, just outside Bude. In 1843, Gurney purchased Hornacott Manor at Boyton, a bit further east, together with Woodley (or Woodleigh) Cottage, a small, Regency-style house. By the early 1850s, he was spending his summers there, draining the fields and conducting experiments in scientific agriculture.[40] This could be seen, of course, as a typical retirement project for a gentleman farmer. But in the course of related activities, he had met Jane Betty, the young daughter of a Devon sheep farmer. Jane was born 24 February 1830, making her only twenty-four in the year when Gurney became an officer of the Houses of Parliament. We have not a shred of evidence about how they became engaged or what the marriage arrangements were. They were wed on 28 November 1854 at the parish church of St. Giles in the Fields (where Gurney's first wife, Elizabeth, was buried) and soon produced a daughter, whom they named Elizabeth Jane.[41] The new couple moved into Woodley Cottage, while Anna remained at Reeds, in nearby Poughhill. Within five years the marriage had collapsed. Divorce was out of the question (it required an expensive petition process in the House of Lords, on grounds of adultery), but when Gurney made a will on 29 October 1859, Jane Betty and her daughter were not mentioned. He must have made some settlement for them, but the will left everything to Anna Jane, who resumed her position within her father's household. "Possibly," remarks Harris, "the stepdaughter was not very friendly disposed to her father's second choice."[42]

Now, the time between his son's death and his remarriage was the period when Gurney was first denied the lighting of Parliament, then asked to investigate its heating and ventilation, and finally appointed its sole officer for all these functions. He was, as he said himself, reluctant to continue his frustrating, uncomfortable, and uncertain career in London when a much more respectable position awaited him in Cornwall. He could not be sure whether the parliamentary venture would last more than a single session. On the other hand, his previous inventions and achievements had proved unsuccessful, ephemeral, or like the Drummond light, known only to an inner circle of experts. We can only surmise that in the spring of 1854, speaking to Cayley's committee about his indecision, he was deeply concerned to create something that would live beyond him. Perhaps he had already met Jane Betty and imagined that he could start over again, with a new family and a new project to "fairly set agoing" in the very heart of British government. If he had not yet considered remarriage, his description of the ventilating system as another "child of my own" implies that he sought a substitute genealogy through his work.

Having accepted the appointment, Gurney finished installing the bulk of the new equipment during the 1854–55 session. The Clock Tower was still unfinished (the great bell known as Big Ben had yet to be cast), but he set up a steam-jet furnace at ground level to create the necessary draft and connected it both to the ventilating system and to a noisome sewer that had been discovered running lengthwise under the New Palace. Windows, shut tight for years, were pried open; Reid's offending steam pipes were replaced by warming stoves; and the old lights gradually changed over to the patented Bude design. A cache of twenty-eight hundred pounds of old candle ends, discarded over the years by footmen, was discovered and removed as a fire hazard. Gurney trained a team of workmen to maintain each part of the arrangements, continued experimenting during sessions to improve them, and of course responded to frequent requests or complaints from individual members. He even gained a grudging respect from the new First Commissioner of Works, Sir Benjamin Hall, whose first act upon his appointment in 1855 was to issue a scathing critique of almost everyone and everything previously connected with the office.

In a few years, Gurney was to suffer some of the same nit-picking interference and inquiries that drove other Office of Works contractors to despair. But the facilities he constructed for Parliament endured. In the 1860s, after his retirement, a new study by Dr. John Percy (1817–1889) showed that the current of air flowing through the buildings needed to be doubled or tripled for optimum ventilation and that heat from the Gurney warming stoves and Bude lamps was collecting under the roof, slowly roasting it towards the point of spontaneous combustion. After correcting those problems, Percy moved the ventilation intake shafts to the Members' Terrace by the River Thames, whose waters, once reeking with effluvia, had been

The Clock Tower at Westminster, showing Gurney's steam-jet furnace mounted for ventilation of the Houses of Parliament. Drawing by Christine Porter. Porter collection.

cleaned up by the new London sewer system. Finally, he hired an architectural draftsman and two skilled assistants to map the rabbit warren of pipes, vents, chimneys, valves, and tunnels created over decades by Reid, Barry, Gurney, and other contractors, and translate the mess into a set of rational drawings. With that in hand, he streamlined the system to produce a steady flow of fresh air at a relatively uniform temperature, and with his modifications, it lasted into the twentieth century. The Bude lamps burned for fifty years, until they were replaced by electric lights.[43] Gurney's "child" was indeed a credit to its father.

12

The Steam-Jet Furnace and the Sewers of London

When EXPERIMENTING WITH VENTILATION AT THE HOUSES OF PARLIAMENT, GUR-ney naturally took note of conditions in the neighborhood. Barry's New Palace was erected on the built-up banks of the Thames as the river looped northward around Pimlico and then between Westminster and Lambeth before resuming its eastward journey to the sea. The southwest side of the building, crowned by Victoria Tower, over-looked a crazy quilt of cement and lumber wharves, crowded tenements, and workshops along narrow, muddy Abingdon Street. Directly to the west, across from the main entrance and street approaches, stood medieval Westminster Abbey and St. Margaret's Chapel, lately flanked by a broad new street named for the young queen. Along Great George Street, to the northwest, stretched a great office block, today the home of the Treasury, but filled in the 1850s with offices for engineers and their parliamentary agents. Whitehall and Scotland Yard lay directly northward, set off from the river by private gardens. There, the Thames banks had been built up over the centuries with walls, pilings, stairs, and docks, fitting company to the old humpbacked Westminster Bridge, which was slated for replacement. The strong, straight embankment and regular walls of the New Palace provided a sharp contrast to its neighborhood.

The factories, wharves, tenements, traffic, and river banks produced an always changing, but invariably noxious, array of problems for Parliament's ventilation officer. Smoke, horse droppings, ashes, dust, and putrid river mists could be drawn into the premises. The main offenders were the sewers, which in many places were simply open drains. The New Palace itself enshrined a sewer, laid lengthwise from south to north, right through the center of the foundation level.[1] It was linked to sewers in Great George Street and Parliament Street, and a large new sewer along Victoria Street was under construction. These drains and sewers emptied into the Thames through large pipes that crawled like snakes out into the river bed.

The Thames is a tidal river; the water level rises and falls about twenty-six feet, twice a day. The sewer discharge pipes ended somewhere between the high- and low-water marks. Each pipe was equipped with hinged leather or iron flaps to prevent gases from rising over the sewage level and escaping out the end. At high water the pipes became tidelocked: the Thames flooded up into them, forcing the accumulated sewer gas, and often the sewage itself, back into the neighborhood sewers, where it leaked into riverside buildings or out of the street gully-holes. At low water, the pipes discharged rainwater and raw sewage into the Thames, usually leaving a trail of stinking muck along the mud banks. In theory, the river would carry this sewage down to the sea, and in fact it did work in that direction. But twice a day the tides returned upstream, bringing part of the sewage along with them; when they came to rest before ebbing back toward the sea, they precipitated their odoriferous burden along its banks. Sewer gas seeped into the chambers of Parliament, backed up in the streets, made people and horses nauseous, and in several cases caused instant death to sanitation workers who attempted to enter the drains.

Gurney was very much aware of how dangerous sewer gas was. In 1852 he had been called to perform autopsies and give evidence at an inquest into the death of five men in a Pimlico sewer. He noted how quickly the men were suffocated, and he remembered that when the sewer was opened from the street to get the bodies out, someone carelessly lit a match, and the flame blew twenty feet high.[2] But he thought he had a remedy: having successfully applied his steam-jet furnace to drawing off coal damp from polluted mine shafts, he considered that it would work for sewer gas as well. In fact, he visualized the metropolitan sewer system laid out like a large, shallow mine with multiple main shafts and miles of tributary galleries. If the system could be made airtight, with the exception of one intake opening and one exhaust pipe linked to a furnace, it could be cleared of dangerous gases in a short time.

Now, when mines were ventilated, the offending gases were allowed to dissipate over the surrounding countryside. The smell was nauseating and sometimes alarmed nearby farmers, but it only lingered for a few hours. Continuous ventilation of sewer gas into the atmosphere of the city, already famous for its "pea soup" quality, would be catastrophic. Gurney, however, hypothesized that the gas could be rendered odorless and safe by passing it through a steam bath just before burning. From the works of J. J. Berzelius, one of the foremost inorganic chemists of Europe, and from more recent experiments in Paris and Belgium, he had learned that steam could lower the temperature needed to burn various gases from 1,200 to 300 degrees. But steam also seemed to attack organic "animalculae" in the gases, leaving them vulnerable to decomposition in the flame. It was, he said, "like a flux in the reduction of metals."[3] He could not express this idea in terms of germ theory, for that was not introduced locally until the publication in 1855 of the second edition of John Snow's *On the Mode of Communication of Cholera*. Even then, "germs" as a concept remained more metaphor than fact for some years. However, prevailing theories of water quality did link contamination to the decay of microsopic animal matter, even of specific types of organisms.[4] Gurney's belief that "bad" organisms shielded themselves by some kind of coating, which was impervious to dry heat but not to steam, was only an informed guess. It was consistent with contemporary disease theory but so original as a hypothesis, and so far in advance of experimental data, that hardly anyone bothered to comment on it. Dr. Lewis Thompson, who helped Gurney with many of his experiments at the time, testified later that the process was "quite original—I never heard of it before and it has never, I believe, been thought of before."[5]

Gurney's theory about noxious gases, like so many of his ideas, grew out of research for his lectures on chemistry in the early 1820s. It was further developed in 1832 when he studied the possible chemical origins of cholera, which had just made the first of several incursions into England. In a letter to Sir Anthony Carlisle, which the latter published, he noted that medical men were completely divided about the disease, but suggested that the most likely course of inquiry would be a chemical analysis of the "poison" that carried it. Every specific poison must be a chemical compound, he wrote; this one arose from animal decomposition, and was contagious. "On ultimate analysis, we shall find phosphorous forming a component part in all animal matter in some state of combination." Phosphorous was even more dangerous to organisms than nitrogen (the most popular culprit among contemporary medical theorists), and, in various combinations, could be the root cause of plague, typhoid fever, smallpox, and cholera. The chemistry of phosphorous was at that time little known, so Gurney proposed a research program to identify as many of its compounds as possible and test their effects on animal health. If the right "poisons" could be found, it should be possible to destroy or decompose them with appropriate chemical antidotes.[6]

Gurney's medical hypothesis proved as groundless as those proposed by many other physicians and surgeons of the time, whose confidence in their profession was shaken by the intractability of cholera. It is just as well that he was occupied in other scientific and technical pursuits during the 1840s. However, his ideas about decomposing gases were not forgotten. In July 1849, while he was lighting the temporary House of Commons, but before he became light and ventilation officer of the New Palace, he was asked to investigate a variety of bad odors in the neighborhood of Parliament. He wrote to Lord Ebrington at the nearby Law Courts for permission to experiment with one or more sewers in the vicinity and applied to the newly formed Metropolitan Commission of Sewers for assistance in closing the various traps and gullies.* "Means are at hand," he wrote, "by which the Sewer might afterward be efficiently ventilated at little expense. I believe the effluvia arising from every sewer in London may by the same means be drawn out to given points, decomposed, and rendered perfectly inoffensive." The Sewer Commission's assistant engineer, John Grant, thought that the sewers near Parliament would be inappropriate for the experiment, because there were so many street gullies and other openings on private property that it would be well-nigh impossible to stop them all up. By August, however, Grant had targeted a more isolated sewer in Friar Street, in the Blackfriars Road area south of the river in Southwark, which had been closed due to a buildup of raw sewage and lethal gas. Gurney estimated that it would cost about £10–20 to ventilate if a high-pressure boiler were available, and offered to do the work for expenses only. The MCS solicitor, E. H. Woolrych, rejected this offer, allowing a flat £25 for the experiment.[7]

According to Gurney's report of 30 October 1849, the Friar Street sewer was 1,500 feet long and typically egg-shaped, three feet wide by five feet high. It had been backing up since its construction two years previously, so that about 12,000 cubic feet of sewage had accumulated. The side gullies had been covered to prevent gas from leaking into the street, and the men who ordinarily flushed out drains had sealed it up to prevent fatal accidents from inhaling its fumes. Gurney was spending the parliamentary recess at Hornacott Manor, his experimental farm near Launceston, but he rode back to London in September, collected the necessary equipment and chemicals, made several experiments, and then (with the help of William Keene, who had worked with him on steam carriages in the 1820s) installed his steam jet at the mouth of the sewer. As soon as it was fired up

---

*The gullies were rain and sewage runoff collectors located at the sides of streets. They drained into the central sewer line, which ran under the street through pipes fitted with S-shaped traps, similar to those under a kitchen sink; the traps prevented fumes from escaping back to the surface. Some older gullies were not trapped and would have to be covered with oiled cloth for the experiments.

with coke, a strong downward draft was felt at the far end of the sewer where air was being sucked in. Five minutes later the flushing men entered, discovered the air fresh enough to work, and spent the next three days clearing sewage out of the back end. The draft was strong enough to put out a candle flame, said Gurney, and when the furnace was shut down from time to time, the men had to leave the sewer within five minutes to avoid suffocation.[8]

Keene reported to the MCS on 11 October that the sewer was "effectually cleared of all its offensive gases," and Gurney wrote a week later (from Keene's London house), "I can now speak to the absolute certainty of being able practically to draw all the gaseous products found in the sewers of London . . . to one great point, or more convenient points, and there to break down their chemical affinities, and effectually decompose them before they can escape or pollute the atmosphere."[9]

Gurney was to quote his own report several times in subsequent years as proof that his system worked when given a fair trial. However, he had a later exchange of letters with the MCS that casts a different light on the Friar Street experiment. In November 1849, after receiving polite thanks from the MCS, Gurney wrote to its solicitor, Woolrych, that the undertaking had been risky because the sewer was so choked with lethal material and because cholera had raged in the area not long before. Although he had no patent on the steam jet and therefore no pecuniary interest in promoting its use, he wished to note that he had paid over £68 out of pocket to conduct the tests. This was a clear hint that some compensation would be appreciated, even though he only requested a copy of his report from the MCS "as a record of history in my exertions in thus settling an interesting public question." Woolrych duly sent the report and asked for particulars of the expenses so that he could bring them to the attention of his superiors. He got not only a list of expenses (now grown to the sum of £108), but also an expansive claim that Gurney had spent six weeks in the capital, taking precious time away from his experimental farm and his duties as a Cornwall and Devon magistrate. Woolrych delayed replying until the following April, when he offered £49 in payment. That brought Gurney to London for an interview, after which he again pressed his case in writing. But Woolrych had now received a second report from John Grant, stating that Gurney had actually arrived in London only two weeks before the jet was put into operation and that it had only worked for about an hour, on 6 October. Gurney had then gone off to Exeter until the tenth, put the jet back into service from the eleventh through the thirteenth, and conducted experiments with decomposing sewer gases from the sixteenth through the twentieth. The jet was then removed by Gurney and replaced by an ordinary steam pump. The sewer itself was about one-third cleaned by that time. Grant finished the job by flushing it out with water from a separate drain discovered at the rear of Friar Street.[10]

Gurney was neither the first nor the last consultant to experience the frustrations of recovering expenses from bureaucratic offices, and in view of his later adversary relations with the MCS, one could be suspicious of Grant's version of events. But Grant had a reputation as an affable, "exceedingly painstaking" engineer. He had once challenged his own supervisor on the accuracy of statements made to the public about a pending project. His detailed notes on Gurney's operations are typical of the close attention he gave to sewer construction all during his long career, so there is no reason to doubt them. Grant did give Gurney credit for showing how to clear out an isolated sewer, and he advised the Law Courts that the sewers in their vicinity might be ventilated through the furnaces of local manufacturers, if such could be persuaded to cooperate. But he concluded that the sewer system as a whole had so many openings from street gullies and house drains that a sufficient draft could never be created by steam jets operating at only a few points.[11] This view became an article of faith at the MCS, and it was repeated in testimony to Parliament with regard to Gurney's later efforts.

When Gurney was appointed supervisor of lighting, heating, and ventilation for the House of Commons in 1854, he immediately set about reversing Dr. Reid's system of ventilation, which had drawn air from the Clock Tower through the buildings, to be exhausted up the central tower. As mentioned previously, he installed a steam-jet furnace near the bottom of the Clock Tower (the bell had yet to be installed, so the upper floors were only roughed in), drawing air into the palace through a number of ground-level apertures and thence through the chambers of the New Palace. Based on his experience in Friar Street, he believed that this furnace could also be used to burn off pestilential gases from nearby sewers.

The scheme of integrated sewer lines that would soon become famous as the London Main Drainage System was then in the planning stages, awaiting legislative resolution of the inevitable arguments over jurisdiction and financing. What lay below ground around Westminster in 1854 was a warren of private and public drains, installed sporadically during the previous three hundred years. Some were clay pipe, others brick or cast iron; the oldest were hollow cedar logs. Some ran directly down to the river, but many fed haphazardly into intercepting sewers. In the midst of this warren, Gurney discovered a set of connections that appeared somewhat integrated and autonomous. The sewer line that ran under the Houses of Parliament joined a main sewer, running along Westminster Bridge Street, just to the north. That, in turn, was fed by a line that ran south to Abingdon Street through New Palace Yard (between Parliament and Westminster Abbey) and joined another sewer coming off from Wood Street, just south of the Victoria Tower. The four drains made a sort of rectangular grid that Gurney believed could be closed off from other parts of the metropolitan system by installing traps or flaps at strategic points. The Bridge Street sewer was also connected to a new line that ran up Victoria Street, past Buckingham Palace. This line was not yet in operation, so it could also be stopped up for experimental purposes.

The noxious odors reported in 1848–49 had now returned, along with warnings about the return of cholera. In July 1854, Gurney applied to H. M. Office of Works, the agency in charge of the New Palace, for permission to try ventilating the sewers. He was referred back to the MCS, which delayed action on the matter until the Prime Minister, Lord Palmerston, intervened with a personal letter.[12] In December a young engineering clerk, William Booth Scott, was assigned to help install the necessary flaps and hook up the local grid to the Clock Tower furnace via a short, ten-inch-diameter pipe. Another flap was installed to allow shutting off the ventilation of the Houses of Parliament, so as not to compromise the experiment. In view of the later MCS challenge to the efficacy of the steam jet, it is interesting to note that the MCS chief engineer demanded that it be run at full power during the positioning of the flaps, so that their workmen would not suffocate in the sewer lines.[13]

With most of the air intakes covered, Gurney waited until the sewers were tidelocked and opened the pipe from the sewers to the steam-jet furnace. The whole grid was shortly cleared of effluvia. Gurney's assistants were sent out to check the sewer lines, where they discovered a "strong intake" down those gully-holes which had not been trapped. Despite these leaks, which had earlier concerned engineer Grant, a pressure gauge still indicated a "considerable" extracting draft in the sewer line. Gurney then ordered the stop valve removed between the Bridge Street and Victoria Street sewers, so that the latter was open to the effects of the furnace. He reported to the MCS that a draft was detected a half-mile away where Victoria Street met Vauxhall Bridge Road (near the present Victoria Railway Station), and despite the absence of traps on almost eighty gully-holes on this line, he claimed that sewer gas was drawn through the Clock Tower furnace at the rate of twenty-five thousand cubic feet per minute. He also suspected that the toxic animalculae in the gas had been decomposed, but he reserved judgment about this until an expert could investigate.[14]

As a result of these experiments, Gurney recommended trapping all the gullies around Parliament and extending the mouths of all large sewers outward below the low water line, so that the sewer gas could be drawn off through a furnace rather than leak into the atmosphere. A few of the sewers were, in fact, extended by the MCS. However, in 1855 that agency was superceded by a new Metropolitan Board of Works, which was specifically charged to build a main drainage system for all of London. The new system would intercept all sewage flowing down toward the river and carry it far to the east of the metropolis. Gurney's plan was put aside.

So far Gurney had concerned himself only with the gaseous effluvia emanating from sewers, not with the sewage itself, and he had not extended his investigations to the River Thames, into which all the sewage flowed.[15] His concern was simply with those elements disposable in the steam-jet furnace. He was soon drawn into the wider issues, however, and in the worst possible circumstances. He was caught up in a quarrel between two government agencies led by strong-minded politicians and engineers.

The Metropolis Local Management Act of 1855, which created the Metropolitan Board of Works, was written by Her Majesty's First Commissioner of Works, Sir Benjamin Hall. A successful draper, and Member of Parliament for the London borough of Marlyebone, Hall had led the fight by local governments in the 1840s against Edwin Chadwick's plans for a centralized sanitation authority. A firsthand look at the cholera outbreak of 1854 abruptly changed his attitude. His Local Management Act of 1855 was intended to consolidate over three hundred agencies—parish overseers, paving boards, lighting boards, sewer commissions—comprising more than ten thousand commissioners who applied, with varying degrees of accuracy and efficiency, some 250 acts of Parliament to the metropolitan region. It also proposed to include the City Corporation, that curious square mile of original London which had its own medieval guild officers and regulations. The Metropolitan Commission of Sewers, organized in 1848, had been a feeble attempt to overcome this fragmentation, but it had never had the authority it needed to levy rates and secure rights-of-way for construction. Hall's legislation swept away the MCS and most of the parish boards and provided for the election of delegates from each parish or district, including several from the City Corporation, to the new Metropolitan Board. The MBW, unlike the

MCS, could finance its works out of a share of the local rates, and it could borrow capital from the Treasury against future revenues.[16]

Although the MBW was supposed to be autonomous, Hall retained the power to review large-scale MBW projects. He had, unfortunately, a tendency to denigrate the work of his predecessors and to criticize subordinates, even in technical matters. When the MBW's experienced chief engineer, J. W. Bazalgette, produced plans for the new London Main Drainage in the spring of 1856, Hall pronounced them unacceptable. He demanded extensive changes, which would raise the cost of the project. The MBW objected; Hall appointed a panel of engineers to review Bazalgette's plans and design a new system; the MBW appointed a rival review panel, which published a scathing attack on the first panel's design; and nothing was done to improve London's sanitation.[17] In the autumn of 1856, Hall asked Gurney to undertake an independent study of the Thames and recommend his own plan for disposing of the sewage. Because Gurney's appointment as lighting and ventilating officer of Parliament came through the Office of Works, Hall's request was officially justifiable, but it was also unorthodox. It is difficult, from our vantage point, to tell whether it was a genuine effort to break out of the impasse, a gambit to put pressure on the MBW, or just a way of stalling for time. Gurney, for his part, certainly took it seriously.

Most people in the 1850s still thought of the Thames as a giant natural drain. Its currents ran toward the sea; whatever fell into it ought to be taken along. The tides complicated this process because they carried a good deal of sewage back up through London, and the irregular shoreline allowed ugly deposits to form. At low tide, for instance, Hungerford Bay, a shallow, twenty-acre bulge in the river where it curved eastward from Westminster to Waterloo, turned into a seething expanse of pestilential muck. Some engineers argued that the river could be streamlined by straightening its shorelines and narrowing its channel. It would then develop a faster current and greater "scour," thus discharging its polluted waters more efficiently. A detailed plan for doing that had been worked out in 1840 by Captain James Walker,[18] but the wharf owners refused to abide by the line he established. Other plans for reconstructing the banks of the Thames were proffered almost yearly. The First Commissioner of Works funded construction of a mile of river wall between Chelsea and Pimlico in the 1850s and floated designs for a more extensive project. But commercial interests, legal battles, and parliamentary stinginess undermined every venture. Over the years, fouled by the flushings from a million cesspools and water closets, and receiving waste from tanning factories, chemical works, and breweries, the river became so polluted that it threatened the health of everyone who lived or worked nearby. By 1856 it was receiving over eight million gallons of sewage daily.[19] The London water companies were forced to move their intake pipes farther upstream, but scientists could not decide whether, or to what extent, the water supply was still polluted. Raw sewage precipitated along the extensive mud banks near the Strand and Charing Cross and fermented in the sunshine. One expert told Parliament that the Thames produced "such a mixture of gases, that I should think it would puzzle all the chemists in the world to define what they are."[20] Fortunately (said the newspapers), the Houses of Parliament lay directly on the river, next to some of the largest sewer outlets in the region. Members could not help noticing the nauseating stench.[21]

Gurney therefore had several incentives for investigating the problem. He enlisted the help of Dr. Lewis Thompson and an experienced medical chemist, William Maugham, to test the air near Parliament for noxious gases, oxygen content, and drafts through various drain openings. He made a survey of the river and all the drains that fed into it, although Sir Benjamin Hall denied him funds to make detailed drawings. Several committees and royal commissions had recently investigated the problems of water quality and drainage, so there was plenty of technical information at hand. Gurney tried out a new water purity gauge based on the refraction of light, invented by his friend Sir George Cayley.[22] He also consulted his old Cornish notes on tides, river currents, sediments, fertilizers, and mine ventilation.

In common with many chemists of his day, he believed that the dangerous elements in sewage formed from decaying organic matter. Decay was then transmitted to human bodies; sickness and disease were but special types of the same process. Some believed that gaseous miasmas and bad water predisposed people to illness by weakening the body's general constitution. Others followed the German theorist Justus von Liebig, who had begun to target specific agents of decomposition, such as hydrogen sulfide, even linking them to specific illnesses. Since these hypotheses were argued before parliamentary committees and reported in the newspapers, the public grew sharply critical of the state of its water supply. It was alarmed even more by the publication of drawings taken from microscope slides, showing hideous creatures living in their drinking water. The problem with the theories of decay or putrefaction was that chemists were generally unable to distinguish the various types of organic matter in water or to describe the process of putrefaction that made them dangerous. Nor could they account for the apparently random appearances of typhoid and cholera, some of which occurred in neighborhoods with "clean" water. In 1856 one of von Liebig's students, August Hofmann, president of the newly established Royal College of Chemistry, admitted to the Board of Health that chemists were incapable of determining whether or not water was immediately harmful to health. This conclusion was echoed by sanitary engineers assigned to monitor the condition of the Thames upstream from London. All they measured, said Hofmann, was the amount of nitrogen present, which might be taken as a sign of the water's potential for putrefaction.[23]

The failure of chemical analysis had two important consequences for Gurney's investigations. First, public officials concluded that sewage, in and of itself, was not necessarily harmful except as a medium of decay. So long as the process or the products of decay could be treated, therefore, there was nothing wrong with dumping sewage into the Thames. A number of people, in fact, thought that sewage could safely be turned into fertilizer, and in 1855–56 several private companies were offering to collect London's entire supply for commercial purposes. Gurney, however, had tried such fertilizers during the 1840s on his farm near Launceston, and found them too expensive to be feasible.[24] He therefore concentrated his attention on the flushing action of the Thames, seeking to contour its bed and shoreline for more efficient sewage disposal. He recalled that when the tides came up the Camel River in Cornwall, they shifted sand and gravel along the bed to fill in any holes left by dredging, but never added material after that. In the Thames, regular dredging and shifting currents created holes, trenches, and gravel ridges that attracted sewage; they could be eliminated by proper contouring. The irregular banks of the river also dragged on the current, forming eddies ("retrogrades") and vertical whirlpools that encouraged precipitation—the same phenomenon ("vena contracta") he had discovered in the currents of air drawn through mine shafts. As an experiment he applied a smooth grade of gravel to a small section of Thames shoreline, near Parliament, and noted how the muck and sewage readily slid off into deeper water. In numerous boating trips down the river, he discovered that contrary to current opinion, sewage was not exactly lighter than water. Most of it had a specific gravity halfway between that of fresh water and salt water. It was carried downstream in suspension, gradually sinking, until it ran into the saltier water coming in from the sea, which floated it back up towards London. If it could be channeled along the bottom of the river, it might escape this process.[25]

All of these considerations led Gurney to two recommendations: (1) that all the sewer lines along the Thames be extended to discharge below the low-water line, thus preventing exposure to air, which caused putrefaction, and (2) that the bed and banks of the Thames be dredged and contoured in a very specific manner. The smaller irregularities of the shoreline were to be removed and the bed narrowed, so that the river kept a uniform current of 225 feet per minute or more. The banks would be scraped smooth, at a constant slope of one in sixteen (three to four degrees) from the top down to the low-water line, and lined with gravel so that sewage would slide or wash off easily. Where the river widened and grew shallow, as at Hungerford, the slope would extend below low water to a channel dredged into the river bed, nine feet deep by fifty feet wide. Two channels, one on each side of the river, would collect the sewage and encourage the natural scouring of the current.[26]

While Gurney was pursuing his investigations, the public grew increasingly restive. Although officials had concluded that sewage was not intrinsically dangerous, the average London resident made the reasonable assumption that if the water looked bad, smelled bad, and tasted bad, it probably *was* bad. Furthermore, residents knew from experience that the fumes from sewer pipes were not only nauseating but dangerous. They demanded that the water companies filter their supplies, which was done, and that the fumes be suppressed. Hundreds of tons of deodorizing chloride of lime were spread over the river and its mud banks during the summers of 1857 and 1858, and people hung lime-soaked cloths over their windows to freshen the air.

Gurney, who of course shared the popular fear of sewer gas, proposed to Commissioner Hall that it could be drawn off through a dozen or so large steam-jet furnaces, each working in a chimney about ten feet in diameter and sixty feet high. These would be hooked up to the sewer system at strategic points around London. Since the drains running to the Thames would be extended beyond low-water level, they would always remain covered with water and thus sealed off from gaseous discharge. Only the street gullies would remain open. If they were properly trapped (the technology was simple, although the application would be tedious) the furnaces could easily and cheaply deodorize the whole metropolis. They would do even more: Dr. Thompson had discovered that the steam jet actually decreased the proportion of nitrogen and increased that of oxygen in the air, just as rain showers were thought to do. This, according to Hofmann's theories, should render the atmosphere healthy as well as odorless.[27]

Gurney carried on his research during the spring and summer of 1857 and made a final report to Sir Benjamin Hall on 3 November

1857. During this time he and his mechanic, John Blight, moved the steam-jet furnace 180 feet up into the Clock Tower. The tower was still under construction, with timber braces and building materials crowding the space, which required the venting shafts and chimney to be mounted at awkward angles. Despite this circumstance, he used the furnace to ventilate the Houses of Parliament and experimentally burned sewer gases drawn from the nearby drains.

Still at loggerheads with the Metropolitan Board of Works and their main drainage scheme, Benjamin Hall sent Gurney's report to the House of Commons to be reviewed by a select committee. Lord Palmerston's Whig-Liberal ministry fell in February 1858, however, and Hall was replaced by Lord John Manners, an experienced former commissioner, who had the backing of the new prime minister, Benjamin Disraeli. The Tories, anxious to build popularity, supported the idea of cleaning the Thames, but not along the lines suggested by Gurney. Lord John Manners got on well with the Metropolitan Board of Works and was familiar with their plans for the main drainage, which now included an embankment along the Thames to enclose the low-level intercepting sewer. The committee to consider Gurney's proposals was not selected until May 1858, did not meet until June, and did not issue a report until 19 July, much too late in the session to take any action. Among its members were Manners and Hall, Palmerston, London alderman William Cubitt (a successful contractor, suspicious of the Metropolitan Board of Works), Joseph Locke, and William Tite (who had been involved in previous schemes to embank the Thames), Edward Cayley, and Robert Stephenson, the railway engineer (who supported the MBW's sewer plan).[28]

The timing and personnel of this committee are important because the Thames pollution reached crisis proportions in the summer of 1858, known as "the summer of the Great Stink." In May, after six weeks of drought, a sudden severe rainstorm flushed all the sewage of London into the river. Then, drought resumed, leading to "the hottest June on record, save one." Temperatures remained eight degrees above average, and a peak of 113 degrees was reached on 16 June. The Thames shrank. Its muddy banks grew ever larger, and when the temperatures rose into the nineties, the sewage covering the banks actually began bubbling and hissing.[29] A sulfurous mist rose from the water. Fish died, horses staggered, and coach passengers had to use smelling salts to cross the Thames bridges. Boatmen and wharfingers suffered nausea and cramps, swollen sore throats, and "utter mental confusion." The Law Courts at Westminster adjourned to the country. "Gentility of speech is at an end," cried the *City Press*. "It stinks. And whoso once inhales the stink can never forget it, and may count himself lucky if he live to remember it."[30] Members of Parliament beseiged Gurney with demands for relief from the heat and stench, and he rushed about, covering open windows with lime-soaked cloths. On 21 June, the Lords abandoned their committee rooms, claiming that they "stunk abominably."[31] Meanwhile the Metropolitan Board of Works took advantage of the situation to push for a bill giving them the autonomy and the financial resources they needed to implement their version of the main drainage without interference from the First Commissioner of Works. Although many members thought the MBW incompetent and the drainage plans wasteful or shortsighted, they were desperate enough to vote for anything that promised immediate action. Lord John Manners introduced the bill while Gurney's committee was still sitting. Prime Minister Disraeli spoke strongly in favor of it, and it was passed on 2 August.[32]

When the select committee of Commons met on 3 June to examine Gurney's proposal, it was already very uncomfortable in the committee rooms, and members might have been forgiven for short tempers. But in fact, they treated Gurney with respect. He explained his plans to reshape the river, citing the experiences and experiments that had led to his conclusions. The committee ascertained from other witnesses that the proposed alterations would not preclude embanking the river at a later date. Gurney then recalled his application of the steam jet to the Friar Street sewer in 1849. Dr. Thompson explained how the steam eliminated noxious organic matter at lower temperature, and William Maugham described the experiments they had made with the sewers near Parliament in 1856. Although Maugham lectured regularly at the Royal Hospital, his testimony was rather shaky (Gurney himself corrected it at one point). The committee concluded that a new set of tests was required to prove whether the furnace did in fact ventilate a given length of sewer. They asked the Metropolitan Board of Works to assist Gurney in making the arrangements, to check the equipment, and to verify the results.

With characteristic naïveté, Gurney approached these hearings in the guise of a disinterested public servant who had no pecuniary interest in the designs he put foward, but sought only due recognition of his inventive imagination and efforts. He again convinced himself that the problem as he defined it, and the particular solution he devised, needed only to be understood to be accepted. These attributes indeed went a long way in parliamentary committees, where class and confidence were everything. But as we have seen before, Gurney had little talent for strategic alliances. He did not know how to orchestrate support for his schemes or defend them against unscrupulous attacks. In this case he ran into opponents who did both with great relish.

Because Gurney's plan was similar in many respects to one put forward in 1840 by Captain James Walker, he had discussed its features with that engineer, and Walker was called to give evidence before the committee at an early date. Walker acknowledged reading Gurney's report and agreed that shaping the banks of the river was the right thing to do. He did not think that the two channels in the river bed would work, because the naturally winding current of the river would cut through them. The plan would be a total failure unless the width of the river was made constant throughout, a degree of construction Gurney was not prepared for. Walker, in fact, no longer believed that simple dredging would do. Like most other engineers, he now favored construction of a walled embankment.[33]

A few days later, Gurney reappeared before the committee at his own request, because the newspapers had published details of Walker's evidence against Gurney, but none of Gurney's own explanation. He was sure that this was done with Walker's connivance, and though members who attended the committee hearings knew the truth of the matter, those who had not attended, along with the House of Lords, would be prejudiced. He wished to make a public statement because "there are reporters behind me who will see it is unfair to publish one part and not the other." The newspapers had written that Walker denied reading Gurney's report, but Gurney read a letter from him in which he had commented on the report's features. "This last observation," Walker had written, "coming from a gentleman of such known scientific attainments, and so eminently successful in the lighting and ventilating of the Houses of Parliament, after many very expensive but unsuccessful attempts by others, is surely deserving of attention at a time when millions are proposed to be expended upon the modes of purifying the river."[34] Gurney asked that these words be entered into the record and requested the committee's protection from further misrepresentations. He then produced a new report on the state of the river with a model of the river bed as he would have it shaped, explaining the whole plan once more. "The facts are clear," he said acidly, "and the remedy simple; but I am afraid the remedy I have proposed is so simple that it is doubted, and thought too inexpensive to be successful."[35]

"The facts," as Gurney presented them, were not so clear as he thought. The committee continued to puzzle over the mechanics of his plan and the assumptions behind them. But his final comment, even if intended as sarcasm, was true enough. His remedy, based on questionable assumptions about the tidal regime of the river, was

not only simple, but technically simpleminded, and his cost estimates were mere guesswork. In the eyes of professional engineers,
his ideas seemed naive and misdirected. Yet these men, too, were
prejudiced. Some of them were veterans of the engineering staff of
the Metropolitan Commission of Sewers, who had developed the
plan for constructing intercepting sewer lines along the banks of the
Thames. When the MCS was superceded by the Metropolitan Board
of Works in 1855, the engineering staff, headed by J. W. Bazalgette,
transferred to the new agency, expecting to implement their scheme
immediately. After Sir Benjamin Hall rejected it, Bazalgette recruited
fellow engineers Thomas Hawksley and George Parker Bidder to help
him counterattack. All were members of the Institution of Civil Engineers, an increasingly powerful club for professional men, located
in Great George Street near Parliament. James Walker had been president of the ICE in 1835, Sir William Cubitt in 1849, and Robert Stephenson in 1855. Joseph Locke, a member of the select committee,
was the current president, and G. P. Bidder was his vice president.
Gurney, lacking an engineer's training, had been granted associate
status at the ICE. He attended meetings when papers of particular
interest were read, such as on mine ventilation, gas lighting, or hot-
air engines, but he was neither an insider nor an officer. Although
the rules of the ICE prohibited discussion of current contracts during
regular meetings, all of the Great George Street engineers were well
aware of the MBW main drainage scheme, and many of them had
contributed ideas to it at one time or another. They were also involved
with contractors, hoping to win a share of the extensive construction
work it promised. In short, there was a large and vested interest
among the elite of the London engineering community in the MBW's
plans for the main drainage and for a Thames embankment.[36] By the
time Gurney came along, this professional elite had already decided
that London's sewage was not going into the river. It was to be sent
underground, out of the metropolis, and therefore would produce
no effluvia to be burned off by Gurney's steam–jet furnaces.

Joseph William Bazalgette was a formidable adversary. Son of an
admiral who fought in the Napoleonic Wars, he was apprenticed to
the eminent engineer Sir John Macneill, and came of age during the
railway mania of the 1840s. A man of slight build and uncertain
health, he nevertheless carried an extraordinary workload. He was
probably better at synthesizing and applying the ideas of others than
at original thinking. He had a gift for organizational management,
and his serious grey eyes and large muttonchop whiskers gave him
an air of authority. Having to appear constantly before government

committees, he developed a stern, confident manner that seemed to admit no possibility for error or doubt.

Gurney had applied to Bazalgette in 1854 for help with his experiments on the sewers near Parliament and received, as he wrote at that time, "cheerful cooperation and assistance."[37] Bazalgette had even agreed to extend several sewer lines below the low-water line in the Thames as Gurney recommended.[38] Four years later Bazalgette hardly remembered the incident, since he had to read or prepare dozens of reports every month; but the assistant he sent on that occasion, William Scott, testified that the chief engineer had penciled a cautionary note about it:

> To obtain useful deductions from this experiment, it is necessary to ascertain what amount of fuel was being consumed in a given period during the experiment, first without the jet, and then with the jet; what number of jets were there, of what size, and what pressure of steam per square inch? The openings of the sewers should be shown upon the plan, and if a further opportunity of trying an experiment offers, all the inlets for air should one after another be stopped by laying sacks or sand-bags over the gullies, to try how far the current can be extended from the furnace, and what effect this has upon the flaps at the mouths of the House drains.[39]

By laying out criteria for a successful experiment, Bazalgette essentially dismissed Gurney's 1854 results and set the stage for the confrontation that was to follow. The note was not made known to Gurney in 1854, nor were the recommended procedures communicated to him after the parliamentary committee requested Bazalgette to assist him with a new experiment. Bazalgette had his mind made up and did not expect to change it. As witnesses to his investigation he recruited Thomas Hawksley, his ally in the fight with the Office of Works, and William Haywood, chief engineer for the City of London, with whom he had a long and close working relationship.

Even before the experiment took place, Bazalgette and his associates attacked Gurney's plan. The chief engineer told the parliamentary committee that the analogy of sewer lines to mine shafts had been popular years ago, when he was at the Metropolitan Commission of Sewers. At that time he had investigated several devices, including Gurney's, had visited mines in Wales and Newcastle, and had read Nicholas Wood's treatise on mine ventilation (in which Gurney's furnace was at that time favorably described). He had concluded that the analogy with mines was faulty and that ventilating furnaces consumed enormous amounts of fuel.[40] When George Parker Bidder took the witness chair, he declined to discuss details of the plan, and left the steam-jet furnace for the chemists to ponder. "But my short answer is, that it is out of the question; it is merely trifling with the thing. To suppose that, by covering the shores with a stratum of gravel, and making those two little channels, he will cure the evil complained of, and the impurity of the Thames, is a proposition that I can hardly treat seriously."[41] William Haywood ridiculed the notion that sewers could be ventilated like mine shafts. Mines have only downshafts and upshafts, he pointed out, but counting the street drains and access shafts for workmen, there must be a million openings to the metropolitan sewer system. The City of London alone had forty-eight miles of sewers, with 1,065 air shafts and 2,810 gully openings. Putting traps in all of them and pumping that expanse of air would be far too expensive. Despite a complete lack of experience with Gurney's furnace, Haywood estimated that a set of them would cost from £60,000 to £100,000 per year to operate. And despite contrary evidence from the Friar Street sewer, he claimed that the draft needed to pull the gas out would be so strong that his maintenance men could not work in it.[42]

Having offered this barrage of criticism in advance, Bazalgette, Haywood, and Hawksley prepared to test the steam-jet furnace mounted in the Clock Tower. The furnace could be connected either with the sewer under the Houses of Parliament or, by an alternate flap, with the six miles of metropolitan sewers linked together in a nearby grid. Bazalgette claimed at first that he would need at least a month to seal all the openings in that area, but when pressured by the committee, he agreed to undertake some tests in the next week. Gurney, no doubt with many reservations, agreed to let the MBW engineers view the mechanism and measure its effects on the nearby sewers. He chose to stay away from the building at this time, either from some misguided feeling that it would make the experiments more objective or from fear of becoming implicated in the results. There are two versions of what happened. Bazalgette testified that he asked Gurney to make the trials at low tide, on Saturday evening, 10 July. Gurney demurred, as the House was not sitting and the furnace would be turned off. Bazalgette, Hawksley, and Haywood went on Saturday anyway, and examined the furnace in the presence of Gurney's workmen. They then canvassed the neighborhood sewer lines to check on air currents.

On Monday the twelfth, the three engineers met again at the Clock Tower and with the help of Gurney's foreman, Mr. Kelly, started the furnace and connected it to the flue leading to the neighborhood sewer lines. After measuring the air current through the furnace, Bazalgette and Haywood went outside, leaving Hawksley to continue observations. At the sewer opening in Great George Street, about one hundred yards from the Clock Tower, they found no detectable current of air and sent a workman into the sewer, towards its junction with the Houses of Parliament. The workman discovered an iron flap covering the junction, shutting off the sewer system from the intake pipe for the furnace. Checking his records, Bazalgette found that the flap had been constructed in 1842 by the parliamentary architect, Sir Charles Barry. It was propped open when the MBW's William Scott helped Gurney with his experiments in 1854, but only temporarily. It had been closed ever since then, claimed Bazalgette. Therefore all the currents of air in the Clock Tower must have been drawn from the Houses of Parliament, rather than from the sewers.[43]

The workman who found the flap also observed that a quantity of coal gas had leaked in from an adjoining pipeline, filling the sewer junction. When he raised the flap, there was a loud explosion on the other side. Hawksley, checking the instrumentation up in the Clock Tower, heard and felt the blast, and thought that his fellow engineers were done for. But Bazalgette and Haywood were outside the sewer, and their assistant emerged unharmed. On Tuesday morning they returned to retest the current of air at the furnace and found that its velocity was higher than before the flap was opened. They then checked all the neighborhood sewers but found the drafts perfectly normal. In fact, the draft in the Victoria Street sewer was passing away from the furnace, not toward it. Curious at this discrepancy, they returned to the Clock Tower and discovered that the vent from the Houses of Parliament had been reopened the previous evening, by Gurney's direction. Thus, the experiment had been compromised. Bazalgette sent an assistant on Wednesday to repeat the tests, but Gurney refused permission, saying that the House ventilation system was in operation.[44]

The chief engineer sent this report to the select committee, accompanied by a set of calculations showing that the local sewers were too voluminous to be ventilated through the relatively narrow intake pipe to the Clock Tower, even if it had not been blocked. The current of air measured at the furnace, 542 feet per minute, translated into a draft of only six feet per minute in the larger area of the sewers, less than the current produced by atmospheric conditions alone. Given these data, he calculated that 230 furnaces would be needed to ventilate all the sewers of London, requiring a capital outlay of £460,000 and an annual operating budget of over £200,000. "I have only to add," he concluded, "that my inquiry on this occasion has led me to the same result, to which I have been led by extensive inquiries on many previous occasions, namely, that the sewers of

London can never be effectually ventilated by furnaces constructed for that purpose; and I am only sorry that Mr. Gurney was not with us to see these experiments tried." Asked by the committee if he considered this a fair test of the equipment, given Gurney's absence and the apparent confusion over venting arrangements, Bazalgette responded: "It was one labouring under difficulties, but I think a sufficient one to establish the conclusions I have come to."[45]

After listening to Bazalgette's testimony, Gurney gave his own version of events. He had directed his workmen to make the furnace available for examination as requested by the committee, he said. On Saturday the tenth, the sewers were tidelocked at the appointed time, so nothing could be done, and the workmen left the building. The MBW engineers asked to come on Sunday, but Gurney objected, so they agreed to come on Monday morning before nine o'clock. When Gurney arrived, just after nine, his ventilating assistant told him that "some tricks had been played." There was some stoppage in the vent to the Victoria Street sewer, which had been open for the past two or three years, and the furnace would now only draw from the Houses of Parliament. Gurney then sent for William Woodcock, a qualified engineer who was helping him produce commercial heating stoves, to check the sewer. By ten o'clock, Woodcock had made his way up to a grating that separated the parliamentary sewers from the Victoria Street sewer and saw, some distance away, a large piece of iron plating, fixed so as to shut off the flow of air. Thinking that this must be part of the experiment, he left for an hour. When he returned he found the obstruction apparently gone. If this inexplicable phenomenon was some kind of accident, Gurney advised the committee, it was regrettable. But if it was intentional, it was a plain case of sabotage; and as a report of the failed experiment had appeared in Tuesday morning's paper before it had been heard by the committee, he had to believe there was "a great animus" working against him. He reminded Lord John Manners that the MBW had recently been working in the Victoria Street sewer and had, from time to time, diverted its flow into other lines near Parliament, so they had had plenty of opportunity to alter the flaps and other arrangements. He had written to Lord John about it, requesting an investigation. Since he had no access to the area sewers, he could not guarantee the conditions for the most recent experiment, but it was obvious that "there has been a good deal of negligence, or a want of fair play in this matter."

He added that soon after the explosion, when Hawksley had finished checking the furnace, Gurney was told that the flow of air had been diverted underneath the burner unit rather than over it, with the result that the burners began to overheat and melt the grating. He had put the furnace back in working order, and since the House of Commons was to meet that night, he had told his workmen to hook up the House ventilating system again. Other than that, he said, "I studiously avoided interfering" with the MBW engineers.

When asked to comment on Bazalgette's calculations, Gurney replied that they were simply absurd. The intake pipe, which Bazalgette claimed was too small to be effective, had in fact been ventilating the Law Courts and the whole of the Palace Yard for several years at the request of the First Commissioner of Works. When it had been installed, the Metropolitan Commission of Sewers, under Bazalgette's supervision, had come around to trap all the gullies in the area. Bazalgette had grossly distorted the amount of fuel used by the furnace, and the number of furnaces needed to ventilate London's system, to arrive at his outrageous cost figures. Gurney thought that his system should be tested by more competent and disinterested parties. In the absence of such, he would stand on the results of his previous experiments, which had been verified by the MBW's own engineer.[46]

At the end of this remarkable exchange, Sir William Cubitt told Gurney: "You have given evidence, proving to the satisfaction of my mind, that [your furnace] could, and did, ventilate the sewers." Other members of the committee were not so certain. The evidence was contradictory, and the arguments could only be resolved by another set of experiments, which would take more time. The session was nearly at an end, and both the public and members of Commons were clamoring for action. As a last resort, the committee reexamined William Scott about the experiments he conducted with Gurney for the MBW in 1854, the only ones to have shown positive effects. Scott was a poor witness. It came out that he had had little experience with sewers. He admitted that he had not measured the current of air coming into the Clock Tower with the furnace off, and when he did take measurements, his anemometer wouldn't work, so he judged the current by the angle and color of a candle flame. The committee observed that a draft sufficient to ventilate the sewers would have blown out the flame. In answer to the most crucial question, Scott could not remember whether he had left the flap at the sewer junction up or down when he finished.[47]

It was now 15 July. The "Great Stink" continued unabated, and government had introduced its bill to give the MBW complete authority to build the main drainage according to their own plans. The select committee chairman, Nicholas Kendall, sought a graceful way to extricate Gurney from a lost cause. He proposed a report, which said:

> That the evidence and experiments submitted seem to substantiate, in most particulars, the theory of Mr. Gurney, as to the causes of the existing evils; and too much praise cannot be given to him for his deep research and deductions; but as a great difference of opinion exists as to the practicability, durability, and even temporary efficiency of the remedial measures proposed, as much conflicting evidence has been submitted, the Committee do not feel justified in recommending the adoption of any portion of the said remedial measures.

The new Main Drainage Bill, he concluded, appeared to make any further investigation by his committee superfluous.[48]

Had Kendall's draft been approved, members of Parliament and the public might have been tempted to look into the "conflicting evidence," and rally behind one or the other side in the matter. Gurney himself, though failing to win approval for his scheme, would have received credit for his scientific investigations, and his steam-jet furnace would no doubt have attracted a great deal of attention. But such possibilities were crushed by the committee's majority. Lord Palmerston, a surprising convert to the MBW's point of view, penned an alternative report which refuted all of Gurney's assumptions and remedies, point by point. "Your committee cannot recommend the adoption of any part of Mr. Gurney's plan," he wrote. "They consider that part of it which relates to the river to be founded upon an erroneous assumption, and they think that part of it which relates to the burning of gases would be of very doubtful efficacy." The steam-jet furnace might work for a small area that could be made airtight, but it was wholly unsuited for the metropolitan sewer system. The sewage really needed to be carried downriver before discharging, as the MBW recommended, and the muddy banks of the Thames could best be improved by a walled embankment as described by some of the "eminent engineers" examined by the committee.[49]

Palmerston's draft was adopted by a decisive vote and the report issued to a House of Commons already eager to make the MBW its agent of deliverance. The newspapers ignored it; the Lords were not interested. Bazalgette got the authority and financial support he needed to build the main drainage system and set to work immediately. A few years later, Parliament added funds for building the great embankment, which transformed a filthy commercial waterfront into an architectural wonder. Despite the usual construction delays, cost overruns, and claims of incompetence by politicians and journalists, the project proved extremely successful. The odors abated, the noxious muck disappeared from the Thames banks, deaths from pollution-related diseases dropped, and the public strolled through flowered gardens reclaimed from Hungerford Bay. The Metropolitan Board of Works enjoyed a brief but intense popularity for its achievement. Bazalgette was knighted. Gurney, bitter and disillusioned, went back to providing heat, light, and ventilation to those who had rejected his proposals.

13

Recognition and Decline

Iₘₘₑᴅᵢₐₜₑₗᵧ ᴀfᴛᴇʀ ʜɪѕ ɪɢɴᴏᴍɪɴɪᴏᴜѕ ᴛʀᴇᴀᴛᴍᴇɴᴛ ᴀᴛ ᴛʜᴇ ʜᴀɴᴅѕ ᴏf Bᴀᴢᴀʟɢᴇᴛᴛᴇ and his parliamentary allies, Gurney was drawn into another arena of public controversy, this time over a claim to his most celebrated and important invention. In 1857, Samuel Smiles published the first edition of his *Lives of the Engineers.* Trying to portray engineers as cultural heroes, he attributed the achievements of many individuals to a few leading figures. The late George Stephenson, for example, was credited with inventing most of the features of the standard railway locomotive, including the steam jet that gave it enough power to haul large loads at high speed. Scores of outraged inventors who had contributed ideas and improvements to early locomotive design challenged Smiles in letters to the *Times* and the *Morning Chronicle.* An expert named Hedley, who had witnessed the first railway trials in 1829, refuted Smiles, point by point, in an 1859 book, *Who Invented the Locomotive Engine?* Encouraged by the support given by Hedley and others, Gurney rushed into print an *Account of the Invention of the Steam-Jet or Blast and Its Application to Steamboats and Locomotive Engines.*[1] Edward Cayley, so familiar with the history of that invention, edited the pamphlet, adding selections from the printed evidence of parliamentary committees, Sir Charles Dance's account of the trip to Bath, contemporary reports by Nicholas Wood and other experts, and even the testimony of George Stephenson himself. The evidence was conclusive, wrote Gurney. Before the adoption of his steam jet by Timothy Hackworth in 1829, and its subsequent addition to Stephenson's *Rocket,* the highest speed estimated for railway locomotives was six miles per hour, while Gurney's steam carriage had already attained speeds of twenty or more. "All the facts on record, and the testimony of living witnesses, show that Mr. Richard Trevithick was the inventor of the Locomotive Engine, and that Mr. Goldsworthy Gurney was the inventor of the Steam Jet—emphatically called by engineers the 'life and soul' of its locomotion."[2]

The attack hit its mark. Smiles was forced to retract or modify his claims in subsequent editions. Nevertheless, his biography of Stephenson became standard reading for generations of British schoolboys and was translated into dozens of languages, while the arguments of the critics gradually faded.[3] Today Stephenson is recognized, not so much for original inventions, but for having brought together the main features of the railway enterprise: a company operating its own self-powered locomotives and stock on its own track, built with joint-stock capital, under statutory authority, with regularly scheduled public service.[4] The many inventors who made the locomotive possible, like those who later developed the mechanics of the automobile engine before Henry Ford, have been largely forgotten.

In the meantime Gurney continued supervising the ventilation and lighting of Parliament from his office quarters in New Palace Yard. The steam-jet furnace in the Clock Tower had to be removed and refitted when Big Ben was finally hoisted up to its belfry. Also, Gurney began designing a special arrangement for artificial lighting in the Lords' Library. On the whole, however, the system of heat, light, and air regulation he had established could be attended by skilled workmen with a minimum of supervision. Thrifty with materials and careful to cut costs where possible, he began to delegate small purchases and wage payments to his foreman, rendering his accounts in the aggregate in the manner of an independent contractor instead of a government employee. He came up to London only when Parliament was in session, and attended the House only when it was actually sitting.

More and more of his time was spent on the friendly coast of Cornwall. For a while he continued his agricultural experiments at Hornacott Manor, working with the properties of plant fibers and natural fertilizers. As president of the Launceston and Stratton Agricultural Society, he was said to conduct meetings with "great charm." In addition, he was the senior resident magistrate, presiding over the Stratton area petty sessions. It is easy to imagine him, now over sixty years old, somewhat jowly and genial, back in a social element that gave him respect. Although his separation from Jane Betty and Elizabeth, some time before 1860, led him to sell Hornacott Manor and Woodley Cottage, he continued his public appearances at local affairs. He now lived at Reeds, where Anna Jane resumed the role of daughter and companion so reluctantly relinquished in 1854. As before, she observed and assisted with her father's experiments and helped him prepare his various papers and pamphlets. In 1862 the local newspaper noted their attendance at the annual Stratton and

Bude Poultry and Cottage Garden Society exhibition at the Acland estate near the Castle.[5]

Disappointed in so many ventures, Gurney turned his back on the London scientific and technical establishment, but he continued to pursue several lines of enquiry. He presented papers to the Royal Institution of Cornwall, where he had been a longtime member, and communicated other results to appropriate experts and officials. In the summer of 1859, he applied for a patent on an electrical conductor for telegraph lines, proposing a flat ribbon of copper instead of the round wire then used.[6] At the same time he investigated the problem of signaling between ships and shore, which was part of a larger concern for the scandalous number of shipwrecks around the British coast, which continued despite years of maritime and lighthouse legislation.[7] The Admiralty had proposed to lay a telegraph line around the entire coast for effective communication between naval stations. Ships would be able to link up to the telegraph by sending visual signals during daylight, but they could not do so at night. Gurney visited the naval station at Plymouth at the invitation of authorities, and on 7 July 1859, he proposed a system of flashing lights, analogous to the dot-dash telegraph code. He then devised a version of the Bude light with a concentric burner that produced a powerful, focused beam, using any of several types of oil. This light was apparently tried first in the Bude lighthouse, where its power was quickly appreciated.[8]

In his usual way, Gurney extended the concept of flashing signals to related instruments and processes. He realized that lighthouses could be more readily identified, especially at night, if each one flashed its beam of light on a predetermined frequency: eight flashes for lighthouse number eight, twelve flashes for number twelve, and so on. A simple pendulum, attached to a valve in the fuel line, would keep the frequency constant. The lights could also be programmed for double or triple flashes or in dot-dash code. The frequency and location of each lighthouse could be entered on mariners' maps for ready reference. Gurney further proposed that each lighthouse be equipped with a second light, mounted a standard forty feet higher than the first in a vertical line. Such an arrangement would enable a seaman to calculate his distance from shore by simple triangulation, using a sextant or even a practiced eye. This system of identifying location and distance was the subject of a patent granted on 3 June 1862. It was described and explained in a pamphlet Gurney wrote that same year, but the manuscript remained unpublished until 1864, when Anna had a few hundred copies printed to distribute to various scientific and technical societies.[9]

As explained previously, Gurney's remuneration for services in Parliament and at the Law Courts had been a complicated and exasperating problem ever since he had been appointed supervisor of heating, lighting, and ventilation in 1854. He believed, as he had believed in 1838, that his patent rights in the Bude lamp and warming stove should be recognized and compensated separately from the work of installation and daily maintenance. But Parliament and the Office of Works proved singularly uncharitable in this regard. He had also forgone his salary from time to time while the Treasury, the Office of Works, and the chairs of parliamentary committees dithered over which of them was responsible for his position. On the question of establishing a government pension plan, the Office of Works treated him as an independent contractor or consultant, but in matters of installation and maintenance, they harassed him about filing detailed accounts, as if he were a salaried clerk. When his friends Sir William Molesworth and Lord John Manners had been First Commissioner, these matters were resolved with civility, if not with great haste. But Sir Benjamin Hall was intent on rooting out corruption, real or imaginary, and treated all contractors accordingly. Gurney penned a detailed explanation of the terms of his appointment to Hall in 1855, but the Works staff challenged every one of Gurney's claims, offering conflicting and insulting compromises or referring him back to the sergeant at arms of the House of Commons, who had no real jurisdiction.[10] A sort of truce was reached in 1859, after a change of ministry had brought Manners back into office. The Works staff recalculated everything due since 1854, added an annual lump sum to cover wages and incidentals that Gurney had paid his workmen, and reimbursed him a total of £682.[11] When the Whigs returned to power later that year, they appointed William Cowper, an intelligent manager and deft conciliator, as First Commissioner of Works.[12] Under Cowper things ran more smoothly, but Gurney never recovered his enormous investment of time, money, and patent rights in the Houses of Parliament.

In 1851 *The Mining Journal* had proposed formal state recognition for Gurney's important contributions to mine ventilation, but as these soon became shrouded in controversy, the idea lay fallow. It was revived in 1863, the year that Gurney turned seventy. On 11 August the *London Gazette* announced that Queen Victoria had bestowed upon him the dignity of Knight Bachelor of the United Kingdom. He was henceforth to be known as Sir Goldsworthy Gurney of Bude in the County of Cornwall.

Although some of Gurney's friends might have prompted such an initiative, there is no evidence for such action, and one can only

Sir Goldsworthy Gurney, ca. 1863. Drawing by Christine Porter, from an old photograph. Porter collection.

surmise that senior officials found it a convenient way to encourage his retirement. The Houses of Parliament and the Law Courts were now illuminated, heated, and ventilated in tolerable fashion with a minimum of day-to-day supervision. Those who had supported Gurney's experiments and installations or had worked with him to finish the New Palace were now gone. Sir William Molesworth had died in 1855, Sir George Cayley in 1857, Sir Charles Barry in 1860, and Edward Cayley, who, as M.P. for Yorkshire, had worked out the terms of Gurney's position and had assisted him as editor and friend, in 1862. Although William Cowper was a charitable man, he was bound to take note of Gurney's decreasing presence at Westminster, and the ventilation supervisor's annual retainer of £1,000 could not have escaped William Gladstone's penny-pinching scrutiny of government expenditures at the Exchequer. On the other hand, both of those men had been in government since 1832 and were familiar with Gurney's many achievements, most of which had enriched the kingdom rather than himself. Cowper, in particular, had been at the Treasury and the Office of Works for a dozen years and held several large folios of memoranda which detailed Gurney's long record of invention and service at Westminster as well as his frustrating efforts to obtain adequate recognition. The honor was certainly justified.

Gurney's contract, annually renewed, was set to run until July 1864, and it is likely that he would have retired at that time. Tragically, however, on 11 October 1863, he suffered a severe stroke which left his right side paralyzed, his speech impaired, and his memory uncertain. Anna took him to Plymouth in hopes that the warm sea climate would restore his health, but after almost a year there, it was clear that he would recover very slowly, if at all. As with many people in his condition, the uncertainty of his memory and language caused him great anxiety and bouts of depression. Lacking the means or the will to hire attendants and being the only person who could understand her father's garbled utterances, Anna attended him around the clock, searched for missing accounts among his disorganized papers, and drafted his correspondence, which he signed with a shaky left hand. In September 1864, she moved him with great difficulty back to Reeds, where his extended family and friends could provide some support and relief. Over time, he realized from his own medical knowledge that his condition was probably intractable, and he became both less irritable and less attentive to business. Anna, like many another woman in that age and since, dedicated the next twelve years to the care of an invalid parent.[13]

She mounted a campaign to squeeze some sort of pension out of the government. The Office of Works had made it clear as early as 1854 that Gurney was employed as a consultant, on a temporary basis, and pointedly did not deduct retirement contributions from his salary. Nevertheless, despite two decades of reformist attacks on government patronage, there were still plenty of precedents for awarding pensions, honoraria, or sinecures to former employees or to men and women with long records of public service.[14] And Anna was no shrinking violet. She had witnessed her father's chemical and steam experiments as a child. In the 1830s, after her mother died, she had become his hostess, secretary, and, no doubt, his laboratory assistant at the Castle and then at Reeds, where so many inventions were first born. She had functioned as his companion in both Cornish and London society. She was convinced of her father's genius and determined that the public should not forget him.

On 19 July 1864, two days before his contract expired, Anna sent a letter of resignation signed by her father to William Cowper. It noted that the Office of Works had, over a period of twenty to thirty years, asked his advice regarding many different subjects beyond his principal work at the Houses of Parliament and the Law Courts, to which he had always paid close attention. His exertions on behalf of the public were in great measure responsible for his present state of health, Gurney argued, and he trusted that the First Commissioner would bear that in mind when presenting his case to the Lords of the Treasury [that is, the prime minister's office]. Cowper sent regrets and a request for a detailed memorial, then turned the matter over to his experienced secretary, Alfred Austin. The latter must have written on his own to express his condolences, for Anna replied by private note to thank him for his concern. "My father," she said, "is as unable to memorialize as he is to continue his official duties. He has attempted many times to dictate a letter to you, calling attention to his arrangements in the Houses of Parliament, which he seems to say now almost regulates its temperature according to its own requirements, but generally becomes puzzled and fatigued and says, 'But he knows it all himself—they all know it.' I have asked my father several times about the things in his rooms [his office at Old Palace Yard], but he seems to think this too trifling a subject, & it only worries him."

Nevertheless, she gathered what documents she could find and asked questions whenever her father seemed responsive. For his part, Austin made notes from the office files and gave advice about preparing the memorial to Charles Gurney, son of Goldsworthy's uncle Gregory, who visited the Office of Works several times at Anna's request. Within a week she had cobbled together a substantial document, penned closely on two sheets of paper, which she sent off with trepidation on the twenty-fifth. "My father was very anxious it should go then, as he knew every one would soon be leaving town," she wrote to Austin. As a result, the sheets were not fastened together, the memorial was not dated, and it omitted the key request, that his salary of £1,000 a year be continued to him as a pension. Austin thought the results "suitable," but Anna was not satisfied and asked him to return the pages for revision. "The facts related in the Memorial are chiefly from my own knowledge & recollection," she advised him on 2 August. "My father's performance for the Office of Works I am not so well acquainted with, and should have to gather this especial information from papers which it may not be even in my power to get at, as my father cannot be moved, & I cannot leave him. Could I have any assistance from the Office?"

Austin sent what information he could gather, but Gurney's condition in August and September 1864 was in "a very precarious state," and Anna, complaining that she could find no one to help her nurse him, was unable to amend the Memorial. On 23 September she returned it to Austin, saying that Gurney had "fretted and wasted considerably" since sending his letter of resignation, had secluded himself in his bedroom, and was now under the illusion that his quarterly salary would soon be arriving as a pension payment. The document was forwarded to the Treasury by Cowper in the first week of October, with a letter noting Gurney's "very satisfactory" performance and recommending a favorable response. This occasioned a choice bit of bureaucratic shuffle. Treasury ruled that the case did not fall under the statutory pension rules for the Office of Works because Gurney was only a consultant, under renewable contract. However, if he could be regarded as a salaried officer of the House of Commons, he could be eligible for retirement benefits from that source. The Speaker of the House said that Gurney's work had been "efficiently and zealously performed," but that he was in fact not an employee of theirs. Sir Thomas Peel, at Treasury, then authorized on his own authority a pension of £333. 8s. 6d per annum.[15]

A pension of one-third of an official's annual salary was the standard allowance for all government employees of Gurney's rank, but given the sums he had earned in years previously and the general inflation that marked the mid-Victorian economy, it was not much, and Anna was not satisfied. She penned a flurry of notes to Austin, rehearsing all of her father's achievements and arguing that his scientific contributions to public welfare, plus "the great mental exertion & constant application required for his services" in Parliament, deserved greater recognition. In February 1865 she forwarded a new petition, but the Treasury refused to grant any additional allowance.

Alfred Austin continued to correspond with Anna for several years. He advised her on the procedure for obtaining power of attorney to sign her father's signature, which enabled her to dispose of minor questions in the various accounts for which Gurney had been responsible, and he forwarded to the Treasury officials a copy of Gurney's last pamphlet, the one on lighthouse signals, which she had enclosed for his perusal. Although Anna's constant duties as nurse and secretary sometimes drove her to write disjointed, complaining letters, the secretary's responses were always, as she acknowledged, "kind and considerate."

Sir Goldsworthy Gurney died at Reeds on 28 February 1875. "There is now a sad blank!" wrote Anna. His will, proved on 31 March, left everything to Anna, but there was only £300 in the estate, hardly enough to see her through her final years. Twenty years earlier, soon after he had sold the Castle and moved to Reeds, he had told a parliamentary committee, "Money would not be my price—I do not need it—I have independent means." He had, moreover, been paid £1000 per year for nearly ten years, a salary higher than that of the senior assistant engineers at the Metropolitan Board of Works. It is quite possible that Hornacott Manor, as an experimental farm, may have swallowed his considerable investment in it, and at least some of the profits from its sale in 1859 must have gone to support his estranged second wife and daughter. But he should have had enough for a comfortable retirement, even on the modest pension allowed by the government, had not a dozen years of miserable illness drained his resources.

The will, however, cannot be taken as a true measure of Gurney's estate. Anna Jane appears to have had the funds to ensure that his memory was literally etched in stone, and fairly expensive stone at that. She buried him in her mother's family plot (Elizabeth's own grave was at St. Giles in the Field, London) next to the wall of picturesque St. Swithin's Church at Launcells, providing a massive granite cover decorated with a large relief cross. Around the edge are the words: "To his inventive genius the world is indebted for the high speed of the locomotive, without which railways could not have succeeded and would never have been made." Five years later she donated £500 in her father's memory toward the building of the new Truro Cathedral, with an inscription that perfectly epitomizes the late Victorian blend of missionary Christianity and worship of technology. She gave the sum "as a thank offering to almighty God for the benefit of high speed locomotion whereby His good gifts are conveyed from one nation to another and the word of the Lord is sent unto all parts of the world." In 1889 she provided £110 to place a chiming clock in the tower of Poughhill Church, where it can still be seen, with a plaque that claims, after the usual dates and titles of her father's life, "His inventions and discoveries in steam and electricity rendered transport by land and sea so rapid that it became necessary for all England to keep uniform time." This hyperbolic reference to electrical discoveries was repeated in the inscription for a stained-glass window that Anna donated to St. Margaret's Chapel at the side of Westminster Abbey in memory of both her parents. There she claimed that among other achievements, "he originated the Electric Telegraph." T. R. Harris accurately summarized these inscriptions as "the compositions of an adoring daughter."[16]

Obituaries and tributes poured into Reeds from the many associations with which Gurney had been connected and from periodicals that had once reported his inventions. The Rev. R. R. Wright, J.P., conveyed the sympathy of the Stratton Petty Sessions to the daughter of their senior magistrate, speaking in court about his fame and pleasant personality. The *West Briton and Cornwall Advertiser* carried biographical notices, perhaps supplied by Anna, emphasizing the "affectionate solicitude of his daughter" during his last years. "His home has been hers for more than 60 years," said the writer; "she has been his companion, and has always taken the greatest interest in his discoveries and inventions." A more technically oriented memoir appeared in the *Minutes of Proceedings* of the Institution of Civil Engineers, where he had engaged in so many lively debates. *The Engineer* for 12 March noted his "considerable eminence as an inventor. . . . his career was invested with peculiar interest for engineers by his connection with steam locomotion on common roads." The same point was made by *The Atheneum* on the twentieth, adding a tribute to his threefold contributions to the Houses of Parliament. At the spring meeting of the Royal Institution of Cornwall, where he had been a corresponding member of long standing, Dr. Jago, F.R.S., recalled several of his contributed papers, concluding: "By his sound qualities, and as a man of science, he was an honour to his native county."[17]

Anna also continued for several years to proclaim her father's genius in print. The obituary she wrote for the *Times,* printed on 26 December, attributed so many discoveries to him that it occasioned a sharp attack from Samuel Smiles and an acrimonious exchange between them.[18] She sent reprints of old pamphlets to various scientific and technical institutions, with handwritten comments in the margins, pointing out the circumstances and significance of key measures. And she frequently reminded the Office of Works that her father's services had never been adequately rewarded. When the House of Commons decided in 1881 to try out the new electric light, she sent an effusive warning to the First Commissioner of Works, Mr. Shaw Lefevre, not to jeopardize the apparatus of her father's unique and successful lighting apparatus by haphazard experiments. She noted that the old fixtures were placed, with great difficulty, so as to eliminate shadows, and were integrated with the system of ventilation in such a way that a change in one might interfere with the other. Furthermore, she added, both systems were installed with the understanding that her father would be compensated for the equipment and patent rights by vote of the House, *in addition to his regular salary.* This had not been done and was a debt due to her as his heir.

Dr. John Percy, who was then the superintending engineer for heating, lighting, and ventilation at Parliament and had been responsible for modifying and improving many of Gurney's arrangements, replied in a memorandum to Shaw Lefevre. He confused the Bude light with the previous Drummond, or limelight, and thought that it had never been used in the House; he ignored the issue of patent rights; he claimed that Gurney's only innovation had been the ventilating steam jet, and that he had abandoned that as impracticable; and he even disputed the fact that Gurney had invented it. Percy concluded that in his judgment Anna's claim for compensation "is not for a moment to be entertained." The Works secretary concurred. Shortly thereafter Anna received a curt letter summarizing Percy's views and informing her that the Office of Works would recognize no further claims of any kind. Her latest letter to Alfred Austin was also returned with a note that he no longer worked at the office. It gave no forwarding address.

She wrote a rebuttal. She cited the relevant technical refinements to the Bude light with a degree of detail and accuracy completely at odds with the stereotype of the fluttery, domestic Victorian spinster. Admitting that the patent rights to the light were no longer valid, she raised the issue of the warming apparatus, or Gurney stove, whose royalties Gurney had in fact reserved for himself. It was a strong letter, but it earned her only a stony silence from the Office of Works.

Anna Jane lived until 1896. She had seen the Bude light and magic-lantern limelight replaced by electric lamps, and lived long enough to hear about the invention of the internal combustion engine and the motorcar. The steam railway had been extended to Holsworthy, ten miles from Bude, bringing crowds of summer tourists to the picturesque coastline and salubrious air. A few miles away at Reeds, time slowed down, even reversed, as she clung to the memories of her father's accomplishments.

There is a local tradition that Anna burned all of Goldsworthy Gurney's papers before she died, either in the hope that her own memorials would remain the sole reminders of his fame or to ensure that her stepmother and stepsister could never enjoy them. It is just as likely, given Anna's laments during her father's illness, that they were left in considerable disarray and were disposed of by the estate agent or next occupant. Many other records were left in his offices at Old Palace Yard when he suffered his attack of paralysis in 1863; they were not kept by the Office of Works. But if Anna did indeed plan to deprive her stepmother of her inheritance, she was bound to be disappointed. Jane Betty Gurney secured a burial plot just across the path from Sir Goldsworthy's grave at St. Swithin's church, and upon her death on 11 December 1911, her daughter raised a stone there, identifying her as Lady Jane Gurney, second wife of Sir Goldsworthy Gurney, with the motto: "My Grace is sufficient for thee."

Information about Lady Jane's daughter, Elizabeth Jane, has been hard to come by. Gurney's obituary notices mentioned neither of them, and although Anna was identified late in life as his "elder" daughter by his "first wife," the names and location of Jane Betty Gurney and Elizabeth were not given. From newspaper notes and local directories, it appears that at the time of her mother's death, Elizabeth Jane was married to James Crocker, Fellow of the Royal Institute of British Architects, of 11, College Road, Exeter. I have not been able to trace either the husband or wife after that. In 1930 a Mrs. John James of Glan Mor, Truro, noted in correspondence to the *West Briton* newspaper that she was related to Gurney on her mother's side, and that Elizabeth Jane was still living. In such situations a biographer always hopes that the publication of his work will alert a descendant to the possibility that "those old family papers in the closet" deserve to be made public. Otherwise we must remain ignorant of many fascinating aspects of Sir Goldsworthy Gurney's private life, scientific investigations, and wide-ranging correspondence.

14

Science, Technology, and Invention in the Early Nineteenth Century

Sir Goldsworthy Gurney's life spanned the revolution in chemistry, the establishment of steam power in British industry, the coming of the railways, the replacement of oil lamps by gaslight, the expansion of deep coal mining, and the discovery of electromagnetism. The astonishing thing is not that these occurred between his birth and death, but that he was involved with all of them, and in some cases significantly so. The focus of his career may be dramatized by comparing a list of events that happened during his life span but never drew his close attention or participation: the Napoleonic Wars, Catholic Emancipation and the Great Reform Bill, the Factory Acts, the great Irish famine, and the advent of Free Trade. These were momentous changes, to be sure, but their impact on Gurney's career and relationships is barely noticed in the surviving records. His life is defined almost wholly by his scientific and technical pursuits.

Almost, but not quite. For he was a Cornishman from first to last, and a gentleman in that county, if not always in London. At the age of twenty-seven, he set off to make his mark in the great metropolis, seeking status and money as a surgeon, lecturer, inventor, and manufacturer. After a decade he returned to his provincial roots to build the Castle and carry out many of his most successful experiments. It is not surprising that his first wife, Elizabeth, was a young woman of local family; his second wife, Jane Betty, hailed from nearby Devonshire, and his retirement years were spent near Bude rather than in some suburban London villa. He took an active role in Cornish agricultural improvements and served as magistrate in the local courts.

Gurney's status as a younger son of Cornish gentry ensured that he would not inherit an estate, and his unusual early interest and training in science and mechanics led him into medicine instead of into the church, where his brother and many of his uncles and cousins found places. His subsequent career may be understood as the subtle and often frustrating interplay between this provincial background and the emerging professionalization of science and technology in nineteenth-century Britain. He was by no means the last of his kind—a largely self-taught gentleman scientist, whose commercial instincts were always lagging behind his boundless enthusiasm for learning and invention—but the species was in decline. The careers of Davy and Faraday signaled the future for scientists as early as 1820, while the intervention of engineers like Bazalgette, Haywood, and Hawksley in the 1840s and 1850s demonstrated the growing authority of professional men.[1] Where previously an individual mechanic or scientific experimenter could hope to succeed as a freelance entrepreneur or find an outlet for his talents within a small workshop or laboratory, now he was increasingly drawn into competition with larger, well-organized teams of experts, who possessed political as well as commercial influence. Gurney was ill equipped to deal with this gradual change in the contexts of innovation. His social milieu favored personal attachments over organizational power; his upbringing in Cornwall was devoid of experience with large-scale commerce or industry; and his unique personality, marked by voluble swings between enthusiasm and despair, a fertile imagination, and a sometimes naive optimism, did not fit easily into the emerging institutional framework of British politics and enterprise. In Truro, Wadebridge, or Bude, he could play the surgeon, magistrate, or local genius to an appreciative audience. There, his social status depended more on his family origins and personal connections than on skilled achievement. Among the experts and authorities in London, however, the same type of behavior sometimes appeared amateurish and pretentious. Hence Gurney's defeat in Parliament at the hands of a powerful network representing agricultural, horse transport, and railway interests. Hence his eventual displacement in the field of mine ventilation by Nicholas Wood and the North of England Institute of Mining Engineers. Hence the sabotage of his steam-jet sewer furnace by the engineers of the Metropolitan Board of Works.

The evolution of this institutional, professional framework for British science and industry should not, of course, be overstated. When Gurney retired in 1863, the Metropolitan Board of Works had not yet won public confidence for its engineering prowess, the scientific establishment was still fragmented, gentlemen amateurs were confidently ruling over a vast colonial empire, and simple partnerships or family firms were by far the most common form of business or industry. The empiricism of British natural philosophy was carried over into the training of engineers and research scientists, where practical apprenticeship remained more popular than academic study. Even at midcentury, Gurney's ramshackle theories and trial-and-error methods were commonly employed by so-called professionals. However, knowledge and practice were becoming more refined and were regulated by hierarchies of self-proclaimed experts. The mid-Victorian world was not the world into which Gurney was born. If we want to understand why he was so successful in his early years and increasingly frustrated later in life, we need to acknowledge these subtle but profound changes.

While giving an account of Gurney's life, I have tried to indicate particular instances of institutional and professional development as they impinged on one or another of his enterprises. I have also indicated contemporary individuals and ideas to show that Gurney, like most inventors, did not operate as an isolated genius. In doing so I may have appeared to be denigrating his achievements. Such was not my intention. Rather, I hoped to put his life and work in context, so that it might be accurately and meaningfully evaluated. For example, many people have celebrated Gurney's invention of the Bude light, and a few have pointed out that it was used in the Houses of Parliament for almost sixty years before being replaced by electric lamps. But how many understand just how the Bude light worked and how it differed from the dozens of other "improved" oil and gas lamps then being patented and offered to the public? Investigating the technical aspects of the invention, while surveying Gurney's competition, helps us assess his contributions to a collective enterprise.

Again, it is recorded that he was invited to try out the Bude light in the temporary House of Commons as a result of his experiments at Trinity House under Michael Faraday and his acquaintance with an influential member of Parliament, Joseph Hume. These connections might be taken as evidence that he was unfairly favored over other inventors, that personal prejudice replaced objective judgment. In reality, as we have seen, Faraday's recommendation was based on Gurney's imaginative and persistent investigation of the original lime-light, or Drummond light, and his realization that an entirely different principle would yield superior results. Moreover, the notion that science and technology proceed without personal prejudice and patronage has been thoroughly discredited by modern research.

Much of what we know about science and technology in the past comes from the work of specialists in various fields, such as chemists or engineers, who are concerned to explain the inner logic of scientific or technological development. The expert assumes a pattern of continuous progress, gained by solving a series of problems presented by the environment, or more commonly, by previous discoveries. Using this approach, it is possible to show why and how the steam carriages were developed by Gurney, Squires, or Gordon, and why they ultimately failed, both as reliable inventions and as systems of transport. In other words, one can explain the physics of steam propulsion and the steam jet, and behind the publicity attending trial runs and the hyperbole of parliamentary arguments, one can find evidence of how frail and temperamental the carriages were to operate on the rough roads of the day, how much care and repair they required from trained engineers, and how few passengers they could actually carry compared to the railways. Specialists might also pay attention to experiments with alternatives to steam power, such as Sir George Cayley's hot-air engine or the early ammonia gas models, which standard histories never mention.

Other major sources of technology history are biographies of leading men and women whose discoveries or inventions made them famous: Thomas Telford, George Stephenson, Humphry Davy, and Michael Faraday. The biographical approach to science and technology, made famous by Samuel Smiles's *Lives of the Engineers*, has yielded more complex studies, because even geniuses like Telford and Stephenson, Lavoisier, Davy, and Faraday had to put up with interference and interruption from the political, commercial, and social worlds in which they operated. Still, biography tends to be limited to the immediate interests and problems of an individual. As we have seen in the case of Smiles's life of George Stephenson and in Anna Gurney's vigorous memorials to her father's career, biographers feel a constant temptation to claim for their subjects more than is really due and to neglect subtle relationships with rivals and associates, natural philosophers and patrons, families and financiers. They also tend to forget that their readers may not readily identify and understand the terminology and mechanics of bygone scientific instruments or technology. The result is often a record of achievement that leaves us full of admiration for the person, but deficient in understanding what exactly they did and the circumstances in which they did it.

In the past twenty years, scholars have developed a sociological approach to the history of technology, which joins the "expert" and the biographical approaches to a wider view of the social contexts in which inventors work. This approach is allied with social studies of science, which developed out of the insights of Thomas Kuhn in his pathbreaking book, *The Anatomy of Scientific Revolution* (1962, 1970). Kuhn, a trained physicist, argued that changes in scientific thinking, such as Galileo's shift from an earth-centered to a solar-centered astronomy, do not emerge automatically from the logic of scientific research. Instead they arise when traditional assumptions, and the experiments that derive from them, arrive at an impasse—when the usual methods will *not* yield a solution to a significant problem. Then, scientists have to fashion a new hypothesis on the basis of new assumptions. At this point the veil of scientific secrecy and elitism is drawn aside, because new hypotheses about the material world are often linked to assumptions about religion, politics, and commerce (as Priestley's career demonstrates) and to practical matters like patronage, government funding, or access to equipment and capital. The chemical revolution that shaped Gurney's early career involved radical changes of this type. One of those changes was initiated by Lavoisier, who perceived, in current experiments with combustion, a new principle of attraction between chemical elements. Another was generated (literally) by Humphry Davy when he realized that the primitive battery, known as the voltaic pile, was capable of isolating the elements of metallic compounds. Davy turned an entertaining artifact into a significant tool for research, opening up a whole new field of knowledge. At the same time, the voltaic pile was being interpreted by other people as a marvelous medical instrument, as a possible source of light and heat, or as a revelation of divine power. France and England devoted scarce resources to the construction of rival piles, and Davy himself used it to procure a lion's share of resources for further research.

What happens in science also happens in technology. Textbook accounts of the industrial revolution give the impression that steam power developed logically, almost inevitably, from Savory and Newcomen's original pumping engines, through Watt's crucial improvements, to Trevithick and Stephenson. Each inventor adds something new to the device, and change, while incremental and sometimes uneven, is always progressive. Any episode in the life of Goldsworthy Gurney is sufficient to show how deceptive this view is. Take, for example, his invention of the tubular boiler. In the first place, he didn't invent it: tubular boilers had appeared at least two decades before 1824, but had failed to work. In the second place, Gurney's various modifications to his original design did not always improve it, and rival designs were deemed superior by several experts. In the third place, the primary advantage of the tubular boiler, namely its light weight, was of little or no consideration when applied to the requirements of railway transport, which consequently adopted a different design. However, the high ratio of heating surface, facility in recycling water, and ease of access for maintenance that the tubular boiler offered turned out to be advantageous for stationary engines, which did not have to suffer the jolts and vibration of carriages on common roads. Stationary tubular boilers were therefore refined and used for long periods after the original vehicular application had been abandoned.

A second instance of irrational and discontinuous development was the assumption that steam-carriage wheels could not generate enough traction to go up hills. Gurney himself shared this assumption, but it was based on his childhood observation of a Trevithick road locomotive, and he abandoned it as soon as his new model carriage conquered its first hill. Those whose belief in the intractability of the wheels stemmed from hearsay or theory, on the other hand, refused to admit that they were wrong, even after practical experience disproved the point.

As indicated in the Introduction, this kind of disjuncture between theory and practice, between scientific principle and industrial application, has been the subject of intense debate among historians of nineteenth-century science and technology. Gurney's career indicates that the boundary between empirical experiment, which occupies the great majority of scientists most of the time, and the craft-oriented pattern of technological development typical of British industry in the early nineteenth century was always vague and constantly shifting. His trial-and-error improvement of the oxyhydrogen blowpipe and his experiments with coal mine ventilation are but two instances where theory and practice interacted advantageously, with neither having logical precedence.

The more significant contrast in his work lies in the scale of the projects and the nature of the sociopolitical communities in which they occurred. He advanced successfully in the relatively specialized world of London scientific research and lecturing around 1820 and in the relatively intimate world of Parliament in the 1840s. Both communities operated through personal contacts and patronage, so that self-confidence, enthusiasm, manners, and the cultivation of friendships paid real dividends. The projects they appreciated were limited in scale, appropriate for individual supervision. In contrast, the worlds of steam locomotion and metropolitan sanitation operated on the basis of large-scale finance and legislation, which required the aggressive recruitment and coordination of technicians, bankers, landed aristocrats, government officials, and engineers. The men who triumphed in these fields seldom understood scientific research or its specialized results, but they appreciated its worth and knew how to apply its principles. They had arrived at the early stages of what Tom Peters calls "technological thinking," the ability to perceive the construction of machines, railways, and related artifacts as complex processes, requiring the same kind of design as the objects themselves. Moreover, they considered Parliament not as a community of friends and possible patrons, but as an arena for the negotiation of power and exclusion. Gurney never understood their way of thinking, and, I believe, never understood why he could not compete in their emerging world. Like his friend George Cayley, he remained a gentleman mechanic, as he had been a gentleman scientist.

To explore the political, commercial, and cultural contexts in which invention and industrial organization take place, without ignoring the achievements of outstanding individuals or the purely technical aspects of development, has proven difficult for historians of technology. For a biographer the trick is to show enough of the subject's background and connections with contemporary movements to indicate the sources of his inspiration and technical knowledge, the sometimes mistaken assumptions he shared with rivals and assistants, and the causes for his success or failure in particular ventures, without losing the uniqueness and the continuities of his personal life and career. For acknowledged leaders in a field, this is not so difficult a feat, because their negotiations and diversions appear to coincide with the larger endeavor.[2] But for a scientist-inventor of the second rank, one whose interests are diverse, and whose resources and ambition remain less sharply focused, the task is daunting. A comparison of a provincial gentleman scientist like Goldsworthy Gurney with his contemporaries shows how up-to-date he was in many regards, how closely he followed experimental reports in London and on the Continent, and how involved he was with leading experts like William Wollaston, John Farey, and Michael Faraday. Yet it must also disclose, as biographies of Davy and Faraday don't often do, how misdirected and unsystematic his efforts could be.

The work of famous scientists and inventors is also easier to explain, perhaps, because readers recognize the names and functions of the main inventions, even if they cannot always follow the supporting chemistry, engineering, or calculus. Voltaic piles became batteries, which we have all seen, and railway locomotives just grew larger. An "oxyhydrogen blowpipe" is a different sort of artifact. Few people have even heard of blowpipe analysis, and nobody practices it anymore. Introducing the blowpipe as a sort of proto-acetylene torch is not very accurate, but it is probably the most useful analogy for most readers. Describing how it was constructed presents other problems. Gurney was not consistent in his description of its parts, particularly regarding the water-filled tube, mounted behind the jet, that prevented the flame from backing up into the gas chambers. In some accounts he called the tube a "gasometer," because the water level indicated gas pressure; in others he called it a "pyrometer," a device to measure heat expansion. But he also used "pyrometer" to designate a different device that he invented at the same time. The Bude light offers another problem in definition. Originally a sort of Argand lamp augmented by a stream of oxygen, it was later designed to burn ordinary air through multiple rings of flame. Even after it had been installed in the Houses of Parliament for several years, people confused the later type with the earlier, and even with its quite different predecessor, the Drummond light. A memorialist, interested only in celebrating Gurney as an unsung genius, might be excused for consolidating such apparently minor changes and dating the invention by reference to Gurney's description of it before the Commons Committee of 1839. Historians trying to discern the links between technical change and human behavior must be more exact.

Like many scientists and inventors who converse and correspond frequently with other experts, and who focus their efforts strenuously on an object of curiosity or ambition, Gurney found it awkward to describe and explain his work to laymen. In a pamphlet or paper composed at leisure, he could be clear enough, but oral exchanges often went awry. Newspaper reporters and members of Parliament were forever repeating ignorant questions and misunderstanding or misrepresenting his answers. The famous trip to Bath, for example, was reported in some periodicals with a drawing of his earlier steam carriage, rather than the "drag" that actually made the journey, and more than once, periodicals announced the inauguration of service on a new carriage line, "with the inventor himself piloting the maiden voyage," without any basis in fact. Gurney explained mine ventilation to at least five different parliamentary committees and still found his arguments and data completely twisted in debate, where he could not reply.

Such experiences are common enough in all times and places, but to a man of Gurney's sensitivity (perhaps to any Cornishman), they appeared as pieces of a thoroughly despicable conspiracy. As I have argued above, Gurney himself had little inclination for political organization, preferring the gentlemanly art of personal influence. He also believed, as many people still believe, that new scientific ideas and technical inventions need only be demonstrated to the public to be accepted. He was therefore surprised, then shocked and dismayed, when vested interests, competitors, and politicians raised obstacles to the realization of his projects. By 1858 he had become familiar with the pattern, but not much better at dealing with it. When his plan for deodorizing London's sewage fell victim to political infighting between Sir Benjamin Hall and the Board of Works engineers, he publicly castigated a parliamentary committee for allowing his testimony to be suppressed in favor of his critics', and refused to cooperate further with the charade of "professional" evaluation.

Gurney's frustration with the perversity of laymen and vested interests has to be balanced against the encouragement and assistance he received throughout his life from friends, patrons, and genuine admirers of his work. He was fortunate in the appointment of Thomas Hogg as schoolmaster at Truro. He was lucky to have a father with the income to support his surgical apprenticeship and the acumen to place him in a position so suitable to his talents. Prominent scientists, such as Sir Anthony Carlisle and William Wollaston, accepted his experimental work as interesting and reliable and helped procure his appointment as lecturer at the Surrey Institution. The members of Parliament from Cornwall, particularly Sir William Molesworth, advocated his interests in every committee and debate. Sir George Cayley and his nephew Edward offered constant political, technical, and moral support, which Gurney warmly reciprocated. This network of associates, friends, and patrons was crucial to his success, and it must be said that Gurney cultivated it enthusiastically. He showed a genuine interest in the work of others and repaid their assistance with dedicated, painstaking effort. The stereotype of the inventor as isolated genius is nowhere so misplaced as in his case.

It is unfortunate that his achievements were documented mostly through the minutes of parliamentary committee hearings and debates, in self-justifying petitions and pamphlets, in partisan newspaper reports, and in the memorials of a zealous daughter. These records, by their very nature, lean toward hyperbole and inconsistency, which tends to cast suspicion on claims to originality and significance. By placing them in appropriate contexts, I have tried to establish a more reliable assessment of his contributions. They were, I believe, less dramatic, but more substantial, than Anna Jane appreciated.

The Surrey Institution lectures in chemistry were neither better nor worse than other published surveys of the time, but the fact that they were innovative and solid enough to be recommended for publication in a competitive market reflected Gurney's remarkable curiosity and extraordinary investment in experimental research. Had he not been lured away by the grail of steam locomotion, the lectures might have gone through many editions. As it was, they provided the soil from which all of his other projects grew. Decades later he would refer to his lecture preparations as the inspiration for a particular device or concept. For the young provincial surgeon, making his debut in a great imperial metropolis, they were an enduring achievement.

The oxyhydrogen blowpipe he perfected for laboratory use provided a safe, efficient instrument for mineralogical analysis. Donated to the public through the Society of Arts, it was destined to undergo many improvements and alterations. Its most enduring application, however, was one Gurney had foreseen in a moment of speculative musing. As the source of limelight, it powered the magic lanterns and lit the theaters of Victorian England.

The steam jet deserves a history of its own, if only to contrast the many ways in which Gurney tried to make use of it with the one application that made it famous, and for which he received scant credit. Based on contemporary accounts and on Beasley's careful research in private documents, it seems clear that Gurney first invented the steam jet and used it in his early carriages; that Timothy Hackworth, among others, realized its potential for railway engines at the Rainhill trials in 1829; and that George Stephenson's immediate adaptation of it for the *Rocket* enabled that and all subsequent locomotives to attain the speeds required for successful railway transport. Gurney's later experiments with steam-jet ventilation in coal mines and in the Houses of Parliament were apparently successful, but like his several steam carriages, required too much personal attention and maintenance for long-term utility.

His arrangements for heating, lighting, and ventilating the Houses of Parliament performed to the satisfaction of members during the ten years he served as supervisor under the Board of Works. Because the immense collection of chambers, corridors, offices, and vaults had been built by committee and underwent frequent alterations and changes of function, no system of utilities could ever be considered permanent. Although Gurney came to delegate much of the day-to-day work to trained assistants, he was often obliged to modify the path of air currents, raise or lower the lighting fixtures, or deal with invasions of alien odors. It is not surprising, then, that his successor made a great many changes. But the lighting remained in place until the 1880s, and the ventilating system continued its basic functions until the end of the century. Given the chaotic, dysfunctional installations produced by Barrie and Reid before Gurney was put in charge, this continuity of service is remarkable.

The Gurney stove seems a minor artifact. Yet both the large, fluted barrel produced for commercial use and the earlier, finned steam radiator show a keen insight into the advantages of maximizing surface radiation. He also grasped the principle of central heating and built functioning boilers for the purpose. It was not his fault that the

British proved more reluctant than other Europeans to give up their traditional fireplaces. The reality was that for many large buildings it proved easier to maintain a Gurney stove than to retrofit the structure with a modern heating system. As a result, a half-dozen stoves continue in daily operation, almost a century and a half after they were installed.

The Castle at Bude is an appropriate monument with which to conclude our evaluation. It is richly ironic that the most enduring legacy of a man passionately devoted to steam-powered transport, who spent his career perpetually commuting between Cornwall and London, is a solidly entrenched stone building. Like many of Gurney's inventions, it was motivated by a combination of scientific curiosity, social emulation, and the Cornish equivalent of chutzpah. Its outward appearance was purposely anachronistic, in tune with the medievalist fantasies of the early Romantic era, but its foundation incorporated the newest technology, and its interior was designed to be lighted by a system Gurney was still trying to perfect. The building site, dredged out of the dunes between the mouth of the Neet and the Bude Canal, was shunned by traditional householders. Now it anchors the town center, its pleasant gardens overlooking the library, the museum, and the civic assembly hall.

It would be nice to report that the Castle stands unaltered from its original construction. But like most of Gurney's discoveries and inventions, the integrity of its basic design was compromised by generations of improvements. Occupants remodeled the interior of the Castle so often that the floor plan of 1830 disappeared. Only a few panes of original glass remain in the windows, and the casings have all been replaced. Central heating and electric lights were installed, which Gurney would have approved. But the exterior, despite some unfortunate extensions along the back wall, remains faithful to its first owner. Like the early steam carriages, it is bulky and heavyset, more energetic than graceful, an old-fashioned body equipped with a new frame and functions. Its charm lies in its friendly bravado, its enthusiasm for scientific novelty mixed with social pretension, incongruous with its environment, but demanding appreciation on its own terms. It is a fitting memorial to the man who built it.

Notes

U. K. House of Commons *Sessional Papers* are abbreviated as H. C. *Sess. Pap.* and cited by session year, command number, volume and title. Page references are to the original report, as the sequential pagination in different collections may vary.

INTRODUCTION

1. Leonard G. Wilson, "Science by Candlelight," *The Mind and Art of Victorian England* ed. Josef Altholz (Minneapolis: The University of Minnesota Press, 1976), 94–105, argues that amateur scientists made notable contributions in spite of, or perhaps because of, the lack of government support and supervision. Morris Berman, *Social Change and Scientific Organization: The Royal Institution, 1799–1844* (Ithaca: Cornell University Press, 1978), ch. 4, "Toward a Rational Society," traces the trend from gentlemanly science to professional discourse in the leading experimental institution of the day. Roy Porter, "Gentlemen and Geology: the Emergence of a Scientific Career, 1660–1920," *The Historical Journal* 21, no. 4 (1978): 809–36, discusses the nineteenth-century resurgence of the gentleman amateur tradition in a related field. The first generation of geologists included medical practitioners, like Gurney, and clergy, like other men in his family.

2. A. E. Musson and Eric Robinson, *Science and Technology in the Industrial Revolution* (Manchester, U.K.: Manchester University Press, 1969), preface. The debates of the 1960s were reviewed by Neil McKendrick in "The Role of Science in the Industrial Revolution: A Study of Josiah Wedgwood as a Scientist and Industrial Chemist," *Changing Perspectives in the History of Science: Essays in Honour of Joseph Needham,* ed. Mikulás Teich and Robert Young (London: Heinemann, 1973). McKendrick, although recognizing Musson and Robinson's leadership in the field, argued that the enthusiasm for scientific discussion and experiments shown by entrepreneurs like Wedgwood was still not the same as applied scientific thinking (279).

3. Musson and Robinson, *Science and Technology,* preface: 2–3, 251–337. Cf. Berman, *Social Change and Scientific Organization.* David Knight, *Humphry Davy: Science and Power* (Oxford: Blackwell, 1992): 454, remarks that Davy's first successful paper at the Royal Institution was a discussion of the processes of tanning, and that his *Elements of Agricultural Chemistry* (1813), written for the improving landlords who formed the core of the RI's first generation of members, went through four editions. Michael Faraday began his apprenticeship with Davy by studying sugar beets.

4. On Faraday, see Joseph Agassi, *Faraday as a Natural Philosopher* (Chicago: University of Chicago Press, 1971), and L. Pearce Williams, *Michael Faraday: A Biography* (New York: Basic Books, 1965). On Dalton's theory, see Knight, *Humphry Davy,* 76–7, and L. A. Whitt, "Atoms or Affinities? The Ambivalent Reception of Daltonian Theory," *Studies in History and Philosophy of Science,* 21 (1990): 57–89.

5. Thomas Kuhn, *The Structure of Scientific Revolutions* (Chicago: The University of Chicago Press, 1962; 2d ed., 1970).

6. For Kuhn's description of "normal" science, see ibid., 25–30. Kuhn argued that the image of random experimentation is most prevalent during periods of scientific revolution, as in the chemical revolution, but others have noticed the difference between laboratory practice and subsequent reports and textbooks. See Maurice Crosland, *Gay-Lussac: Scientist and Bourgeois* (Cambridge: Cambridge University Press, 1978), 69; Jan Golinski, "The Theory of Practice and the Practice of Theory: Sociological Approaches in the History of Science," *Isis* 81 (1990): 494; and Bruno Latour and Steve Woolgar, *Laboratory Life: The Social Construction of Scientific Facts* (Beverly Hills and London: Sage Publications, 1979), 15–41.

7. Musson and Robinson, *Science and Technology*, 2–3.

8. The stages of development in nineteenth-century technological thinking are clearly set out in Tom F. Peters, *Building the Nineteenth Century* (Cambridge, Mass: MIT Press, 1996), which also notes the close link to analytical chemistry (66). See also A. Rupert Hall, "What Did the Industrial Revolution in Britain Owe to Science?" in his *Science and Society: Historical Essays on the Relations of Science, Technology and Medicine* (Aldershot, U.K.: Variorum, 1994), part III, 147–8.

9. Cf. *The Social Construction of Technological Systems: New Directions in the Sociology and History of Technology,* ed. Wiebe Bijker, Thomas Hughes, and Trevor Pinch (Cambridge, Mass: MIT Press, 1987).

Chapter 1. Gurney's Cornish Background

1. Claude Berry, *Portrait of Cornwall,* 2d ed. (London: Robert Hale & Co., 1971), 13. See also W. G. V. Balchin, *Cornwall: An Illustrated Essay on the History of the Landscape* (London: Hodder and Stoughton, 1954). Tourism did not become a major industry until the completion in 1859 of the Saltash Bridge, which linked the locally developed Cornish railways to the trunk lines of England. It was coincidental that the pilchard runs began to disappear around that time.

2. Harris, T. R., *Sir Goldsworthy Gurney, 1793–1875* (Penzance, Cornwall: The Trevithick Society, 1975), 9–10. Mary Peter's family was descended from Peter of Harlyn, whose father acquired his surname and Cornish estates through marriage in the time of Queen Elizabeth. John de Harlyn had built the first bridge over the River Camel at Wadebridge in 1485. C. S. Gilbert, *Historical and Topographical Survey of the County of Cornwall* (London, 1820), vol. 2: 228. After his marriage to Mary, Gregory Gurney remained vicar of Tregony, some fifty miles away, although it is probable that like many churchmen of his time, he appointed a curate to carry out the actual duties of the parish. His nephew Richard inherited the living at Tregony but combined it with a similar position at St. Paul, with the rectorship of St James and St. Cuby, and with the deaneries of Powdre and Penwith. Cf. ibid., 71, table of parishes.

3. Ibid., 652.

4. Harris, *Gurney,* 10. Trevithick was also described as a "vivacious, lovable, blue-eyed giant."

5. Berry, *Portrait of Cornwall,* 178. Although Trevithick is usually pictured driving a "drag," or locomotive, he also built two self-propelled steam carriages, and it is likely that one of these was driven around his Cornish cottage. Cf. Ian McNeil, *Joseph Bramah: A Century of Invention, 1749–1851* (Newton Abbot, U.K.: David & Charles, 1968), 177. In a pamphlet published in 1859 to defend his claim to original-

ity in steam invention, Gurney described himself, as a boy, experimenting with a teakettle in Trevithick's presence and suggested that he gave the older man the idea for the high-pressure steam exhaust used in Trevithick's early locomotives. One can only point out that Gurney was ten or eleven years of age at the time.

6. Berry, *Portrait of Cornwall,* 139.

7. Nickolaus Pevsner, *Cornwall,* rev. Enid Radcliff (Harmondsworth, U.K.: Penguin, 1951), 19–23.

8. Berry, *Portrait of Cornwall,* 176.

9. Richard Polwhele, *The History of Cornwall* (5 vols., 1806: reprint, London: Kohler and Coombes, 1978), 5: 60–65.

10. Ibid., 65. Cardew's double loss may be attributed to the fact that a principal trustee of the school endowment, John Borlase, was also deeply involved in Truro borough politics. Humphry Davy was, briefly (1793–94), a student at Truro School, but Cardew later admitted to Davies Gilbert that "I could not discern the faculties by which he was afterwards so much distinguished." *The Dictionary of National Biography* s.v. "Davy, Humphry."

11. Polwhele, *History of Cornwall,* 5: 66. Hogg also raised the annual fees by six shillings. Polwhele, a Truro "old boy," regretted the intrusion of science and hoped "that Mr. Hogg will soon come to his senses," restoring the classics to their primary place.

12. Harris, *Gurney,* 10.

13. Dorothy Porter, "Medicine and Industrial Society: Reform, Improvement, and Professionalization," *Victorian Studies* 37, no. 1 (Autumn 1993): 130–34. Gurney would also have been aware of the deplorable reputation of most Cornish apothecaries in his day.

14. For the relation of science to medicine, see Gwendy and Alban Caroe, *The Royal Institution: An Informal History* (London: John Murray, 1985), 19. The relative status and numbers of physicians and surgeon-apothecaries are discussed by Berman, *Social Change and Scientific Organization,* 102–3. Davy's apprenticeship is reported by the Caroes, (*The Royal Institution, 21*) and by Knight, *Humphry Davy,* 2, 16–17. Anne Treneer, *The Mercurial Chemist: A Life of Sir Humphry Davy* (London: Methuen, 1963), describes Davy's Cornish background better than other biographies.

15. As in other parts of Cornwall, the bridge and roads had been built and maintained by the sale of indulgences. After the Reformation they fell into disrepair. Until the turnpike era of the eighteenth century, most people traveled on foot or on horseback, but preferably by water.

16. Balchin, *Cornwall,* 116–17.

17. Berry, *Portrait of Cornwall,* 79, 156.

18. C. S. Gilbert, *Historical Survey of the County of Cornwall,* 2 vols. (London, 1817) 1: 92–93.

19. Harris, *Gurney,* 12.

20. W. F. Bynum's comparative survey of medical practice in Europe and America agrees with more localized studies that medicine, in the early nineteenth-century, was more art than science. *Science and the Practice of Medicine in the Nineteenth Century* (New York: Cambridge University Press, 1994), 9–11, 20, 118.

21. A. J. Youngson, *The Scientific Revolution in Victorian Medicine* (New York: Holmes and Meier, 1979), 18–20. For more extensive views on medical practice and its reputation, see Jan Golinski, *Science as Public Culture: Chemistry and Enlightenment in Britain, 1760–1820* (Cambridge: Cambridge University Press, 1992); Ian Inkster and Jack Morrell, eds., *Metropolis and Province: Science in British Culture 1780–1850* (Philadelphia: University of Pennsylvania Press, 1983); and Roger French

and Andrew Wear, eds., *British Medicine in an Age of Reform* (London, Routledge, 1991).

22. Harris, *Gurney*, 12–13. Gurney related his discovery of the fertilizing lime in sea sand much later in life, in testimony before a parliamentary committee, and left the impression that he was the first to notice this quality. But ninety percent of Cornish farmland around Padstow was fertilized in this way, and had been for centuries. The farmers had a traditional, legal right to dig whatever sand they required for their crops. Telford's Bude Canal was built from the coast in 1825, principally to carry sea sand to the agricultural interior. Gurney simply located supplies much further inland than expected. Cf. Berry, *Portrait of Cornwall*, 12.

Chapter 2. London, 1820–1824: Lectures on Chemistry, Part I

1. Donald J. Olsen, *The Growth of Victorian London* (Harmondsworth, UK: Penguin Books, 1976), 40–44. H. J. Dyos, "Urban Transformation: A Note on the Objects of Street Improvement in Regency and Early Victorian London," *International Review of Social History*, 2 (1957): 261, quoted in H. C. Darby, *A New Historical Geography of London After 1600* (Cambridge: Cambridge University Press, 1976), 222.

2. H. C. *Sess. Pap.* 1835 (483) 13, Report from the Select Committee on Mr. Goldsworthy Gurney's Case (second report), 10 July 1835: 19. Sir Anthony had gained fame, with William Anderson, in 1800, by achieving the first decomposition of water into oxygen and hydrogen, by electricity from a voltaic pile. He went on to serve on the Royal Institution committee on chemical research, became lecturer to the Royal Society in 1804, and professor of anatomy at the Royal College of Arts, in 1808. He was knighted in 1820 (Golinski, *Science as Public Culture*, 205, 251).

William Hyde Wollaston (1766–1828), a Cambridge graduate, gave up medical practice to do chemical research in his private London laboratory. He published a total of fifty-six papers on pathology, physiology, optics, mineralogy, crystallography, astronomy, electricity, mechanics, and botany. He was nicknamed "The Pope" for the infallibility of his chemical analyses. A new process for purifying platinum gained him the Copley Medal in 1802 and a substantial royalty income for the rest of his life. David Knight (*Humphry Davy: Science and Power*, 7) described him as shy and cautious, "more anxious to avoid error than keen to discover truth." Wollaston suggested the imperial gallon, adopted by the government in 1824, and served on the Royal Commission that rejected the decimal system. He was an ally of Davy (as was Gurney, apparently) in the argument over who invented the safety lamp. Harris says that he and Gurney formed a "lasting friendship" early in the 1820s.

One other name mentioned by Harris was "a Dr. Luke, who was sixty years of age and in full practice." This was undoubtedly Dr. Stephen Luke, a native of Penzance, who apprenticed with a local apothecary and then practiced as a surgeon in London and Paris. He eventually won a medical degree, married into a prominent Cornish family, and settled in Falmouth. Gurney would have heard of his celebrated diagnostic skills and could easily have known him personally. Cf. Polwhele, *History of Cornwall*, 5: 132.

Gurney's claim that these men attended his lectures may be accurate, but it was made over a dozen years after the event, when he was trying to establish a claim to compensation from the government. It was common in these years to cite eminent names as a guarantee of quality; Davy made a habit of citing the experts in his own audiences as proofs of his experiments.

3. According to Harris, *Gurney*, 14–15, the *Western Luminary* for 7 May 1822

reported that "Mr. Goldsworthy Gurney, surgeon, late of Wadebridge in this county, has been appointed Lecturer in Chemistry and Natural Philosophy at the Surrey Institution, London, a situation for which his well known talents and acquirements so peculiarly qualify him, that we have no doubt he will reflect additional honour on the county of Cornwall." The Surrey Institution's mission was noted in *The Illustrated London News*, XIII, no. 334 (9 September 1848): 151.

4. Golinski, *Science as Public Culture*, 128–35. Cf. Robert J. Morris, "Lavoisier and the Caloric Theory," *The British Journal for the History of Science* 6, no. 21 (1972): 1–38.

5. Golinski, *Science as Public Culture*, 204–10. According to Caroe and Caroe (*The Royal Institution*, 20–28) the galvanic pile was discovered in 1800 by Joseph Banks, founder of the RI. Davy, who had begun his study of chemistry with William Nicholson's textbook, gave his first lecture at the RI on galvanism in 1805.

6. Golinski, *Science as Public Culture*, 189, 214–16.

7. Ibid., 238–42. Gurney could easily have obtained information about the voltaic pile and Davy's achievements with it by consulting Thomas Thomson's reputable *System of Chemistry* (London: Colbrun and Bentley, 1802; 6th ed., 1820); Samuel Parkes's popular *Rudiments of Chemistry* (1810 and subsequent editions); Parkes's shorter *Chemical Catechism* (1818); or William Henry's *Elements of Experimental Chemistry* (1818).

8. Golinski, *Science as Public Culture*, 269–70.

9. Ibid., 272–73.

10. G. Gurney, *The Elements of Chemical Science* (London: G. and W. B. Whittaker, 1823), 246–49.

11. Golinski, *Science as Public Culture*, 275–78. The instrument for measuring crystalline angles, called a goniometer, was invented in 1809 by William Hyde Wollaston. The goniometer's accuracy and convenience was praised by Gurney's predecessor at the Surrey Institution, Thomas Accum. The convergence of physical and chemical approaches to crystallography is explained as part of a general dynamic between the disciplines in Evan Melhado, "Chemistry, Physics, and the Chemical Revolution," *Isis* 76 (1985): 195–211.

12. Golinski, *Science as Public Culture*, 273–75.

13. Ibid., 263. It did not help that Dalton resided in Manchester and used crude, simple equipment for his research. A true disciple of Priestley—independent, humble, and honest—Dalton spent more time with private pupils than with the public, and his experiments often failed in lectures. Davy, who was working on an alternative theory, rejected atomism and persuaded other metropolitan scientists to do likewise.

14. Knight, *Humphry Davy*, 76–77; Golinski, *Science as Public Culture*, 265–68.

15. Golinski, *Science as Public Culture*, 59–61. Evan Melhado ("Chemistry, Physics, and the Chemical Revolution") claims that the chemical revolution was "powerfully affected by physics," which contributed the concept of positive and negative attractions between particles and their relation to the theory of heat. One can find a good many principles of physics in Gurney's lectures on chemistry.

16. J. N. Hays, "The London Lecturing Empire, 1800–50," in Inkster and Morrell, eds., *Metropolis and Province*, 91–119.

17. Golinski, *Science as Public Culture*, 253–54. Cf. J. N. Hays, "Science in the City: The London Institution, 1819–1840," *The British Journal for the History of Science* 7, no. 26 (1974): 146–62, and Jessie E. Milton, "Lectures and Lecturers in the First One Hundred Years of the Royal Institution," *Proceedings of the Royal Institution* 50 (1978): 133–44.

18. Harris, *Gurney*, 14. In 1835, Gurney recalled that he made "the most profit"

from his private chemistry class at Argyll Street rather than from the Surrey Institution lectures. At the time he gave the figures, he was demanding compensation from Parliament for income lost in the pursuit of steam carriage manufacturing, for which he gave up his medical practice and lecturing career. Cf. H. C. *Sess. Pap.* 1835 (483) 13, Report from the Select Committee on Mr. Goldsworthy Gurney's Case (second report), 10 July 1835: 19.

19. Hays, "Science in the City," 149.

20. Hays, "The London Lecturing Empire, 1800–50," 98–100. Repeating essentially the same lectures at several locations, almost always at an elementary level of knowledge, could also become very boring, and many lecturers of the time, like teachers today, considered the work pure drudgery.

21. Ibid., 100–102.

22. The London Institution, the largest of the Royal Institution's imitators, also justified its science lectures on the grounds of "utility, natural theology, casual amateurism, and edifying amusement." Hays, "Science in the City," 146.

23. Golinski, *Science as Public Culture,* 11–12.

24. Ibid., 8.

25. Ibid., ch. 3, "Joseph Priestley and the English Enlightenment," especially 75–85. See also George Porter, "Joseph Priestley and His Contemporaries," *Journal of General Education* 27, no. 2 (1975): 91–100. Gurney would also have understood by that time what Priestley learned from sad experience, that reading descriptions of experiments in textbooks, no matter how detailed, was no substitute for hands-on training in the laboratory.

26. Golinski, *Science as Public Culture,* 166–75. Beddoes was dismissed from his post as professor of medicine at Oxford because of his radical views. He and Davy then discovered the euphoric effects of nitrous oxide ("laughing gas") and, with Priestley, began promoting it as a liberating elixir, much as marijuana was promoted in the 1960s.

27. Ibid., 6–10, 191–95.

28. Ibid., 258–9; Knight, *Humphry Davy,* 6; George A. Foote, "Sir Humphry Davy and his Audience at the Royal Institution," *Isis* 43 (April 1952): 6–12.

29. Golinski, *Science as Public Culture,* 8–10, 200–226.

30. David Gooding, "In Nature's School: Faraday as an Experimentalist," *Faraday Rediscovered: Essays on the Life and Work of Michael Faraday, 1791–1867,* ed. David Gooding and Frank A. J. L. James (London: Macmillan, 1985), 105–35. As in other fields, there were practical electricians outside the Royal Institution who challenged Faraday with Priestley's concept of experimentation as a fundamentally democratic process. Iwan Rhys Morus, "Different Experimental Lives: Michael Faraday and William Sturgeon," *History of Science* 30 (1992): 1–28.

31. Golinski, *Science as Public Culture,* 243.

32. Ibid., 246. In 1819, Accum published *A Practical Treatise on Gas Lighting.* Humphry Davy, who hated commercialization, labeled Accum "a cheat and a Quack."

CHAPTER 3. LECTURES ON CHEMISTRY, PART II

1. The lectures were published in London by G. and W. B. Whittaker, Ave-Maria Lane. Gurney's preface is dated 2 July 1823, at no. 7, Argyll Street. A copy may be found in the British Museum Library. The *Monthly Magazine* for 1 July (55, no. 383): 549, advised that Gurney's lectures were now being printed. "They will comprise the

bases of the new theory of crystallization, and diagrams to illustrate the elementary combinations of atoms, particularly theories of electrical influence and of flame, with a full description of the author's blow-pipe when charged with certain gases, etc."

2. Caroe and Caroe, *The Royal Institution*, 31, quote Davy: "In seeking brilliant impossibilities, they [alchemists] sometimes discovered useful realities." Knight, *Humphry Davy*, acknowledges that Davy and other chemists were fascinated by alchemy because they saw, underneath its strange practices, a vision of science unified by analogy (78). Thomas Thomson's popular *History of Chemistry* also began with a short catalog of alchemists' works, but Thomson did not feel it worthwhile to study them.

3. See Morris, "Lavoisier and the Caloric Theory," for a full exposition of the concept and its central place in Lavoisier's physics and chemistry. Although Lavoisier admitted that caloric could not be demonstrated or measured experimentally, he believed it to be an essential fact of nature.

4. Gurney, *Elements,* lecture 6, 139. Gurney's entry in the *Dictionary of National Biography* gives the essential information, but discreetly says only that observation of the needle's behavior "is claimed as unquestionably Gurney's" and that he therefore "anticipated the principle of the electric telegraph." The remark, addressed to Sir Anthony Carlisle, was made at a contemporary experiment by Sir W. Snow Harris, having to do with ships' lightning conductors. Harris, *Gurney* (19), mixes the experiment up with the lectures, making the remark seem more significant than it really was. The principle of alternating electromagnetic action was discovered in the eighteenth century and had been considered as a possible method of signaling before Gurney was born.

5. Gurney's demonstration of the properties of flame anticipated, by a quarter-century, Faraday's famous lecture on "The Chemical History of a Candle," inaugurated in 1848 and given as a children's Christmas lecture in 1860. Cf. P. W. Atkins, "The Candle Revisited," *Proceedings of the Royal Institution* 65 (1994): 1–14.

6. Chlorine was called "dephlogisticated muriatic acid" when first discovered, in 1774, but Lavoisier and other French chemists named it "oxymuriatic acid," and its salts, the "oxymuriates." Hydrochloric acid was long known as "muriatic acid." These were the terms used by Gurney in 1822.

7. Harris, *Gurney,* 16.

CHAPTER 4. NEW DIRECTIONS

1. That scientific knowledge was often gleaned from the process of technical invention, especially in chemistry and steam power, is shown by Musson and Robinson, *Science and Technology*, 6–7, 251–337, and by Peters, *Building the Nineteenth Century,* 66.

2. Walter Weldon, *Popular Explanation of Chemistry* (?1825), quoted in Golinski, *Science as Public Culture,* 255.

3. Cf. M. Jeanne Peterson, *Family, Love and Work in the Lives of Victorian Gentlewomen* (Bloomington: Indiana University Press, 1989), 35–37.

4. In February 1823, in a letter to the Society of Arts, Gurney gave his address as Charles Street, Soho Square, a quarter-mile east of Argyll Street. It is not known whether the family had moved there after John was born, or whether Gurney had leased rooms for experimenting with the oxyhydrogen blowpipe and steam jet, which were both explosive.

5. Harris called it a "finger organ," which was probably one with a keyboard but no pedals. According to musicologist Dr. Cecelia Porter, English organs did not have pedals until the eighteenth century. However, the years around 1820 are notable for the enthusiastic adaptation of all kinds of musical instruments and contraptions, and there is an absence of technical documentation on organs in that period. From the description, it is possible that Gurney used the pedals on the piano for both instruments. In his lectures Gurney said that he constructed the organ "Some years since, when a very young man," and conceived the idea of connecting it to a piano when still "flushed with this success." Harris, however, quotes a report from the *Royal Cornwall Gazette* for 17 September 1819 that suggests that it was new at that time, when Gurney was twenty-six years old.

6. Harris, *Gurney*, 13. The report cited "a gentleman in the neighborhood of Wadebridge."

7. Ibid., 18. The glass piano was described, along with other instruments, in an 1823 issue of *Gill's Technical Repository*.

8. H. C. *Sess. Pap.* 1835 (603): 5, Gurney testimony question 67. In that testimony Gurney said that he received a gold medal from the Duke of Sussex for this work, but that is incorrect; it was given for his work on the oxyhydrogen blow pipe, a related but quite distinct apparatus.

9. Harris is again confusing here. He claims that Gurney "demonstrated the effects of a jet of high pressure steam" at the time of his lectures (19), and that it was used, by 1827, for ventilating "the Ophthalmic Hospital, in Albany Street." In another chapter he says that in 1825, Gurney obtained a lease of premises in Albany Street, "originally built as an eye infirmary for Sir William Adam, the celebrated oculist." We should probably assume that these buildings are one and the same, and that Gurney used his new steam jet to ventilate his own workshop and possibly the attached residential rooms.

10. Golinski, *Science as Public Culture*, 140–42.

11. Harris, *Gurney*, 20. Harris cites the Society's *Register*, but the appropriate publication was the *Transactions*. The early mechanical pyrometers soon gave way to a different device for measuring very high temperature, the type of pyrometer known today. Examples of both may be seen in the Science Museum, Kensington.

12. The development of the laboratory blowpipe is credited to Johann Gahn, whose assistant, the great Swedish analyst Berzelius, described it in a treatise on chemistry. Wollaston translated the treatise and made several improvements in the instrument. See Thomson, *The History of Chemistry*, 240–47.

13. Golinski, *Science as Public Culture*, 269–70, 279–81.

14. Gurney, *Lectures*, 273–74.

15. D. R. Oldroyd, "Edward Daniel Clarke, 1769–1822, and His Role in the History of the Blow-pipe," *Annals of Science* 29 (1972): 213–35.

16. The valve also had a water-level gauge, which in combination with the one-square-foot pressure platform permitted measurements of gas volume. This feature was described in a separate publication as a "gasometer" (cf. *Lectures*, 283–89).

17. Harris, *Gurney*, 20. Interestingly, Humphry Davy had published a notice in 1817 of his experiments with an oxyhydrogen blowpipe, including the heating of lime and other minerals to produce an intense light. David Knight, who reports the notice, says that "this was the principle of limelight," without reference to Gurney's well-known claim to the discovery. Knight, *Humphry Davy*, 124–27.

18. Minutes of the Joint Committee of Chemistry & Mechanics, 11 April 1823, Royal Society for the Arts archives. The joint committee, forty-four members strong, was chaired by Henry Coxwell, Esq. It included Samuel Varley, the scientific instru-

ment maker and founder of the London Philosophical Society, and John Bostock (1773–1846), an Edinburgh graduate, who was a physician at Guy's Hospital. Bostock had reviewed Davy's *Elements of Chemical Philosophy* for the *Monthly Review* (1813) and published a survey of galvanism (1818).

19. "An Improved Blow-pipe," *Transactions of the Society of Arts,* 41 (1823–24): 70–77, with two plates. This article does not detail all of Gurney's failures in developing the instrument. The Gold Isis medal was about two inches in diameter; an example is on display in the foyer of the society's building in John Adam Street, London. Gurney's Isis medal has been presented to the Truro Museum by his descendants, Peter and Michael Gurney.

20. Prior to 1853 the inventor had to petition the Home Secretary for a patent. The petition was referred to one of the law officers for a report, which was then returned by the inventor to the Home Office, to be assigned once again to the law officer, who prepared a parliamentary bill, which in its turn, after complex formal procedures had been completed, resulted in a grant-of-letters patent. However, the patent could be challenged in court at any time. Cf. the Public Record Office Information sheet #17, on patents. According to his biographer, Thomas Telford remarked that he had once taken out a patent, but it caused him so much trouble that he never bothered with another. Sir Alexander Gibb, *The Story of Telford* (London: Alexander Maclehose, 1935), 268.

21. Joseph Kahn's waxworks museum, opened in 1825, offered a mix of medical education and thinly veiled eroticism. He introduced the oxyhydrogen 'microscope' in 1833, and it proliferated, as entertaining "educational" shows gradually superceded the older scientific lectures. Cf. R. D. Altick, *The Shows of London* (Cambridge, Mass.: Harvard University Press, 1978), 338–42. Models of oxyhydrogen magic lanterns are in the Science Museum, Kensington, and an early version is shown and described in *The Magazine of Science and School for Arts* 92 (January 2, 1841). The French military authorities in Paris, under siege by the Prussians in 1870–1, used an oxyhydrogen lantern to enlarge and view miniature photograph negatives of enemy positions, taken by French reconnaissance balloons and sent back to Paris by carrier pigeon. As late as 1890, a lecture series for workingmen, which toured England, was accompanied by an extensive oxyhydrogen magic-lantern show.

CHAPTER 5. INVENTING THE STEAM CARRIAGE

1. Alexander Gordon, *A Treatise on Elemental Locomotion,* 3rd ed. (London: Thomas Tegg & Son, 1836), 31. This statement is not in the published edition of Gurney's lectures. It may have been based on Gurney's testimony before Parliament in 1831–32, or on some other contemporary report.

2. Gordon, *Treatise,* 31–2; Harris, *Gurney,* 22. The patent was dated 24 May 1825. In 1831, Gurney recalled that many scientists and inventors were trying out "explosive and äeriform bodies" in engines.

3. Alexander Gordon was a civil engineer, living in Westminster, who personally inspected and rode on most of the steam carriages of the day. Gurney's *Account of the Invention of the Steam-Jet or Blast* was written in 1859, and according to Anna Gurney, it was revised by Edward Cayley, M.P., a longtime family friend, in the next year or two. It was prepared to contest a statement by Samuel Smiles, in his biography of George Stephenson, that Stephenson invented and first applied the steam jet, a vital component of steam engines. Cayley's death in 1862 and Gurney's para-

lytic stroke in 1863 prevented publication at that time, but Anna published it privately in 1881 and sent copies to eminent survivors from that period, as well as to all the major scientific and technical institutions. A copy, with her penciled notation, is in the Institution of Civil Engineers Library and Archive, London. Several claims to inventive precedence were made in this publication and accepted by subsequent biographers, including Harris. In view of its purpose and the amount of time that had elapsed after the events it described, it must be used with great caution.

4. *The Suppression of the Automobile* was published in New York by the Greenwood Press, 1988.

5. W. David Lewis, "Goldsworthy Gurney," *Great Engineers and Pioneers in Technology,* ed. Roland Turner and Steven Goulden (New York: St. Martin's Press, 1981), 434.

6. Beasley, *Suppression of the Automobile,* 12.

7. C. St. C. B. Davison, *History of Steam Road Vehicles* (London: H.M. Stationery Office, n.d.), chapter 1. Davison writes that Watt and his partner Matthew Boulton dissuaded Murdock from continuing his experiments. Watt appears to have been chiefly concerned to keep anyone else from developing such a vehicle, and even put a covenant into the lease for his house, prohibiting anyone from bringing a steam carriage near it. Given the state of roads at that time, it would probably not have been feasible in any case.

8. Gordon, *Treatise,* 46. According to McNeil, *Joseph Bramah,* 178, the Griffith carriage was fitted out first with a passenger barouche body, then an omnibus frame, and finally a three-ton wagon body, making it the first known freight locomotive. Like Gurney's later designs, it used a rear-mounted, water-tube-type boiler to provide steam to two cylinders, and a condenser to return used steam to the boiler. Timothy Bramah, the younger of the sons, became the firm's steam expert and rode on a Gurney carriage, rebuilt by Sir Charles Dance, in 1833.

9. Gordon, *Treatise,* 27–29, 51. Brown's gas-vacuum engine proved too expensive to keep in operation. Cf. Gordon's testimony on his father's inventions, in H. C. *Sess. Pap.* 1831 (324) VIII: 74–76.

10. Gordon, *Treatise,* 32–33.

11. Ibid., 39.

12. Robert Stephenson, memoir, *The Illustrated London News* XVII, no. 451: 309.

13. Ibid.

14. Francis T. Evans, "Roads, Railways and Canals: Technical Choices in 19th-century Britain," *Technology and Culture* 22, no. 1 (January 1981): 19–21.

15. Gordon, *Treatise,* 200–201. For a review of the flurry of articles on roadbuilding, carriage design, canal improvements, and railway experiments in the first two decades of the century, see Evans, "Roads, Railways and Canals," 1–6.

16. Gordon, *Treatise,* 44–45.

17. Ibid., 46–47. The principle was later used by the Cornish engineer Samuel Moyle to transport heavy goods through a swamp in South America. Part of the load was a set of iron plates, which Moyle riveted together into a large cylinder, apparently driven with a cogwheel engine like Gordon's. The cylinder was loaded with the rest of the goods and rolled across the swamp to its destination, where the plates were dismantled and put to other uses. Harris states (23) that Gurney consulted Moyle about traction in 1825. They may have known each other previously, since Goldsworthy's cousin Thomas had married Lydia Moyle.

18. Gordon, *Treatise,* 46, 51. The Seawards' many enterprises are described in the *Dictionary of National Biography,* s.v. "Seaward, John."

19. Harris, *Gurney,* 23, describes the experiments with traction. Cayley's tractor

tread, called the "Universal Railway," was first suggested by him in 1823, patented in 1825, and described in *The Mechanic's Magazine,* no. 127, 28 January 1826. J. Lawrence Pritchard, *Sir George Cayley: The Inventor of the Aeroplane* (London: M. Parrish, 1961), 146–47.

20. Quoted in Gordon, *Treatise,* 79. Gurney said that for ice, "a little roughing of the wheels is necessary, in the same manner as you rough horses' hooves." Otherwise ice made a smooth surface that reduced drag on the carriage.

21. Alexander Gordon described David Gordon's "horse legs" in great detail (with illustrations) in his *Treatise,* 47–50. Gurney's adaptation is mentioned by Harris, *Gurney,* 23.

22. Gordon, *Treatise,* 55. For John Farey, see his entry in the *Dictionary of National Biography.*

23. Gordon, *Treatise,* 125, 162–63. The formation of explosive compounds is mentioned by Gurney in testimony before the 1831 parliamentary committee on steam carriages, H. C. *Sess. Pap.* 1831(324) VIII: 28–29.

24. For Gurney's boiler development, see Gordon, *Treatise,* 139–62. Gurney's own partial description is in H. C. *Sess. Pap.* 1831 (324) VIII: 28–29, and 1834 (483) XI: 5, Report of the Select Committee on Mr. Gurney's Case. For Evans and other Americans, see Angus Sinclair, *Development of the Locomotive Engine* (1907; Cambridge, Mass: the MIT Press, 1970), 17. Sinclair was interested in railway locomotives; he did not mention Gurney.

25. Gordon, *Treatise,* 140–1, and plate XI, facing 168. The "natomy" anecdote is from Gurney's *Account of the Invention of the Steam- Jet or Blast* (London: G. Barclay, 1859, reprint 1881), 6.

26. Gordon, *Treatise,* 141–42. The thin metal plates might be thought susceptible to the flame, but they were attached directly to the water pipes, which distributed the heat so evenly that the plates lasted for up to three years. Gurney found, however, that the weight of additional coils of tubing for the cold water supply was greater than the amount of heat saved.

27. Harris, *Gurney,* 27. The standard commercial iron pipes of the day were only six feet long, while those in the Gurney boiler were about eight feet, so Gurney had to manufacture his own.

28. Gordon, *Treatise,* 163. The plugs were made of a soft metal that would melt if the tubes overheated, acting as miniature safety valves. The same principle was proposed for the boiler connections of a central steam heating system designed by Gurney in 1841.

29. H. C. *Sess. Pap.* 1831 (324) VIII: 19.

30. Gordon, *Treatise,* 146. The caption for the model of Gurney's steam boiler in the Science Museum, London, claims that Marc Seguin of France invented the first pipe boiler. However, Gurney's design is fundamentally different from Seguin's and from the boilers built by the Stephensons for their railway engines. The latter used a series of pipes to carry hot air from the firebox through a large tank of water, rather than forcing steam through pipes wrapped around the firebox. The basic idea, that of increasing the surface area for efficient heat transfer, was the same, but because railway engineers did not need to worry about the weight of the boiler, they could fill it with water. Illustrations in Marie-Hélène Reynaud, *Marc Seguin: du Pont de Tournon aux Premiers Chemins de Fer* (Paris: Editions du Vivarais, 1986), 155 and 165, show the difference. Cf. Evans, "Roads, Railways and Canals," 29–30.

31. Gurney, *Account of the Invention of the Steam-Jet,* 5. In this publication Gurney claimed that at the age of eleven, he had either witnessed or assisted Trevethick's

discovery that the heat from an oil lamp would dissipate the steam from a teakettle spout—the same principle used in the locomotive.

32. Ibid., 6. The syntax of the sentences in this passage is quite confusing. William Keene testified before a committee of the Lords in 1849 that he had witnessed the experimental use of the steam jet in workshop chimneys, but that was in 1826.

33. Ibid., 19.

34. Harris, *Gurney*, 25.

35. Gurney, *Account of the Invention of the Steam-Jet*, 6–8, quoting William Keene's evidence before a committee of the House of Commons in 1849. One of the American observers later got the parliamentary report of 1831, on steam carriages, reprinted by Congress for the use of American engineers.

36. Ibid., 6–8.

37. Beasley, *Suppression of the Automobile*, 10.

38. Gordon, *Treatise*, 61–63.

39. Ibid., 63–64. The *Observer* report of 9 December 1827 is reprinted in *The Engineer* vol. 80 (30 August 1895): 215. The note on Sir John Ross comes from Gurney's testimony in the Report of the Select Committee of the House of Lords, on repealing turnpike tolls on steam carriages, House of Lords *Journals* 1836: 68, Appendix 7: 310–38.

40. Quoted by Gordon, *Treatise*, 140. Dr. Dionysius Lardner, LL.D., Fellow of the Royal Society, had published articles on steam engines and wrote on the subject for the *Edinburgh Review*. A "flamboyantly fashionable" professor of natural philosophy at the new University College, London, Lardner testified for Gurney before the House of Commons Select Committee of 1831 on the problem of excess turnpike tolls on steam carriages. J. B. Morrell, "Individualism and the Structure of British Science in 1830," *Historical Studies in the Physical Sciences* 3 (1971): 199. In 1834, Lardner offered to give two lectures on "The Progress and Prospects of Locomotion" for the Friday evening lecture series at the Royal Institution, assuring Faraday that he would illustrate them with "very beautiful models." *The Correspondence of Michael Faraday*, ed. Frank A. J. L. James, 2 vols. (New York: Institute of Electrical Engineers, 1981), 1: 28, item 177.

CHAPTER 6. THE STEAM CARRIAGE AS A COMMERCIAL VENTURE

1. The contract was dated 10 September 1827 and signed by William Augustus Dobbyn of Wells, Somerset, and by Gurney's brother, Elias Thomas Peter Gurney, "late of Wine-street, Bristol, now of London." Gurney reserved the right to build carriages for the mail but promised not to supply any other agent for this route. Harris says that he was given £4,500 at the outset, but the contract itself, produced for the Commons select committee of 1834–35, stipulates a £1,800 cash premium, with the rest to be paid for a fourteen-year lease of eight carriages, when built. No further mention is made of this contract or the carriages until July 1835, when Gurney said that he had already returned £2,500 to Captain Dobbyn. H. C. *Sess. Pap.* 1835 (483) XIII: 29.

2. Beasley, *The Suppression of the Automobile*, 15–16. Beasley does a careful job of sorting out the legal and financial terms arranged and rearranged by the Gurney patentees from 1827 through 1831. A patent could be held by a maximum of five persons; the other investors were licensed to run on certain routes with leased carriages. The original patentees agreed to pay royalties by mileage, but when Sir Charles Dance bought Viney's portion and began actual operations, he

asked that royalties be calculated instead on the power of the engine, determined by the quantity of water evaporated in a given period of time. The carriages still required training runs for the crews and, of course, were often paraded around towns for publicity; Dance apparently thought that self-reporting of mileage might occasion suspicion and misunderstanding among the partners. Gurney agreed to the change, but the other patentees refused, whereupon Gurney suggested that the new standard be applied only to those holding licenses outside the original patent. This was agreed to on 1 March 1830. H. C. *Sess. Pap.* 1835 (483) XIII : 28–29.

3. Harris, *Gurney,* chapter 4, gives the periodical notices; the London, Bristol, and Bath route was licensed to Captain William Dobbyn. The term "voyage" is interesting, because Gurney said later that some members of Parliament thought of his machine as a kind of steamboat and applied current legislation regulating steamboats to it, rather than treating it as an alternative to horse-drawn coaches.

4. Ibid., 30–31.

5. The 1827 account is quoted by Davison, *History of Steam Road Vehicles,* chapter 2.

6. Gurney gave different versions of this incident. He told the 1831 Select Committee on Steam Carriages that in coming down the hill, the carriage ran up against a stone and was upset. In 1834, before the subsequent Select Committee on Mr. Gurney's Case, he claimed that the axle dragged the carriage to a safe stop.

7. Harris, *Gurney,* 30–31, probably based on George Croly's account of "steam carriages," in *Blackwood's Edinburgh Magazine* 23 (January 1828): 94–96.

8. "The New Invented Steam Carriage," broadsheet, copy in the British Museum Library, catalogue no. 1899.a.9 (42*). There is also a smaller version (42**) with some of the same material.

9. Harris, *Gurney,* 42–43.

10. Ibid., 33.

11. Ibid., 33–35, 43–45.

12. Report of Sir J. Willoughby Gordon, 23 July 1829, from a copy reprinted in *The Papers of Sir H. Taylor* (London: n.d.), 262–64.

13. Beasley, *Suppression of the Automobile,* 2–6. Harris, *Gurney,* 35–43.

14. A *barouche* was a four-wheeled fancy carriage with a fold-up top, the two internal seats facing each other. A *phaeton* was a light four-wheeler with open sides. The *post carriage* was a smaller, closed carriage, drawn by horses which were rented at post stations and ridden by postboys. The post carriage, in this case, could not keep up with the steam carriage, so another pair of horses was added at Maidenhead, the first stop for coal and water.

15. Ibid., 43. Anna's handwritten note, "remembered by me," is penciled into the margin of Gurney's *Account of the Invention of the Steam-Jet,* 1859, next to his description of the Hounslow event, in a copy preserved in the Institution of Civil Engineers.

16. Harris, *Gurney,* 44. John Herapath later helped Gurney devise an improved braking system. It is not clear whether he joined Gurney after witnessing his carriage trials or whether, like some other military officers, he was involved in the project earlier, and wrote the letter to the Duke of Wellington as a commercial promotion rather than a public service.

17. Ibid., 45.

18. Ibid., 50. The Paris licensee removed the steam separator, which allowed wet steam into the cylinders, ruining the machine for commercial runs. Dance's purchase of Viney's one-sixth share of the patent is mentioned in H. C. *Sess. Pap.* 1834 (483) XI: 20.

19. Susan Imiolczyk and Ray Tucker, *Castle and Cottages*. Cyfarthfa Museum Publication no. 4, n.d.

20. Crawshay's letter to the *Cambrian* is reprinted in Gordon, *Treatise*, 76–78.

21. Ibid.

22. Ibid. Crawshay's son Francis was assigned to run errands for Gurney and "see him get fair play in the fitting shop." In 1878, shortly after Gurney's death, he recalled that "the engine did wonders," so that the Welsh mechanics "broke up all their old engines and substituted new locomotives in their place." Harris, *Gurney*, 48–49.

23. Ibid., quoting the *Cheltenham Annuarie*, various dates.

24. Beasley, *Suppression of the Automobile*, 20, has the details of Ward's contracts. Ward was reported to have lost almost £40,000 on his investment in Gurney's enterprise. Cf. House of Lords *Journals* 1836: 68, Appendix 7: 73, Report from the Select Committee on repealing prohibitory tolls on steam carriages.

25. "The New Invented Steam Carriage," broadsheet.

26. Harris, *Gurney*, 53.

27. Ibid., 52.

28. See Gurney's testimony in the House of Lords *Journals*, 1836: 68, Appendix 7: 20. His main rival, Walter Hancock, thought that a moderate load of freight might be pulled behind a steam drag more efficiently than in horse-drawn wagons, but neither man advocated multi-wagon trains.

CHAPTER 7. OPPONENTS AND RIVALS

1. Stone's steam drag trial was reported in a letter to Gurney, reprinted in *Mr. Gurney's Observations on Steam Carriages on Turnpike Roads* (London: Baldwin and Craddock, 1832), 32–33. The smaller wheels were to give a higher mechanical advantage to the axle crank.

2. H. C. *Sess. Pap.* 1831 (324) VIII: 20–21, 87–88. The exact sequence of events and dates is, as usual, hard to sort out from the many accounts given. Mine generally agrees with that given by Beasley in *The Suppression of the Automobile*, 19. Dance's letter to the trustees is quoted by Francis James, the editor of Walter Hancock's *Narrative of Twelve Years' Experiments (1824–1836), Demonstrative of the Practicability and Advantages of Employing Steam Carriages on Common Roads* (London: J. Weale, 1838), 35.

3. H. C. *Sess. Pap.* 1834 (483) XI: 87–8. Dance's statement is given by Harris, *Gurney*, 54, based on testimony by Gurney in 1831.

4. H. C. *Sess. Pap.* 1834 (483) XI: 20–21. About thirty of the bills were from turnpike trusts and another twenty were private bills from individuals who owned roads outright. The Cheltenham toll is given in the House of Lords *Journals* 1836: 68, Appendix 5. Beasley, *Suppression of the Automobile*, 49–51, gives complete details of the tolls levied on all the steam proprietors.

5. Scotland's legal system was separate from that of England and Wales, and all of Gurney's patents except the one for his tubular boiler were issued for England only. Ward had purchased the Scots patent for £15,000, to be paid in three installments, and hoped to sell it for £32,000 at the time of the negotiations. H. C. *Sess. Pap.* 1834 (483) XI: 48, 88.

6. Ibid., 20–21.

7. Ibid.

8. This argument was attributed to Gurney by Francis James, the editor of Walter Hancock's *Narrative of Twelve Years' Experiments,* 37.

9. John Farey (1791–1851) was noted for his patient industry, meticulous research, and great memory for detail. He invented many new drafting instruments and improved the style of mechanical drawings. From 1826 until his death, he was engaged with most of the novel inventions, patent litigation, and scientific experiments around London. His reputation rested on his "fearless honesty" and his exhaustive search for legal precedents. In both his research and his drawings and specifications, he was joined by his wife, "a lady of rare attainments, who to great amiability of disposition, and a thorough knowledge of the duties of her sex, joined almost masculine scientific attainments." Tragically, his whole library of research notes, drawings, and publications burned to the ground in 1850. Institution of Civil Engineers, *Minutes of Proceedings* XI (1851): 100–101.

10. This investigation revealed that there was no standard measure for horse power. Gurney testified (H. C. *Sess. Pap.* 1831 (324) VIII: 26) that it usually meant a force that could pull anywhere from 150 to 200 pounds at two miles per hour, but nothing was said about the kind of surface over which that weight was pulled. Gurney also pointed out that "horse power" was a very misleading term to apply to steam, since a steam engine could produce the same amount of power all day long, while a horse would soon tire. The committee, therefore, gave up its attempt to rate steam carriages according to horse power.

11. H.C. *Sess. Pap.* 1831 (324) VIII: 3–5, "Report."

12. Ibid. The "encouragement of scientific men" reflected the thoughts of patent expert John Farey, who argued that the group of inventors then introducing steam carriages were not trained engineers. They were essentially skilled and imaginative mechanics, who were crazy enough to waste a great deal of money in the pursuit of a breakthrough which the current patent laws could not protect. Using only trial and error, they could not bring the vehicle to a stage of wide production and common use. An engineer, schooled to seek precise forms and dimensions, and with the experience to see the broad utility of such a vehicle, would not have had the wit to invent it in the first place, said Farey, and would be thought foolish for investing money in it at such an early stage. But now engineers were needed to develop reliable designs, and their interest in steam locomotion depended upon the encouragement of a capital market free from debilitating tolls. Ibid., 44–45.

13. Ibid., Appendix B. Gurney also proposed a sliding scale of tolls, based on the width of wheels (Appendix E).

14. The bill is printed in H. C. *Sess. Pap.* 1831–32 (489) IV.

15. H. C. *Sess. Pap.* 1831 (324) VIII: 31. Gurney estimated that each horse consumed grain sufficient to feed eight people, so a coach-and-four ate up sustenance for thirty-two. He regarded this as proof of the economic deficiency of horses and thought steam carriages would lead to cheap food for all, but of course the agricultural interests considered it proof of the economic disaster (and Malthusian overpopulation) that would be caused by the introduction of steam.

16. See the Report of the Select Committee on Turnpike Trusts and Tolls, H. C. *Sess. Pap.* 1836 (547) XIX, for a catalogue of abuses.

17. See Alexander Gordon's comments on the antisteamer sentiment among "country gentlemen," in H. C. *Sess. Pap.* 1834 (483) XI: 56–57.

18. Harris, *Gurney,* 56.

19. Francis James, *Walter Hancock and His Common Road Steam Carriages* (Alresford, Hampshire: Lawrence Oxley, 1975), 55.

20. H.C. *Sess. Pap.* 1835 (483) XIII: Report from the Select Committee on Mr.

Goldsworthy Gurney's Case, 25, 28. Francis James, *Walter Hancock*, 37–46, uncharitably suggests that Gurney brought the excessive tolls upon himself by his "precipitate action and careless attitude" toward the turnpike trustees; kept Sir Charles Dance from testifying in Parliament because conditions on the Cheltenham Road were in fact quite favorable to continued service; and actually encouraged the "prohibitive tolls" panic so that, in the resulting atmosphere of righteous indignation, he could escape with the capital he had raised from his partners. On the other hand, according to Evans ("Roads, Railways and Canals," 29), the *Mechanic's Magazine* for 24 November 1832 reported that "Sir Charles Dance . . . does not hesitate to say, in private, that he was infinitely obliged to the road trustees for furnishing him with so plausible a pretext as they did for abandoning a losing concern."

21. H. C. *Sess. Pap.* 1834 (483) XI: 30–43, 46–47.

22. *Mr. Gurney's Observations on Steam Carriages on Turnpike Roads,* 43.

23. H. C. *Sess. Pap.* 1834 (483) XI: 19–20, 38, 43, 48, 54. These figures are based on the recollections of Gurney, his foremen, Ward, Bulnois, and Hanning's solicitor, three to four years after the event.

24. Ibid., 33–4, 54.

25. Beasley, *Suppression of the Automobile*, 21, Table 1. Beasley does not cite the sources for this table, which has the appearance of a facsimile document but on closer inspection seems to be a composite, drawn from a variety of evidence.

26. According to William Fletcher, *History and Development of Steam Locomotion on Common Roads* (London: E. Spon, 1891), 86.

27. For the Seawards, see the *Dictionary of National Biography*, s.v. "Seaward, John." Prior to entering the marine engine field, they had constructed a steam carriage propelled by a spiked wheel, described by Gordon, *Treatise,* 47, 51.

28. H. C. *Sess. Pap.* 1831 (324) VIII: 38–41. Hancock thought that his 1831 carriage was "any way from being handsome" because it was designed only for experiments, but it worked so quietly "that I have almost run over people on the road, and they have not heard me" (Ibid., 32–35). He later wrote: "Whatever improvements may result from the mode of generating steam by means of flat chambers, exposing large thin sheets of water to the action of corresponding thin volumes of heated air, through flues formed by alternative chambers placed side by side—the writer claims this as the grand and principal feature of his invention. . . ." Hancock, *Narrative of Twelve Years' Experiments,* frontispiece.

29. Lewis Gordon, *Railway Economy: An Exposition of the Advantages of Locomotion by Locomotive Carriages Instead of the Present Expensive System of Steam Tugs* (Edinburgh: Sutherland and Knox, 1849), 59. Gordon was an engineer on Brunel's Thames Tunnel at the time he rode the Hancock carriage. Later he was appointed Regius Professor of Civil Engineering and Mechanics at Glasgow University. By "locomotive carriages," he meant what, in modern times, was the self-driven "Budd" car, used for commuter trains.

30. Hancock's carriages are described by James, *Walter Hancock and His Common Road Steam Carriages;* by Davison, *History of Steam Road Vehicles,* chapter VII; and by Gordon, *Treatise,* 107–13, with drawings on the frontispiece, plate 1. Hancock's evidence in 1831 was very sketchy, but he gave substantial testimony to a select committee of the House of Lords in 1836; cf. Lords *Journals* 1836: 68, Appendix 7: 316–19. One of his more ingenious devices was a friction drum on the front steering assembly, which locked the wheels on a straight course when activated by the driver's foot pedal. Since most steam carriages took a good deal of strength to steer, this was a real help. Beasley, *Suppression of the Automobile*, 35–36, examines

circumstantial evidence that Hancock was actually in league with the railway interests.

31. Davison, *History of Steam Road Vehicles,* chapter VII; Fletcher, *History and Development of Steam Locomotives on Common Roads,* 144–45.

32. A drawing of the Heaton steam drag, from the *Mechanic's Magazine* 19 (14 September 1833): 417, is reproduced by Evans, "Roads, Railways and Canals," 31.

33. Beasley, *Suppression of the Automobile,* 21–2, quotes newspaper accounts of the sabotage and violence directed at Russell; cf. Davison, *History of Steam Road Vehicles,* chapter 7, and Fletcher, *History and Development of Steam Locomotion on Common Roads,* 92, 132–37. In October 1832, Russell authored an article in the *Foreign Quarterly Review,* claiming that all previous attempts to build steam carriages were utter failures, and explaining the mistaken principles that were followed. This was, however, a thinly disguised promotion of his own design, due out in the next few months. Alexander Gordon subsequently pointed out these misrepresentations. Russell was later the designer and builder of Brunel's steamship, *Great Eastern.*

34. H. C. *Sess. Pap.* 1831 (324) VIII: 69–72, 79–80.

35. H. C. *Sess. Pap.* 1839 (295) IX, Report of the Select Committee for ascertaining how far the formation of Railroads may affect the interest of Turnpike Trusts and the Creditors of such Trusts, 42, q. 511–12.

36. Fletcher, *History and Development of Steam Locomotion on Common Roads,* 104–5. Church's publicity poster for the trial run, showing the steam carriage cruising through the countryside like a great circus wagon, is often reprinted.

37. Alexander Gordon wrote that Gurney considered the carriage merely a modification of his own, but Gordon disagreed, adding, "I incline to think that *if* the Colonel and Mr. Squire have made this carriage out of the *debris* of Mr. G.'s factory, they have the more merit." Gordon, *Treatise,* 114.

38. Beasley, *Suppression of the Automobile,* 27, gives additional details. Maceroni appeared before most of the parliamentary committees on steam locomotion, giving bits and pieces of his history each time. His life and career are covered in Fletcher, *History and Development of Steam Locomotion on Common Roads,* 120–28, and in Davison, *History of Steam Road Vehicles,* ch. 7. Gordon, *Treatise,* 114–16, describes two trips to Windsor in Maceroni & Squires' carriage in September and October 1831 and gives details of the boiler. Maceroni published a work entitled *Steam Power applied on Common Roads* in 1835 and two volumes of *Memoirs* in 1836.

39. Henry Maudslay (1771–1831), "the Great Mechanic," was famous for developing engineered toolmaking machines; he trained James Nasmyth and other mechanical engineers. Cf. Musson and Robinson, *Science and Technology in the Industrial Revolution,* 474–76, 490. Maudslay's partner, Joshua Field, rode on Sir Charles Dance's steam carriage during an 1833 trial run from London to Birmingham. Maudslay also employed William Keene, one of Gurney's early assistants, who helped Samuel Gurney build an early steam packet.

40. Bailey's work for Dance is mentioned in H. C. *Sess. Pap.* 1834 (483) XI: 53.

41. Gordon, *Treatise,* 117.

42. House of Lords *Journals* 1836: 68, Appendix 7: 20. The second quotation is from Gurney's evidence in H. C. *Sess. Pap.* 1834 (483) XI: 12.

CHAPTER 8. MR. GURNEY'S CASE

1. Gordon, *Treatise,* Appendix A, 297.
2. The NIL is profiled by Beasley, *Suppression of the Automobile,* 33–34.

3. The report was printed in the *Morning Chronicle;* cf.Gordon, *Treatise,* 95–96. Gordon was one of the engineers on this journey, as was John Macneill, the engineer for the Holyhead road; Joshua Field, of the engineering firm of Maudslay and Field; and Timothy Bramah, who had built the very first working steam carriage for Julius Griffith in 1821. The trip is detailed in Gibb, *The Story of Telford,* 275–76, who also cites the *Morning Chronicle,* by way of the *Observer.*

4. Gordon, *Treatise,* Appendix (G), 322. I assume "The London, Holyhead, and Liverpool Steam Coach and Road Company," proposed in 1834, derived from Telford's study of the same route the previous year, since several engineers were involved in both ventures, and other names carry over to the 1835 steam drag experiment by Field and Dance. This connection is confirmed by Beasley, who gives details of the company's operations in *Suppression of the Automobile,* 25–27.

5. Henry Maudslay built two of his own design, and his partner Joshua Field constructed another steam drag, with Gurney's steam separator restored, for Sir Charles Dance.

6. Sir William Molesworth (1810–55) was the scion of a family that had represented East Cornwall for several generations. Disfigured by childhood scrofula, he was rejected by his father and bullied by schoolmates, and grew to dislike all authority. In 1827 he was expelled from Cambridge for challenging his tutor to a duel. He was "emphatically a Liberal, from a thorough conviction of the uselessness of much of our restrictive legislation." He soon became one of the Philosophical Radicals, adopted several Chartist planks, and lost his seat by opposing the Corn Laws in 1837. While not a powerful debater, he could speak compellingly from notes. *Illustrated London News* XXVII, no. 767: 489–90, and *Dictionary of National Biography,* s.v. "Molesworth, William."

7. The parliamentary debates are quoted by Gordon, *Treatise,* 97–107.

8. H. C. *Sess. Pap.* 1834 (483) XI, "Report," 17 July 1834.

9. H. C. *Sess. Pap.* 1835 (483) XIII, minutes of evidence, 10 July 1835.

10. Ibid., "Report," 17 July 1835.

11. Cf. H. C. *Sess. Pap.* 1836 (547) VI, 67, "A Bill to repeal such Portions of all Acts as impose prohibitory Tolls on Steam carriages, and to substitute other Tolls on an equitable footing with Horse Carriages," 6 May 1836. Boilers were to be proved at double the proposed normal working pressure and the weight of the carriage to be registered by two justices of the peace on a certificate to be carried by the driver-conductor.

12. Gurney said that "thirty to forty large capitalists" applied for licenses after the Commons passed the bill and the Lords appeared favorable. The Devonport, Plymouth, and Exeter company hired Thomas Harris, Sir Charles Dance's former engineer, to drive its carriages. House of Lords *Journals* 1836: 68, Appendix 7: 60, 71. The *West Briton* notices are given in Harris, *Gurney,* 64. Beasley, *Suppression of the Automobile,* 23–24, gives details of the Plymouth and Devonport Steam Carriage Company and says that it was intended to offer "feeder" service to new railways being built in the region.

13. William Playdell-Bouverie (1779–1869), third Earl Radnor, was an associate of William Cobbett. Unlike Cobbett, he was no orator, but earned the attention of the House by his dedication to social reform. Cf. *Dictionary of National Biography,* s.v. "Bouverie, William Playdell."

14. Cf. Beasley, *Suppression of the Automobile,* 38–39. James Archibald Stuart-Wortley, first Baron Wharncliffe (1776–1845), was an early Peelite Tory, appointed Lord Privy Seal in 1835. Not a man of exceptional ability, he was popular with country gentlemen for his "strong good sense" (*Dictionary of National Biography,*

s.v. "Stuart-Wortley, James."). While he was opposing steam carriages, Wharncliffe also managed bills that promoted railways in the region of Cheltenham and Gloucester. Ironically, in a different committee, the Lords were collecting evidence on the danger of fires caused by railway engines as they passed through towns and dry fields. Cf. House of Lords *Journals* 1836, LXVIII, Appendix 5, Report of the Select Committee on "whether any Danger by Fire is likely to arise from locomotive Engines being used on Railroads passing through narrow streets." The committee examined Gurney, Henry Maudslay, and Dr. Lardner, as well as Robert Stephenson and other railway engineers, and concluded that the fire danger was still very likely. They recommended a clause in all railway bills, giving individuals the right to sue for damages by fire.

15. House of Lords *Journals* 1836: 68, Appendix 7: 82–85. Joshua Field, who built three steam carriages for the Cubitt group, paid his engineer John Braithwaite almost three guineas a week, more than the average salary of a lower-middle-class clerk.

16. House of Lords *Journals* 1836: 68, Appendix 7: 310–38. It may be significant that in 1836, the House of Commons, investigating abuses in turnpike trusts, reported that the trusts had a combined debt of £9 million, and were in danger of bankruptcy from the new railway competition. Since many country gentlemen, allied with the landowning peers, had invested heavily in turnpike trusts, they were especially fearful of losing stagecoach traffic to steam carriages. Meanwhile a concurrent Commons committee on turnpike tolls for Scotland reported out a bill regulating steam carriages, which incorporated Gurney's proposed schedule of tariffs. This initiative, of course, was also thwarted by the Lords' deliberations. Cf. Hansard, *Parliamentary Debates,* 3d series, V (1831): 1265–66.

17. In testimony before a committee on mines in 1853, Gurney said that the principle of the steam jet, or "oelipile," was quite old, the modern apparatus being introduced by Trevithick in 1816 as a way to exhaust waste steam. He implied that he himself had helped Trevithick at that time and developed the powerful jet in 1824–25 at his new factory. H. C. *Sess. Pap.* 1852–53 (820) XX, Third Report of the Select Committee on Accidents in Coal Mines, 72, question 4132.

18. An unsigned, undated letter, written to a peer in the House of Lords, probably in 1836, has come to light among the documents collected for the Gurney exhibition in Bude. The writer claims that the steam jet had been falsely attributed to George Stephenson, who used it on engines for the Stockton and Darlington railway in 1825—the claim subsequently published by Samuel Smiles. The author of the letter suggests that a workman, familiar with the steam jet, left Gurney's employ to join the Stephenson works between the time of the invention and the date of its patent, thus conveying proprietary information to the other engineer. The author then adds that Mr. Gurney considered legal action to protect his patent rights, but "having little or no funds for that purpose, he was obliged to submit to Mr. Stephenson's having the honor and profit of the first use of the discovery."

19. Maurice W. Kirby, *The Origins of Railway Enterprise: The Stockton and Darlington Railway, 1831–1863* (Cambridge: Cambridge University Press, 1993), 64–5. John Farey, in testimony before a select committee of Commons (H. C. *Sess. Pap.* 1831 (324) VIII: 43), said that the jet was invented by Gurney and applied by Stephenson.

20. For Farey's statement see ibid. Smiles's claim was made in his *Life of the Late Mr. George Stephenson* (1857), and Gurney's rebuttal was published as an *Account of the Invention of the Steam-Jet or Blast* (1859). Copies of the rebuttal are in the Institution of Civil Engineers archives, presented by Anna Gurney with copious marginal remarks in 1873 and 1881.

21. Beasley, *Suppression of the Automobile,* 38. The heat-pipe boiler design is clearly shown in Marie-Hélène Reynaud, *Marc Seguin: Du Pont de Tournon,* 155, 165. Cf. Jacques Payen, "Seguin, Stephenson et la Naissance de la Locomotive a Chaudière Tubulaire, 1826–1829," *History of Technology* 6, no. 2 (1988): 145–71. For the transition from barrel to pipe boilers and the adoption of steam jets and horizontal cylinders, see Graham Glover, *British Locomotive Design, 1825–1960* (London: George Allen and Unwin, 1967), 13–15.

22. Cf. Gordon's testimony in the House of Lords *Journals* 1836: 68, Appendix 5: 57–58.

23. Stone's steam drag trial was reported in a letter to Gurney, reprinted in his *Observations on Steam Carriages on Turnpike Roads* (1832), 32–3. The smaller wheels were to give a higher mechanical advantage to the axle crank. The railway examples were given by John Macneill, in H. C. *Sess. Pap.* 1831 (324) VIII, Appendix 1. Beasley (*Suppression of the Automobile,* 148, n. 13) argues that Gurney's engine was more powerful than Stephenson's because it drew a heavier payload in relation to its own weight. But the weight was related more to the amount of water and coke or coal carried than to the bare machinery; the railway engines carried enough for long trips, whereas Gurney's drags could only go seven or eight miles without refueling.

24. Michael Robbins, *The Railway Age in Britain* (Harmondsworth, UK: Penguin Books, 1965), 15. As if to add insult to injury, the third railway run with steam locomotives in Britain, after the Stockton and Darlington and the Liverpool and Manchester, was a line built in 1834–35 from Bodmin to Wadebridge, the town Gurney left in 1820 to seek his fortune in London.

25. Cf. H. C. *Sess. Pap.* 1839 (295) IX, Report from the Select Committee on Turnpike Trusts and the Creditors of such Trusts, 25, 42–43. Beasley states that after 1836, some railways began granting monopoly rights to certain stagecoach proprietors for feeder services, driving all the others out of business. Steam carriages were then promoted in combination with railways for this purpose in southern England. (*Suppression of the Automobile,* 24). Nathaniel Ogle, however, objected (H. C. *Sess. Pap.* 1839 (295) IX: 43, q. 514) that steam carriages were not good for short-distance work because each stop required a lot of trouble, and wasted fuel and water.

26. Robbins, *The Railway Age in Britain,* 16.

27. Beasley, *Suppression of the Automobile,* chapter 6, "Opposition of the Railroad Interests," and chapter 8, "The Interest Group Basis of Restrictive Legislation."

28. Pritchard, *Sir George Cayley,* 81. This view was shared by C. F. T. Young, in *Steam Power on Common Roads* (London: John Murray, 1860), who criticized Gurney for paying little attention to fuel economy.

29. House of Commons *Sessional Papers* 1839 IX (295): 30, q. 388.

30. Evans, "Roads, Railways and Canals," 26–7, quoting *The Penny Cyclopaedia* (1833); W. W. Beaumont, *Motor Vehicles* (1900); J. Copeland, *Roads and Their Traffic* (1968); and Anthony Bird, *Roads and Vehicles* (1969).

31. Evans, "Roads, Railways and Canals," 19–21; Angus Sinclair, *Development of the Locomotive Engine,* annotated ed., John H. White, Jr. (Cambridge, Mass: MIT Press, 1970): 28–32. The argument that steam engineers owed little to scientific research has been made many times: see A. Rupert Hall, "What Did the Industrial Revolution in Britain Owe to Science?" in *Historical Perspectives: Studies in English Thought and Society in Honor of J. H. Plumb,* ed. Neil McKendrick (London: Europa Publications, 1974): 129–51.

32. House of Lords *Journals,* 1836, 68, Appendix 5: Report of the Select Commit-

tee appointed to consider whether any Danger by Fire is likely to arise from locomotive Engines being used on Railroads passing through narrow streets.

33. James, *Walter Hancock*, 101.

34. ICE *Minutes of Proceedings* 5 (1840): 77.

CHAPTER 9. STEAMBOATS, LIGHTHOUSES, CASTLES, AND HOT AIR

1. Sir Thomas Dyke Acland, tenth Baronet (1787–1871), was head of the Church of England religious party in the House of Commons during the debates over Catholic Emancipation in the 1820s. From 1837 to 1857, he represented the Tory interest in North Devonshire while his son and namesake held his old seat of Devonshire.

2. Gibb, *The Story of Telford*, 268–9. The precise material used for Gurney's foundation is not known. He knew the properties of "Devonshire cob," a mixture of clay and natural adhesives, tamped between boards to form building walls in southwest Britain. But that would not have lasted 165 years. Portland cement, which had better hydraulic qualities than Parker's formula, came on the market in 1824. French and German scientists took a typically systematic approach to concrete and cement analysis, while the British remained typically empirical. As a result British concrete construction involved "a substantial amount of uncertainty" until the 1870s. Peters, *Building the Nineteenth Century*, 58–63. Cf. Norman Davey, *A History of Building Materials* (London: Phoenix House, 1961), 106, and Stefi Weisburd, "Hard Science," *Science News* 134 (9 July 1988): 24.

3. Harris, *Gurney*, 46; "Notes on the Castle, Bude and its Setting for the Cornish Gorsedd, 1976," typescript by R. M. Heard of Kilkhampton, 1975; personal observations by the author, who was privileged to witness the dedication of the Council chamber in April 1993. Concrete had been used since Roman times, but in the early nineteenth century, engineers building canals and harbor walls developed new combinations of lime, cement, and gravel, which set up in wet conditions and when cured, withstood hydraulic pressures associated with tidal waters. It is not known whether the concrete foundation was reinforced with iron rods or other material; such a technique was almost unknown at the time.

4. *Dictionary of National Biography*, s.v. "Faraday, Michael." Iwan Rhys Morus comments that Faraday, like Davy, enjoyed the luxury of preparing elaborate and rational lecture-demonstrations after experimenting, not always successfully, in a well-equipped institutional laboratory. Less exalted researchers, Gurney included, often carried out their experiments during the course of public lectures or consulting contracts, using practical, makeshift apparatus of their own design. Morus, "Currents from the Underworld: Electricity and the Technology of Display in Early Victorian England,:" *Isis* 84 (1993): 50–6.

5. *Dictionary of National Biography*. Faraday, son of a blacksmith, never felt comfortable in genteel company. He belonged to a strict Christian sect, the Sandemanians, and avoided wordly entertainments. His meager income at the Royal Institution was supplemented by an endowed professorship of chemistry, established for him by John Fuller, an amateur scientist and member of Parliament, who justified his generosity by claiming that the Royal Institution lecture hall was the best place to sleep in all of London. Caroe and Caroe, *The Royal Institution*, 43–48, 56. The contrasts between Faraday's public persona and his private life have evoked equally divergent interpretations by his biographers. The most thorough account of his scientific research is given by L. Pearce Williams, *Michael Faraday: A Biography* (New York: Basic Books, 1965). Geoffrey Cantor, *Michael Faraday: Sandemanian*

and Scientist (New York: St. Martin's Press, 1991) emphasizes the influence of religion, while his status as public experimenter and lecturer is appreciated by John Meurig Thomas, *Michael Faraday and the Royal Institution: The Genius of Man and Place* (Bristol and Philadelphia: Adam Hilger, 1991).

6. H. C. *Sess. Pap.* 1834 (590) XII, Report of the Select Committee on Lighthouses, Drummond testimony, 31–33, 241–9.

7. Ibid., 246. Drummond's appointment on 16 December 1829 is recorded in *The Correspondence of Michael Faraday,* ed. A. J. L. James (London: Institution of Electrical Engineers, 1991), 177, item 96. Drummond promptly invited Faraday to give a course of lectures on chemistry at the Royal Military Academy for a fee of £200, a sum which enabled him to pursue his research on electromagnetism. Cf. Frank James, "Time, Tide, and Michael Faraday," *History Today* 41 (September 1991): 28–34.

8. Joseph Hume (1777–1855), like Gurney, had been apprenticed to a surgeon as a youth. He was a vice president of the Society for Arts, which had awarded Gurney its gold medal in 1823. He was an indefatigable reformer and served on more committees in the House of Commons than any other member of the early Victorian era.

9. H. C. *Sess. Pap.* 1834 (590) XII: 224, Report of the Select Committee on Lighthouses, Drummond testimony, 8 August. For the committee's rehearsal of defects in the lighthouse system, see "Report," 3.

10. Gurney is not mentioned in any biography of Faraday, nor in the *Correspondence* edited by A. J. L. James. This is not surprising, because Trinity House was bombed in World War II, and all of Faraday's reports and correspondence that had been kept there were destroyed. However, Bence Jones, *The Life and Letters of Faraday,* vol. 1 (London: Longmans, Green & Co., 1870) 87, records Faraday's preparation of experiments with the Bude lamp in 1836, and a note in the following year, "pressing Mr. Gurney, by letter, to give us his best lamp at once, and not lose time." In 1838 and 1839, Faraday reported on the new oxygen-fed Bude lamp, comparing its cost and power with the Argand lamp and with Drummond's original device (ibid., 105).

11. "My house at Bude has a long gallery in it; I passed a stream of reflected light through that gallery; every bedroom entering into the gallery was sufficiently illuminated in every part for a person to pick up a pin. The light in the bedrooms was refracted light [i.e., by the atmosphere], from the reflected light passing through the gallery." Harris, *Gurney,* 47, relates a story that Mrs. Elizabeth Gurney Fry, a visitor to Bude around 1840, claimed kinship with Gurney and asked to see the Bude light demonstrated. Gurney obligingly aimed the large reflector at her room in the Falcon Hotel, some 400 yards across the canal, where the beam of light was strong enough to enable Mrs. Fry to read a letter.

12. Drummond's letter is mentioned in ibid., 66. A search of the unpublished manuscript records in the House of Lords Record Office has not turned up such a letter, either. The later acknowledgement is in H. C. *Sess. Pap.* 1842 (251) XIV, Report of the Select Committee to inquire into the Remuneration due to Mr. G. Gurney for his services in Lighting the [old] House of Commons, 5. As in the case of his other inventions, Gurney was not alone in this field. A man named Gottlieb Boccius erected a model of his improved gas lamp in the Strand, opposite Northumberland House, in October 1842, claiming an eighty-three percent increase in efficiency and brilliance over the standard Argand lamp. Cf. *Illustrated London News,* 15 October 1842: 367.

13. H. C. *Sess. Pap.* 1835 (603) V: 6, Select Committee on Accidents in Mines, minutes of evidence, q. 77–86.

14. As David Knight admitted (*Humphry Davy*, 1), Davy had become "one of the most respected and most disliked men of science ever."

15. Sydney Ross, "Herschel on Faraday and the RS," *Notes and Records of the Royal Society* 33, no. 1 (1978): 77–82. Herschel gained Faraday's loyalty by treating him as a social equal and supporting his candidacy for the Royal Society, when Davy refused to do so.

16. Roy M. MacLeod, "Whigs and Savants: Reflections on the Reform Movement in the Royal Society, 1830–1848" in Inkster and Morrell, *Metropolis and Province:* 55–65. For the perception of scientific decline, see J. B. Morrell, "London Institutions and Lyell's Career, 1820–1841," *British Journal for the History of Science* 9, part 2, no. 32 (July 1976): 132–33. Morrell shows that the BAAS stemmed mainly from Northern regional initiative, rather than from the split in the Royal Society, in "Individualism and the Structure of British Science in 1830," *Historical Studies in the Physical Sciences* 3 (1971), 201.

17. Timothy Bramah, the steam carriage expert, contributed a chapter on warm water heating to the third (1836) edition of Thomas Tredgold's *Principles of Warming and Ventilating Public Buildings.*

18. Harris, *Gurney*, 71. The text of Gurney's paper is in the *Report of the 11th meeting of the British Association for the Advancement of Science, Plymouth, 1841* (London: John Murray, 1842), "Transactions of the Sections," 50–51.

19. H. C. *Sess. Pap.* 1835 (603) V: 8–10, q. 98–109. Gurney also suggested replacing barrel boilers with the tubular kind he had developed for his steam carriages, but added, "I feel delicacy in speaking of this arrangement . . . I possibly am an interested witness; though, unfortunately, I have little interest now, as my patent is nearly out."

20. For Gurney's self-acting feeder, see H. C. *Sess. Pap.* 1849 (613) VII: 61–62, Report of the Lords' Select Committee on Mines, q. 516–18. Gurney, at that time, said he had invented the device "about 20 years ago." Seaward is credited with the same invention, by his memorialist, in the ICE *Minutes of Proceedings* XVIII (1859): 200, which was repeated in his entry for the *Dictionary of National Biography.*

21. Cf. his obituary in the *Times*, 18 December 1857: 7, col. 6.

22. Pritchard, *Sir George Cayley*, preface. Pritchard quotes almost thirty of Gurney's letters to Cayley. These letters were believed to have been deposited in the library of the Royal Aeronautical Society, but Harris could find no listing for them in the library catalogue.

23. Ibid., 81.

24. For the parabolic reflector idea, see H. C. *Sess. Pap.* 1835 (603) V: 6, q. 86. For the colliery measurements taken in April 1846, see Pritchard, *Sir George Cayley*, 138–9.

25. Ibid., 83, plate XII.

26. As in the case of steam engines, there were many inventors who claimed precedence for the principle or practical application of the hot-air engine. Stirling's name was eventually attached to the hot-air cycle, and one can still buy working scale model Stirling engines.

27. Pritchard, *Sir George Cayley*, 82.

28. Ibid., 76.

29. M. Jeanne Peterson, *Family, Love, and Work in the Lives of Victorian Gentlewomen,* (Bloomington: Indiana University Press, 1989), preface, x.

30. This distinction is explored in Peters, *Building the Nineteenth Century*, preface and ch. 4. See also his discussion of chemical engineering, 66.

31. It suited his contemporaries, also: Davy and other chemists believed that analogy was, as Knight puts it, "the key to safe hypothesizing." Knight, *Humphry Davy*, 78.

CHAPTER 10. MINE VENTILATION

1. S. G. Checkland, *The Rise of Industrial Society in England, 1815–1885.* (New York: St. Martin's Press, 1964), 157–62.

2. A. V. Jones and R. P. Tarkenter, *Electrical Technology in Mining: the Dawn of a New Age* (London: The Science Museum and Peter Peregrinus, 1992), 9–11.

3. Report of the South Shields Committee (1843) in H. C. *Sess. Pap.* 1852 (509) V, appendix 4. For a modern description of the various mine gases, see Jones and Tarkenter, *Electrical Technology in Mining*, 14–15.

4. H. C. *Sess. Pap.* 1835 (603) V: iii–vi and 1852 (509) V: v–vi, Reports of Select Committees on Coal Mine Accidents. The number of men killed by explosions was always uncertain, due to faulty coroners' returns.

5. H. C. *Sess. Pap.* 1835 (603) V, Report of the Select Committee on Accidents in Mines: iii–viii.

6. Ibid.

7. He said that he had built "an apparatus" that produced the strong air currents needed to test the lamp, and received a medal from the Duke of Sussex for his work. Harris and other authors assumed that he meant the oxyhydrogen blowpipe, but that had nothing to do with generating air pressure. It is more likely that he adapted one of his first steam jets for the purpose.

8. His steam carriage petition had been remanded to a hostile committee by Lord Salisbury on 18 July. Under the circumstances the application of steam jets to mine ventilation was an opportunity not to be missed.

9. H. C. *Sess. Pap.* 1835 (603) V: minutes of evidence, 284–86, q. 3867–71. Gurney's recollection of the challenge issued by the 1835 committee is in House of Lords *Sess. Pap.* 1852 (613) VII, Report of the Lords Committee on Mines, 50, q. 421.

10. Lord Ashley (1801–85), later seventh Earl of Shaftesbury, led the fight by evangelical reformers to regulate working conditions for factory and mine children and chimney sweeps. He was already agitating to limit working hours for women and children to ten hours, a concession not made until 1847.

11. Report of the South Shields Committee on Accidents in Coal Mines (1843), H. C. *Sess. Pap.* 1852 (509) V, Appendix 4: 184–87.

12. Gurney wrote that he had been on the Continent for six weeks prior to this letter, but he did not reveal his purpose or destination. From other evidence it seems likely that he was inspecting a steam jet, installed in a Belgian mine, which the South Shields committee had heard about. The apparatus turned out to be mistaken in principle and ineffectual in practice.

13. H. C. *Sess. Pap.* 1852 (509) V, Appendix 4, : 184, 187.

14. House of Lords *Sess. Pap.* 1849 (613) VII: 353, q. 3716, and 584, q. 6284. For a description and drawings of Struvé's Mine Ventilator, see the Appendix.

15. Ibid., 50–51, copy of Forster's letter to the *Gateshead Observer*, 11 December 1848.

16. Ibid.

17. Ibid., 266–72, q. 2704.

18. Ibid., 354–55, q. 3716, evidence of James Mather. There is no other informa-tion about these applications of the steam jet. It is likely that Mather himself, in his frequent trips to inspect mines and ventilating apparatus, discovered them and perhaps even suggested them in the first place. The destructive emissions from alkali plants are described by A. and N. Clow, *The Chemical Revolution: A Contribution to Social Technology* (London: The Batchworth Press, 1952), 21, and by Anthony Wohl, *Endangered Lives: Public Health in Victorian Britain* (London: J. M. Dent & Sons, 1983), 224–26. The Alkali Act of 1863 set standards of emission and established a government inspectorate, which showed the alkali industry how to recycle wastes. Cf. Roy MacLeod, "The Alkali Acts Administration, 1863–1884: The Emergence of the Civil Scientist," *Victorian Studies* 9 (1965): 85–112.

19. House of Lords *Sess. Pap.* 1849 (613) VII: 58–59, copy of Darlington's letter to the *Times,* 30 April 1849. Limestone was added to the coal in the furnace to produce a better "damp."

20. Ibid.

21. Ibid., 41–46, q. 315–64.

22. Ibid., 41–59, 93–105.

23. Ibid., 41–62.

24. Ibid., 44, q. 344, and 52, q. 436; H. C. *Sess. Pap.* 1852 (509) V, Report of the Select Committee on Coal Mines, "Definitions and Technical Explanations," xii.

25. House of Lords *Sess. Pap.* 1849 (613) VII: 584, q. 6311.

26. H. C. *Sess. Pap.* 1852 (509) V: 16–17, q. 198–211, testimony of J. Mather. Gurney told a version of this story at a session on ventilation at the Institution of Civil Engineers in November 1850. ICE *Minutes of Proceedings* 10 (1850–51): 54. Although the one account identifies the mine only as "Lord Mansfield's," and the other gives only the name "South Sauchie" and its location, the technical details are essentially the same and must be regarded as referring to the same experience. During a later Commons inquiry in 1854, a member hostile to the steam jet charged that the South Sauchie mine fire had since rekindled and had left the mine as unworkable as ever. This charge was not denied by Gurney's advocates.

27. ICE *Minutes of Proceedings* 10 (1850–51): 47–57.

28. *Mining Journal* 21, no. 848 (22 November, 1851): 562. The *Journal* published regular letters for and against Gurney's inventions all during 1851 and 1852. The most detailed criticism came from Joshua Richardson, a member of the Institution of Civil Engineers, who called the steam jet expensive, capricious, and impractica-ble. Dr. George Fife, a member of the House of Commons select committee, an-swered Richardson much later. *Ibid.* 21, no. 850 (6 December 1851): 582–83, and 22, no. 890 (11 September 1852): 438.

29. *Mining Journal* 21, no. 848 (22 November 1851): 562.

30. H. C. *Sess. Pap.* 1852 (509) V: "Report," iv–v.

31. *Mining Journal* 22, nos. 880–82 (3, 10, and 17 July 1852).

32. The founding of the North of England Institute of Mining Engineers was re-ported in the *Mining Journal* 22, no. 881 (10 July 1852): 332, and 22, no. 890 (11 September 1852): 444. In the July issue, the editor noted that the aim was to test the steam jet and other ventilating equipment by "a disinterested and practical investigation." In the later issue, the editor and at least two correspondents noted that the Institute was announced immediately after a national institution for mine safety was proposed at a meeting in Westminster, and questioned the motives of Woods and his associates. The Westminster meeting was probably initiated by Gur-ney. For the proliferation of engineering institutes after 1847, see R. A. Buchanan, *The Engineers: A History of the Engineering Profession in Britain, 1750–1914* (Lon-

don: Jessica Kingsley, 1989), 88–98. The North of England Institute's derivation from the ICE and BAAS is explained in Jones and Tarkenter, *Electrical Technology in Mining,* 6. The Insititute published extensive comparisons of ventilation systems in its *Transactions* 30 (1880–81).

33. "Wood, Nicholas" in Frederic Boase, *Modern English Biography,* vol. 3 (London: Frank Cass, 1901), 1473.

34. H. C. *Sess. Pap.* 1852–53 (820) XX, Third Report of the Select Committee on Accidents in Coal Mines, 86, q. 4306. A report by John Phillips, FRS, to the Home Secretary in 1850 gave some data, but since the experiments combined steam jets with conventional furnaces, no comparative advantage could be determined. H. C. *Sess. Pap.* 1850 (1222) 23: 24–25.

35. H. C. *Sess. Pap.* 1852–53 (820) XX: 72–86.

36. H. C. *Sess. Pap.* 1854 (169) (258) (277) (325) IX, First, Second, Third, & Fourth Reports of the Select Committee on Accidents in Coal Mines. The conclusions of this committee were confirmed in a report by J. Kenyon Blackwell to the Home Secretary in 1860. Blackwell observed that when the boiler for the steam jet was installed at the bottom of the upcast shaft, usually in connection with the traditional furnace, it was very difficult to distinguish the effects of one from the other. Results from different mines were therefore contradictory. *Sess. Pap.* 1860 (1214) 23: 16–17. A royal commission in 1864 recommended that furnaces be installed in all mines, noting that they were "generally in use" at collieries by this time. The commission made no mention of steam jets. H. C. *Sess. Pap.* 1864 (3389) 24, Part I.

37. See the *Mining Journal* 22, no. 889 (4 September 1852): 426 for letters critical of Gurney's "philosophical jargon." "Plain unassuming people are demolished by the hard words and mysterious innuendos of the man of science," said one.

38. Jones and Tarkenter, *Electrical Technology in Mining,* 19–21. Traditional furnace ventilation remained common, especially in the deeper mines of northern England, throughout the nineteenth century.

Chapter 11. Parliament

1. Lord Duncannon was his courtesy title as son and heir of the Earl of Bessborough. His calm, conciliatory manner proved useful in negotiating political compromises. *Dictionary of National Biography* s.v. "Ponsonby, John William."

2. Cf. Sir Harold Emmerson, *The Ministry of Works* (London: Allen and Unwin, 1956); also, the Ministry of Works, *The History of the King's Works,* vol. 6 (London: n.d.).

3. Joseph Hume (1777–1855) had made his fortune as a surgeon for the East India Company before entering Parliament in 1808 for Weymouth. He was a leader of the Radical party for thirty years and joined the anti-Corn Law movement as early as 1834. He served on more committees than any other member, directing his "boundless energy and patience" toward the exposé of extravagance and abuse in government finances. His position as vice president of the Society of Arts explains his interest in lighthouses and in Gurney's system of lighting. "He spoke longer and oftener and probably worse than any other private member," said the *Dictionary of National Biography,* "but he saw most of the causes which he advocated succeed in the end."

4. H. C. *Sess. Pap.* 1839 (501) XIII, Report of the Select Committee on Lighting the House of Commons, appointed to superintend the Experiment of Mr. Gurney to

Light the House: 7, 15–16, 44–47. Acland's freehold of the Castle grounds is given by Harris (*Gurney,* 70) from the records of the Tithe Commissioners.

5. Centrally supplied gas lighting systems were commercially available after 1812, and the basic techniques for arranging gas lamps were commonly known by the time Gurney began work at the Houses of Parliament. As in any early industry, however, elaborate novelties and hybrid arrangments appeared annually. Cf. M. E. Falkus, "The Early Development of the British Gas Industry, 1790–1815," *Economic History Review* 35, no. 2 (1982): 217–34.

6. The comparison was made using a photometer, a sheet of cardboard with a graded scale for measuring the depth of shadow cast by each light. The wax candle was a standard issue, but there is no indication in the evidence of its exact power. The modern unit of candle power, the candela, was adopted only in 1948. Dr. Ure, the expert on comparative lighting at this time, said that the Bude lamp produced thirty candlepower in his tests.

7. H. C. *Sess. Pap.* 1839 (501) XIII: 3–4, q. 18–35; also, *Sess. Pap.* 1842 (251) XIV, Report of the Select Committee to inquire into the Remuneration due to Mr. G. Gurney for his Services in Lighting the [Old] House of Commons, minutes of evidence, 14. Gurney described the lamp as using either air or oxygen, and it is not clear from his testimony which was supplied to the system he installed.

8. H. C. *Sess. Pap.* 1839 (501) XIII: 25–30, q. 420–90. The agreement with Treasury is reviewed in *Sess. Pap.* 1842 (251) XIV: 3. During the sessions of 1839 and 1840, Gurney spent £777. 2s. 6d. to remove the old candelabra, construct a new ceiling framework, and install the necessary gas lines and lamp fixtures. Accounts and notes are in Public Record Office, WORK 11–26/1: 1–40, hereafter cited as PRO WORK.

9. *Illustrated London News* 1845: 284, cited in Harris, *Gurney,* 71. The four lamps in Trafalgar Square were said to be octagonal in shape, mounted on large bronze pedestals.

10. H. C. *Sess. Pap.* 1842 (251) XIV: 3–7. The patent dates are given by Harris, although the patent titles he lists give little clue as to the precise instruments covered. The minutes of evidence from the select committee of 1842 give the date as 1840.

11. PRO WORK 11–26/1, return of 25 February 1840.

12. H. C. *Sess. Pap.* 1842 (251) XIV: 6. A note in the Office of Works records for 1853 indicates that Gurney did finally win compensation for the use of his Bude lights, in 1839–42, at the rate of £120 per annum. PRO WORK 11–26/3, folio 1, Gurney to Works, 4 January 1853.

13. Harris, *Gurney,* 72.

14. The eduction tube is referred to simply as "the Faraday lamp" in the parliamentary records, but *The Correspondence of Michael Faraday,* 228, item 125, shows that Robert and James developed it.

15. Harris, *Gurney,* 72.

16. Ministry of Works, *History of the King's Works,* VI: 210–11.

17. *Dictionary of National Biography* s.v. "Howard, George William Frederick."

18. Harris, *Gurney,* 74–5. For documents on Gurney's lighting experiments, see PRO WORK 11–26/1 and 11–17/3. Gurney sent a memorial to the Treasury on 14 June 1849 rehearsing his claim to patent royalties. He said that he had declined to sell his patent rights to the Bude lamps in the temporary House of Commons on the strength of assurances that such lamps would be installed in the new House. Since that assurance was not fulfilled, he wanted fair consideration for lost royalties, as given in other buildings where the Bude lamp was used. It was "understood" that

royalties would be calculated as half the annual savings in the Commons' lighting expenditures, which amounted to "upwards of £5000."

19. Harris, *Gurney*, 75. Cf. M. H. Port, ed., *The Houses of Parliament* (New Haven: Yale University Press, 1976), 229. Hume's statement was contained in a lengthy letter to T. W. Phillipps, the secretary at H. M. Office of Works, Woods, and Forests.

20. The *Illustrated London News* 20, no. 555 (24 April 1852): 317, complained that Reid's lights were too bright, ugly, and architecturally offensive. "The appearance of the House is completely spoiled by this arrangement." Reid's original lamps had raised the temperature above the House ceiling from 52 to 104 degrees Fahrenheit.

21. For the reform of Woods and Forests, see the *History of the King's Works*, VI: 249, and Emmerson, *The Ministry of Works*, 16. Parliament found three problems at the office: (1) land revenues of the Crown were shifted into accounts for public works, and vice versa, while contractors might be paid (or not) from two or three different sources; (2) supervision of staff was so loose that the office secretary had been on medical leave for two years, the clerks of works met only once a month, and many employees worked only part-time; (3) the office had become a dumping ground for inconvenient jobs no other government department wanted to deal with, leading to an enormous backlog that overwhelmed what staff there was.

22. *The Houses of Parliament*, 115.

23. *The Houses of Parliament*, 218–19.

24. Stephen Shapin, "Nibbling at the Teats of Science: Edinburgh and the Diffusion of Science in the 1830s," in Inkster and Morrell, *Metropolis and Province*, 163–64. A portrait of Reid, about 1842, is given in *The Houses of Parliament*, 219, plate 142, probably from the *Illustrated London News*.

25. *The Houses of Parliament*, 219.

26. Ibid., 220.

27. Ibid., 221.

28. Ibid., 222.

29. Ibid., 115, and plates 74 and 75. In 1856, Reid emigrated to America, where he became Medical Inspector to the U.S. Sanitary Commission.

30. Ibid., 224.

31. H. C. *Sess. Pap.* 1854 (149) IX: 417–42, First Report of the Select Committee on Ventilation of the House.

32. Ibid., 11, q. 112.

33. *The Houses of Parliament*, 226.

34. Gurney and Charles Barry exchanged curt arguments during the summer of 1854 about the relative efficacy of high-level and low-level air intakes. Barry claimed that his own high-level intake through Victoria Tower left the House of Lords fresh and pure, while Gurney's low-level intakes were inevitably dysfunctional. Gurney replied that studies on the Continent had shown the fallacy of Barry's principle, and pointed out that he was recruited specifically to rectify foul smells in the House of Lords, where even the odors of the members' kitchen were drawn down the intake shaft. Cf. PRO WORK 11–24/13, letters of 24 and 31 July, 4 and 12 August.

35. H. C. *Sess. Pap.* 1854 (149) IX: 5–9, q. 30–70.

36. Ibid.

37. An engineer named William Woodcock helped Gurney set up the company and produce the stoves, beginning in 1848. See Woodcock's memoir in the ICE *Minutes of Proceedings* 39 (1874): 299.

38. H. C. *Sess. Pap.* 1854 (149) IX: minutes of evidence, 7, 8, 11. For Gurney's affairs in Cornwall, see Harris, *Gurney*, 88.

39. Ibid., 91. A draft of the official instructions, sent to Gurney as supervisor of

the Houses of Parliament and the Law Court, is in PRO WORK 11–26/3. He was to (1) supervise the warming, ventilating, paving, lighting, water, drainage, and other utilities of both the Old and New Palaces, including all machinery and apparatus; (2) cooperate with Sir Charles Barry on the design and maintenance of sections yet to be completed; (3) keep an office and residential quarters on the premises, so that he might be in attendance at all times when Parliament was sitting; (4) supervise, and keep wages accounts for, all the relevant clerks and workmen; (5) submit regular accounts for materials, services, etc., obtained from area vendors and prepare estimates for the coming fiscal year.

40. According to Mr. Bryan Stamp's research in local records, Hornacott Manor was listed in the Domesday survey. It descended through the Courtenays of Powderhorn, who sold it in 1774 to George Brown, whose descendent, G. F. Collins Browne of Bodmin, built Woodley Cottage, then sold the estate to Gurney for about £6,000. Gurney sold it to a Captain Knight in 1860, after his second marriage failed.

41. Harris, *Gurney*, 95–96. Jane Betty Gurney's tombstone records her birth year as 1830, but Harris quotes from "another source" that she gave her age as twenty-five when married in November 1854. Her father was James Betty of Sheepwash, Devon. I can only speculate that Gurney met her either through the auspices of Sir Thomas Acland, M.P. for Devonshire, from whom Gurney had leased the land for his Castle in Bude, or through associates in the Devon and Cornwall agricultural societies in which both Gurney and Acland participated.

42. Ibid.

43. *The Houses of Parliament*, 227–28.

Chapter 12. The Steam-Jet Furnace and the Sewers of London

1. Engineers from the Metropolitan Commission of Sewers discovered in October 1848 that the sewer line running underneath the New Palace was actually higher than the level of the underground palace vaults and leaked into them. When they climbed from the sewer into the vaults via a manhole, they found themselves knee-deep in a veritable cesspool. The connecting drains were also judged "defective and opposed to all principles of drainage." *Illustrated London News* 8, no. 340 (21 October 1848): 247.

2. H. C. *Sess. Pap.* 1857–58, (442) IX, Report of the Select Committee appointed to take into consideration Mr. Gurney's report on the River Thames, 244. Gurney often said that he had given up medical practice in 1825 or 1826, when he became absorbed in the steam carriage, but apparently he was still available for special assignments.

3. Ibid., 245.

4. The prevailing theories of sanitation and disease are explored in detail in Christopher Hamlin, *A Science of Impurity: Water Analysis in Nineteenth-Century Britain* (Berkeley and Los Angeles: University of California Press, 1990), especially chapters 4 and 5.

5. H. C. *Sess. Pap.* 1857–58 (442) IX: 46, q. 815. Thompson produced two vials of gas, one taken before entering the furnace, one after. The first had been condensed and stored for three weeks, on the standard theory that contaminated water purified itself over time; this sample had actually produced a large mass of algae and some live insects. The second set was "quite pure."

6. Harris, *Gurney*, 57–59.

7. H. C. *Sess. Pap.* 1850 (480) 33: 467–78, "Correspondence between the Com-

missioners of Sewers and Mr. Goldsworthy Gurney in reference to the Experiment of the steam jet in Purifying the pestilential sewer in Friar Street, Borough, in Autumn Last."

8. A copy of Gurney's report from 1849 was included in his later report of 1855, in H. C. *Sess. Pap.* 1854–55 (105) XIII: 295–301. The MCS's engineer, John Grant, quoted much of this in his own report, H. C. *Sess. Pap.* 1850 (480) XXXIII: 467–78.

9. Ibid.

10. Ibid.

11. Ibid., 470–71, Grant's report of 30 October 1849. For John Grant's character and career, see Dale H. Porter and Gloria C. Clifton, "Patronage, Professional Values, and Victorian Public Works: Engineering and Contracting the Thames Embankment," *Victorian Studies* 31: 3 (Spring 1988): 345–46.

12. According to Gurney, that is: cf. H. C. *Sess. Pap.* 1857–58 (442) IX: minutes of evidence, 1, q. 11. H. M. Office of Works records show that Gurney requested help from the MCS in July 1854 and negotiated details of flap installation and expenses during August and September. Assistant MCS Engineer William Cooper prepared working drawings, to which Gurney objected, and it appears that he hired his own contractor to assist him. In December he complained to the Office of Works that the MCS had sent in an account totalling £42 for sewer inspection and flap installation, which he thought grossly inflated. However, their engineers had been "very attentive, and I believe rendered every assistance in their power; they seemed to take much interest in the success of the experiment."

13. PRO WORK 11–24/13, correspondence of 4 and 9 July 1855.

14. H. C. *Sess. Pap.* 1854–55 (105) XIII: 295–301, "Copy (with drawings) of Mr. Gurney's Report to the Office of Works, on his experiment for withdrawing and decomposing the noxious effluvia from the Sewers in the Neighbourhood of the Houses of Parliament, dated 8 January 1855." The notes and correspondence on which this report was based are in the PRO WORK files, 11–24/13.

15. Except that in 1845 or 1846, Gurney did submit a plan to the MCS for flushing sewage down the Thames at high tide.

16. David Owen, *The Government of Victorian London, 1855–1889: The Metropolitan Board of Works, the Vestries, and the City Corporation* (Harvard: The Belknap Press, 1982), 31–35.

17. Ibid., 52–53.

18. Cf. H. C. *Sess. Pap.* 1840 (554) XII: 283, for a drawing of Walker's embankment design.

19. Based on an estimate by Gurney, H. C. *Sess. Pap.* 1857–58 (442) XI: 131, q. 2115.

20. Ibid., 151, q. 2501, testimony of William Maugham.

21. Gurney confirmed that the worst miasmas rose from the water when the barometer was dropping, and prevailing wind currents drew the gases upriver toward the Houses of Parliament. Cf. PRO WORK 11–24/13, Gurney to Hall, 14 July 1857. Reconstruction of the old Westminster Bridge also churned up the mud banks next to Parliament. Additionally, located directly opposite Parliament on the Lambeth Shore, there was a large bone-burning operation, whose nauseating smells wafted across the river. When Gurney complained about the bone burners, he discovered that legislation authorizing the Metropolitan Board of Works in 1855 had inadvertently created a judicial nightmare: local nuisances had to be reported to the borough police, who would file a complaint with the local justice of the peace, who would report to the Home Secretary, who would forward evidence to the Lords of the Treasury, who would refer the matter to their solicitors in H. M. Office of Works.

22. For Cayley's device, an outgrowth of his study of optics in the 1840s, see the ICE *Minutes of Proceedings* 18 (1859): 204. Testing water "by the abstraction of light," it was reported, was "a process which has lately been used with success in the investigation of the waters of the Thames."

23. Hamlin, *A Science of Impurity*, chapter 5, "Nitrogen and Nihilism, 1852–68."

24. H. C. *Sess. Pap.* 1857–58 (442) XI: 18, q. 281. Gurney said that "some years ago, when I left the old House," he became president of a "society of country gentlemen" formed to carry out agricultural experiments.

25. Ibid., 2, 4, 16, 18, 243 and passim. Gurney's analogy between rivers and mine shafts, with regard to retrograde eddies, was actually made in his testimony before the parliamentary committee on Coal Mines in July 1853. Cf. H. C. *Sess. Pap.* 1852–53 (820) XX, Third Report of the Select Committee on Coal Mines, 74, q. 4157.

26. Gurney probably got the idea for the channels from Alexander Gordon, the engineer who celebrated his steam carriage research back in the 1830s. Gordon testified that his father had successfully channeled a river running through his estate, and calculated that a similar set of dredgings in the Thames would cost about £18,000. Gurney recommended channels only from Vauxhall Bridge to Waterloo. Above Vauxhall the Office of Works' embankment, then nearly finished, would perform a similar function. Below Waterloo the City of London Navigation Committee already contracted for regular dredging to facilitate commercial barge traffic.

27. H.C. *Sess. Pap.* 1857–58 (442) XI: 106, q. 1710. "We know," said Dr. Thompson, "that snow contains air which has an excess of oxygen in it, and hence many old women in the country make snow cakes and snow dumplings; they take a portion of the snow and mix it with the flour, they find it unnecessary to add any yeast to it, the oxygen in the snow throws the flour into a state of fermentation, and the bread is quite light."

28. Ibid., 1–16.

29. *Annual Register of Events*, 1858: 111; also, H. C. *Sess. Pap.* 1857–58 (442) XI: 66.

30. *Times*, 6 July 1858: 10, letter of William Ord; *Hansard's Parliamentary Debates*, 3d series, vol. 149 (1858): 436. *The City Press* is quoted by Owen, *Government of Victorian London*, 53, n. 22.

31. H. C. *Sess. Pap.* 1857–58 (442) XI: 68, q. 1150.

32. Owen, *Government of Victorian London*, 50–5.

33. H. C. *Sess. Pap.* 1857–58 (442) XI: 74, q. 1269 and 187, q. 1445.

34. Ibid., 109, q. 1757.

35. Ibid., 110, q. 1760.

36. Cf. Owen, *Government of Victorian London*, 31–53. Also, Porter and Clifton, "Patronage, Professional Values, and Victorian Public Works," 319–50.

37. H. C. *Sess. Pap.* 1854–55 (105) XIII: 295–301.

38. Metropolitan Board of Works, *Minutes of Proceedings* 1857: 494–510, Mr. Bazalgette's report of 1 July 1857, on Mr. Gurney's report to the First Commissioner of Works, regarding the state of the Thames. Greater London Record Office, MBW 2409, report no. 058.

39. H. C. *Sess. Pap.* 1857–58 (442) XI: 221, q. 3438, and 172–78, q. 2828–916.

40. Ibid., 172, q. 2836–66.

41. Ibid., 117, q. 1871.

42. Ibid., 160, q. 2570–78.

43. Ibid., 207, q. 3297–301.

44. Ibid., 209, q. 3302–4.

45. Ibid., 210–11, q. 3304–28. Hawksley made essentially the same statement.

The tests, he said, were hurried, and "not of that refined or careful character a professional man would desire to make," but they were fair enough to confirm his earlier assumptions (222, q. 3220).

46. Ibid., 214–15, q. 3352–71.

47. Ibid., 219, q. 3424.

48. Ibid., "Report," x.

49. Ibid., "Report," xi.

CHAPTER 13. RECOGNITION AND DECLINE

1. Printed in London by G. Barclay, 1859. The Institution of Civil Engineers has two copies of this pamphlet, one sent by "Miss G" in 1873 (archives, vol. 229), and the second sent in 1881 with Anna Gurney's note about Cayley's editorial help. It is in this pamphlet, written so long after the events, that Gurney first claimed to have demonstrated to Richard Trevithick the principle of steam eduction up the locomotive smoke funnel, by passing the steam from a teakettle over the chimney of a burning Argand lamp. The text implies that this took place in 1804, when Gurney was eleven years old—a somewhat questionable claim, though not impossible.

2. *Account of the Invention of the Steam-Jet or Blast,* 24. Gurney's arguments were anticipated earlier in 1859 by a Mr. Hedley, who had witnessed the first railway trials in 1829, in *Who Invented the Locomotive Engine?*

3. See Robbins, *The Railway Age in Britain,* 23.

4. Ibid., 21.

5. Harris, *Gurney,* 93.

6. Ibid.

7. During the period 1852–60, more than ten thousand ships, both British and foreign, were destroyed in collisions or smashed on the rocky shores of the British Isles. A royal commission, appointed in 1859 after two especially tragic shipwrecks, recommended more stringent standards for ship maintenance, the training of captains and crews, and sea charts. It also circulated a list of questions about the optics of lighthouses to men with special knowledge in the field, including Gurney. Roy MacLeod, "Science and Government in Victorian England: Lighthouse Illumination and the Board of Trade, 1866–1886," *Isis* 60, part 1, no. 201 (1969): 7, 10.

8. Harris, *Gurney,* 92.

9. Ibid. Additional copies of *Observations Pointing Out Means by Which a Seaman May Identify Lighthouses and Know Their Distance from His Ship, in Any Position or Bearing of the Compass* (London: Longman, Green, Longman, Roberts and Green, 1864; 13 pp.) were distributed by Anna Gurney after her father's death in 1881, with a handwritten explanation of how it came to be printed. On the copy in the Institution of Civil Engineers, Anna noted that the patent was lost through her failure to pay the required fees, but in any case, the advent of electric lights made the claim irrelevant. The royal commission that had requested ideas for lighthouse communication did recommend, in 1861, the use of more brilliant lights, the use of double lights for calculating distance, and the introduction of a system for distinguishing between lighthouses. Roy MacLeod, "Science and Government in Victorian England," 11.

10. The claims and responses, too tedious to recount here, are in the Public Record Office, PRO WORK 11–26/3, folio 3.

11. PRO WORK 11–26/3, folio 2, 1 September 1859 to 7 February 1860.

12. William Cowper (1811–88) was Lord Melbourne's nephew and Lord Palmer-

ston's stepson. He was appointed President of the Board of Health under Benjamin Hall at the Office of Works in 1855. Edward Barry, completing his father's design for the New Palace at Westminster, considered him "a man who was quite without official airs . . . considerate and accessible." *The Houses of Parliament*, 177–78.

13. My information about Gurney's condition and Anna's care for him comes from letters she wrote to Alfred Austin, secretary to William Cowper, at H. M. Office of Works in 1864–65 (PRO WORK 11–26/3, folio 4), and from the handwritten comments she added to copies of his published pamphlets, which she sent to various institutions after his death.

14. Government rewarded public benefactors through civil list pensions, but the budget for pensions was limited to £1,200, and pensions were generally given to men in the arts. Occasionally a famous research scientist, such as Faraday, was included, but by 1860 applied scientists and inventors were "categorically ruled out" on the grounds that the fund was too small and that inventors should receive such benefits from the industrialists they had enriched. Roy MacLeod, *Public Science and Public Policy in Victorian England* (Aldershot, Hampshire: Variorum, 1996), part V, "Science and the Civil List, 1824–1914," 11.

15. Office of Works papers, PRO WORK 11–26/3, folio 4.

16. Harris, *Gurney*, 97–98. Mr. Peter Gurney has advised me that the clock in Poughhill Church required winding twice a week, which meant climbing the church tower stairs and giving one hundred turns on a manual crank. As no one has been found to replace the present winder, who is retiring, the church elders have installed an electric timing mechanism. By doing the labor themselves, they reduced the cost to £2,600 (only £2,490 more than the original!). Mr. Gurney dedicated the new clock at the end of July, 1996.

17. Harris, *Gurney*, 96–97. The ICE obituary and the pieces in the *West Briton* provided most of the text for Frederic Boase's later memoir of Gurney in his *Modern English Biography* and for George B. Smith's entry on Gurney in the first supplement to the *Dictionary of National Biography*.

18. See the *Times*, 27 December 1875: 6; 1 January 1876: 6; and 24 January 1876: 11. The son of William Keene, Gurney's former assistant, supported Anna in a letter of 29 December.

CHAPTER 14. SCIENCE, TECHNOLOGY, AND INVENTION IN THE EARLY NINETEENTH CENTURY

1. L. T. C. Rolt, *Victorian Engineering* (Harmondsworth, UK: Penguin Books, 1970) provides an accessible narrative, while the development of the profession is described by R. A. Buchanan, "Gentleman Engineers: The Making of a Profession," *Victorian Studies* 26, no. 4 (Summer 1983): 427–29. Buchanan's book, *The Engineers: A History of the Engineering Profession in Britain, 1750–1914* (London: Jessica Kingsley, 1989), concentrates on the growth of the Institution of Civil Engineers and its offspring.

2. For example, David Knight's *Humphry Davy: Science and Power* interprets Davy's career in the context of competition among different social classes for control over scientific research. L. Pearce Williams's *Michael Faraday* is an earlier, more traditional biography, but it gives a thorough explanation of the chemistry and physics of Faraday's time, discusses the tensions arising from his working-class origins and fundamentalist religion, and shows his long relationship with the Royal Institution. Maurice Crosland's *Gay-Lussac: Scientist and Bourgeois* (1978), examines the social, material and political realities of the scientific career in pre-revolutionary France.

Bibliography

U. K. PARLIAMENT, HOUSE OF COMMONS *SESSIONAL PAPERS*

1831 (324) VIII: Report from the Select Committee appointed to inquire into the proportion of tolls which ought to be imposed upon coaches and other vehicles propelled by steam or gas, upon turnpike roads, and also to inquire into the rate of toll actually levied upon such coaches and other vehicles under an Act of Parliament now in force, and who were instructed to inquire generally into the present state and future prospects of land carriage, by means of wheeled vehicles propelled by steam or gas on common roads; with the minutes of Evidence and Appendix.

1831–32 (489) IV: Bill to regulate the Turnpike Toll on steam carriages.

1834 (590) XII: Report of the Select Committee on Lighthouses.

1834 (483) XI—1835 (483) XIII: First and Second Reports from the Select Committee on Mr. Goldsworthy Gurney's Case, with minutes of evidence.

1835 (603) V: Report from the Select Committee on Accidents in Mines.

1836 (547) XIX: Report from the Select Committee on Turnpike Trusts and Tolls.

1836 (67) VI: Bill to repeal such Portions of all Acts as Impose Prohibitory Tolls on Steam Carriages, and to Substitute other Tolls on an Equitable Footing with Horse Carriages.

1839 (295) IX: Report of the Select Committee for Ascertaining how far the Formation of Railroads may Affect the Interest of Turnpike Trusts and the Creditors of such Trusts.

1839 (501) XIII: Report of the Select Committee appointed to Superintend the Experiment of Mr. Gurney to Light the House of Commons.

1842 (251) XIV: Report of the Select Committee to inquire into the Remuneration due to Mr. G. Gurney for his Services in Lighting the House of Commons.

1850 (480) XXXIII: Correspondence between the Commissioners of Sewers and Mr. Goldsworthy Gurney in reference to the Experiment of the Steam Jet in Purifying the Pestilential Sewer in Friar Street, Borough, in Autumn Last.

1850 (1222) XXIII: Report on the Ventilation of Mines and Collieries, by John Phillips, FRS.

1852 (509) V, Appendix 4: Report of the South Shields Committee (1843) on Coal Mine Accidents.

1852–53 (820) XX: Third Report of the Select Committee on Accidents in Coal Mines.

1854 (149) (270) (483) IX: First, Second, and Third Reports of the Select Committee on Ventilation of the [new] House.

1854 (169) (258) (277) (325) IX: First, Second, Third, and Fourth Reports of the Select Committee on Accidents in Coal Mines.

1854–55 (135) XXI: Report of the Royal Commission on the Cholera Epidemic of 1854—Scientific Enquiries.

1854–55 (105) LIII: Mr. Gurney's Report to the Office of Works on his Experiment for Withdrawing and Decomposing the Noxious Effluvia from the Sewers in the Neighbourhood of the Houses of Parliament, 8 January 1855.

1857–58 (442) XI: Report of the Select Committee on the River Thames.

1857–58 (21) XLVIII: Report of Mr. Gurney to the First Commissioner of Works on the State of the Thames in the Neighbourhood of the Houses of Parliament.

1860 (494) XX: Report of the Select Comittee on the Embankment of the River Thames.

1860 (1214) XXIII: Report of J. Kenyon Blackwell on the Ventilation of Mines.

1864 (3389) XXIV, Part I: Report of the Royal Commission on Mine Safety.

U. K. PARLIAMENT, HOUSE OF LORDS SESSIONAL PAPERS

1836 House of Lords Journals 68, Appendix 5: Report of the Select Committee of the House of Lords appointed to consider a Bill entitled, "An Act to repeal such Portions of all Acts as Impose Prohibitory Tolls on Steam Carriages."

1836 House of Lords Journals 68, Appendix 5: Report of the Select Committee appointed to consider whether any Danger by Fire is Likely to Arise from Locomotive Engines being used on Railroads Passing through Narrow Streets.

1849 (613) VII: Report of the Lords Select Committee on Mines.

1854 (149) (270) (483) IX: First, Second, and Third Reports of the Lords Committee on Ventilation of the New Palace.

MUSEUM COLLECTIONS

The British Museum Library
The Bude-Stratton Museum, Bude, Cornwall
The Greater London Record Office
The House of Lords Record Office
The Public Record Office, Kew
The Royal Institution of Civil Engineers
The Royal Society for the Encouragement of Arts, Manufactures, and Commerce
The London Transport Museum
The Science Museum, Kensington
The Truro Museum, Truro, Cornwall

PERIODICALS

The Annual Register of Events (London)
Blackwood's Edinburgh Magazine
The Engineer
Gill's Technical Repository
Hansard's Parliamentary Debates, Third Series

The Illustrated London News
The London Gazette
The Mechanic's Magazine
The Mining Journal
Minutes of Proceedings. The Institution of Civil Engineers, London
Minutes of Proceedings. The Metropolitan Board of Works, London
The Monthly Magazine
Register of Arts and Journal of Patent Inventions
The Times
Transactions of the Society of Arts

BOOKS AND ARTICLES

Accum, Friedrich Christian. *Description of the Process of Manufacturing Coal Gas for the Lighting of Streets, Houses, and Public Buildings [in London].* 2d ed. London: Thomas Boys, 1820.

Ackerman, R. *The Microcosm of London.* 6 vols. London: Methuen, 1904.

Agassi, Joseph. *Faraday as a Natural Philosopher.* Chicago: University of Chicago Press, 1971.

Altick, R. D. *The Shows of London.* Cambridge, Mass: Harvard University Press, 1978.

Atkins, P. W. "The Candle Revisited." *Proceedings of the Royal Institute of Great Britain* 655 (1994): 1–14.

Balchin, W. G. V. *Cornwall: An Illustrated Essay on the History of the Landscape.* London: Hodder and Stoughton, 1954.

Beasley, David R. *The Suppression of the Automobile: Skulduggery at the Cross-roads.* New York: Greenwood Press, 1988.

Berman, Morris. *Social Change and Scientific Organization: The Royal Institution, 1799–1844.* London: Heinemann, 1978.

Berry, Claude. *Portrait of Cornwall.* 2d ed. London: Robert Hale & Co., 1971.

Bijker, Wiebe, Thomas Hughes, and Trevor Pinch, eds. *The Social Construction of Technological Systems: New Directions in the Sociology and History of Technology.* Cambridge, Mass: MIT Press, 1987.

Boase, Frederic. *Modern English Biography.* London: Frank Cass, 1901.

Boase, G. C. *Collectanea Cornubiensia.* Truro, Cornwall: privately printed, 1890.

The British Association for the Advancement of Science. *Report of the 11th meeting, Plymouth, 1841.* London: John Murray, 1842.

Buchanan, R. A. "Gentleman Engineers: The Making of a Profession." *Victorian Studies* 26, no. 4 (Summer 1983): 407–29.

———. *The Engineers: A History of the Engineering Profession in Britain, 1750–1914.* London: Jessica Kingsley, 1989.

Bud, Robert, and Gerrylynn K. Roberts. *Science Versus Practice: Chemistry in Victorian Britain.* Manchester, UK: Manchester University Press, 1984.

Bynum, W. F. *Science and the Practice of Medicine in the Nineteenth Century.* New York: Cambridge University Press, 1994.

Cantor, Geoffrey. *Michael Faraday: Sandemanian and Scientist.* New York: St. Martin's Press, 1991.

Caroe, G. M., and Alban Caroe. *The Royal Institution: An Informal History.* London: John Murray, 1985.

Checkland, S.G. *The Rise of Industrial Society in England, 1815–1885.* New York: St. Martin's Press, 1964.

Clow, Archibald, and Nan L. Clow. *The Chemical Revolution.* London: The Batchworth Press, 1952.

Croly, George. "Steam Carriages." *Blackwood's Edinburgh Magazine* 23 (January 1828): 94–6.

Crosland, Maurice. *Gay-Lussac: Scientist and Bourgeois.* Cambridge: Cambridge University Press, 1978.

Courtney, W. P. *Bibliotheca Cornubiensis.* vols. 1–3. London: Longmans, 1874, 1881.

Darby, H. C. *A New Historical Geography of London After 1600.* Cambridge: Cambridge University Press, 1976.

Davey, Norman. *A History of Building Materials.* London: Phoenix House, 1961.

Davison, C. St. C. B. *History of Steam Road Vehicles.* London: H.M. Stationery Office and The Science Museum, n.d.

The Dictionary of National Biography. Ed. Sir Leslie Stephen and Sir Sidney Lee. London: Oxford University Press, various editions.

Emmerson, Sir Harold. *The Ministry of Works.* London: Allen and Unwin, 1956.

Evans, Francis T. "Roads, Railways, and Canals: Technical Choices in 19th-century Britain." *Technology and Culture* 22, no. 1 (1981): 1–34.

Falkus, M. E. "The Early Development of the British Gas Industry, 1790–1815." *Economic History Review* 35, no. 2 (1982): 217–34.

Faraday, Michael. *The Correspondence of Michael Faraday.* Edited by Frank A. J. L. James. New York: Institute of Electrical Engineers, 1991.

Faraday, Michael. *Faraday's Diary: Being the Various Philosophical Notes of Experimental Investigation made by Michael Faraday.* Edited by Thomas Martin. 2 vols. London: G. Bell & Sons, 1936.

Fletcher, William. *History and Development of Steam Locomotion on Common Roads.* London, E. Spon, 1891.

Foote, George A. "Sir Humphry Davy and His Audience at the Royal Institution." *Isis* 43 (April 1952): 6–12.

French, Roger, and Andrew Wear, eds. *British Medicine in an Age of Reform.* London: Routledge, 1991.

Fulmer, June. "Technology, Chemistry and the Law in Early 19th-century England." *Annals of Science* 38, no. 2 (1981): 155–89.

Gee, Brian. "The Early Development of the Magneto-Electric Machine." *Annals of Science* 50, no. 2 (1993): 101–33.

Gibb, Sir Alexander. *The Story of Telford.* London: Alexander Maclehose, 1935.

Gilbert, C. S. *Historical and Topographical Survey of the County of Cornwall.* London: Anonymous, 1820.

———. *Historical Survey of the County of Cornwall.* London, Anonymous, 1817.

Glover, Graham. *British Locomotive Design, 1825–1960.* London: George Allen and Unwin, 1967.

Golinski, Jan. *Science as Public Culture: Chemistry and Enlightenment in Britain, 1760-1820.* Cambridge: Cambridge University Press, 1992.

———. "The Theory of Practice and the Practice of Theory: Sociological Approaches in the History of Science." *Isis* 81 (1990): 492–505.

Gooding, David, and Frank A. J. L. James, eds. *Faraday Rediscovered: Essays on the Life and Work of Michael Faraday, 1791–1867.* London: Macmillan, 1985.

Gordon, Alexander. *A Treatise on Elemental Locomotion.* 3d ed. London: Thomas Tegg & Son, 1836.

Gordon, Lewis. *Railway Economy: an Exposition of the Advantages of Locomotion by Locomotive Carriages Instead of the Present Expensive System of Steam Tugs.* Edinburgh: Sutherland and Knox, 1849.

Gurney, Goldsworthy. *The Elements of Chemical Science.* London: G. and W. B. Whittaker, 1823.

———. "An Improved Blow-Pipe." *Transactions of the Society of Arts* 41 (1823–24): 70-7.

———. *Mr. Gurney's Observations on Steam Carriages on Turnpike Roads, with Returns of the Daily Practical Results of Working; the Cause of the Stoppage of the Carriage at Gloucester; and the Consequent Official Report of the House of Commons.* London: Baldwin and Craddock, 1832. Institution of Civil Engineers tracts collection, octavo series, vol. 22, no. 11.

———. *Account of the Invention of the Steam-Jet or Blast.* London: G. Barclay, 1859. Reprint, 1881. Institution of Civil Engineers Tracts, vols. 229, 362.

———. *Observations Pointing Out Means by Which a Seaman May Identify Light-houses and Know Their Distance from His Ship, in Any Position or Bearing of the Compass.* London: Longman, Green, Longman, Roberts and Green, 1864.

Hall, A. Rupert. "What Did the Industrial Revolution in Britain Owe to Science?" *Historical Perspectives: Studies in English Thought and Society in Honor of J. H. Plumb.* Edited by Neil McKendrick. London: Europa Publications, 1974: 129–51.

Hamlin, Christopher, *A Science of Impurity: Water Analysis in 19th Century Britain.* Berkeley and Los Angeles: University of California Press, 1990.

Harris, T. R. *Sir Goldsworthy Gurney, 1793–1875.* Penzance, Cornwall: The Trevithick Society, 1975.

Hancock, Walter. *Narrative of Twelve Years' Experience (1824–1836) Demonstrative of the Practicability and Advantage of Employing Steam-carriages on Common Roads with Engravings and Descriptions of the Different Steam-carriages Constructed by the Author, his Patent Boiler, Wedge-wheels, and other Inventions.* London: J. Weale, 1838.

Hays, J. N. "Science in the City: the London Institution, 1819–1840." *The British Journal for the History of Science* 7, no. 26 (1974): 146–62.

Heard, R. M. "Notes on the Castle, Bude and its Setting for the Cornish Gorsedd 1976." Typescript, 1975. Bude-Stratton Museum.

Herapath, John, *A Letter to His Grace the Duke of Wellington on the Utility, Advantages and National Importance of Mr. Gurney's Steam Carriage.* London: Baldwin & Craddock, 1829.

Hunt, Charles. *A History of the Introduction of Gas Lighting.* London: W. King, 1907.

Imiolczyk, Susan, and Ray Tucker. *Castle and Cottages.* Cyfarthfa [Wales] Museum Publication no. 4, n.d.

Inkster, Ian, and Jack Morrell, eds. *Metropolis and Province: Science in British Culture 1780–1850*. Philadelphia: University of Pennsylvania Press, 1983.

James, Francis. *Walter Hancock and His Common Road Steam Carriages*. Alresford, UK: Lawrence Oxley, 1975. [Includes a republication of Hancock's *Narrative of Twelve Years' Experiments*, q. v.]

James, Frank. "Time, Tide and Michael Faraday." *History Today* 41 (September 1941): 28–34.

Jones, Bence. *The Life and Letters of Faraday*. 2 vols. London: Longmans, Green & Co., 1870.

Jones, A. V., and R. P. Tarkenter, *Electrical Technology in Mining: the Dawn of a New Age*. London: The Science Museum and Peter Peregrinus, 1992.

Kirby, Maurice W. *The Origins of Railway Enterprise: The Stockton and Darlington Railway, 1831–1863*. Cambridge: Cambridge University Press, 1993.

Knight, David. *Humphry Davy: Science and Power*. Oxford: Blackwell, 1992.

Kuhn, Thomas. *The Structure of Scientific Revolutions*. 2d ed. Chicago: University of Chicago Press, 1970.

Latour, Bruno, and Steve Woolgar, *Laboratory Life: The Social Construction of Scientific Facts*. Beverly Hills and London: Sage, 1979.

Lewis, W. David. "Goldsworthy Gurney." *Great Engineers and Pioneers in Technology*. Edited by Roland Turner and Steven Goulden. New York: St. Martin's Press, 1981.

Lord, Todd. "Humphry Davy." *Proceedings of the Royal Institution of Great Britain* 52 (1980): 41–58.

MacLeod, Roy. "The Alkali Acts Administration, 1863–84: The Emergence of the Civil Scientist." *Victorian Studies* 9 (1965): 85–112.

———. *Public Science and Public Policy in Victorian England*. Aldershot, Hampshire, UK: Variorum, 1996.

———. "Science and Government in Victorian England: Lighthouse Illumination and the Board of Trade, 1866–1886." *Isis* 60, part 1, no. 201 (1969): 5–38.

McCase, Irene M. "The Physicians-Cum-Natural Philosophers at the Royal Institution, 1799–1840." *Proceedings of the Royal Institution of Great Britain* 50 (1988): 99–118.

McKendrick, Neil. "The Role of Science in the Industrial Revolution: A Study of Josiah Wedgwood as a Scientist and Industrial Chemist." *Changing Perspectives in the History of Science: Essays in Honour of Joseph Needham*. Edited by Mikulás Teich and Robert Young. London: Heinemann, 1973.

McNeil, Ian. *Joseph Bramah: A Century of Invention, 1749–1851*. Newton Abbot, Devon, UK: David and Charles, 1968.

Melhado, Evan M. "Chemistry, Physics, and the Chemical Revolution." *Isis* 76 (1985): 195–211.

Miller, Arthur. "Unipolar Induction: A Case Study of the Interaction Between Science and Technology." *Annals of Science* 38, no. 2 (1981): 155–89.

Milton, Jessie E. "Lectures and Lecturers in the First 100 years of the Royal Institution." *Proceedings of the Royal Institution of Great Britain* 50 (1979): 133–44.

Ministry of Works. *The History of the King's Works*. London: The Ministry of Works, n.d.

Morell, J. B. "London Institutions and Lyell's Career, 1820–1841." *The British Journal for the History of Science* 9, part 2, no. 32 (July 1976): 132–46.

———. "Individualism and the Structure of British Science in 1830." *Historical Studies in the Physical Sciences* 3 (1971): 183–204.

Morris, Robert J. "Lavoisier and the Caloric Theory." *The British Journal for the History of Science* 6, no. 21 (1972): 1–38.

Morus, Iwan Rhys. "Currents From the Underworld: Electricity and the Technology of Display in Early Victorian England." *Isis* 84, no. 1 (1993): 50–69.

———. "Different Experimental Lives: Michael Faraday and William Sturgeon." *History of Science* 30 (1992): 1–28.

Musson, A. E., and Eric Robinson. *Science and Technology in the Industrial Revolution.* Manchester, UK: Manchester University Press, 1969.

Oldroyd, D. R. "Edward Daniel Clarke, 1769–1822, and His Role in the History of the Blow-pipe." *Annals of Science* 29: 213–35.

Olsen, Donald J. *The Growth of Victorian London.* Harmondsworth, Middlesex, UK: Penguin Books, 1976.

Owen, David. *The Government of Victorian London, 1855–1889: The Metropolitan Board of Works, the Vestries, and the City Corporation.* Harvard: The Belknap Press, 1982.

Payen, Jacques. "Seguin, Stephenson et la Naissance de la Locomotive a Chaudière Tubulaire, 1826–1829." *History of Technology* 6, no. 2 (1988): 145–71.

Peters, Tom F. *Building the Nineteenth Century.* Cambridge, Mass: MIT Press, 1996.

Peterson, M. Jeanne. *Family, Love and Work in the Lives of Victorian Gentlewomen.* Bloomington: Indiana University Press, 1989.

Pevsner, Nickolaus. *Portrait of Cornwall.* Revised by Enid Radcliff. The Building of England Series. Harmondsworth, UK: Penguin, 1951.

Polwhele, Richard. *The History of Cornwall.* 1806; London: Kohler and Coombes, 1978.

Port, M. H. ed. *The Houses of Parliament,* New Haven: Yale University Press, 1976.

Porter, Dale, and Gloria Clifton. "Patronage, Professional Values, and Victorian Public Works: Engineering and Contracting the Thames Embankment." *Victorian Studies* 31, no. 3 (Spring 1988): 319–50.

Porter, Dorothy. "Medicine and Industrial Society: Reform, Improvement, and Professionalization." *Victorian Studies* 37, no. 1 (Autumn 1993): 129–39.

Porter, George. "Joseph Priestley and His Contemporaries." *Journal of General Education* 27, no. 2 (1975): 91–100.

———. "Michael Faraday: Chemist." *Proceedings of the Royal Institution of Great Britain,* 53 (1981): 90–9.

Porter, Roy. "Gentlemen and Geology: The Emergence of a Scientific Career, 1660-1920." *The Historical Journal* 21, no. 4 (1978): 809–36.

Pritchard, J. Lawrence. *Sir George Cayley: The Inventor of the Aeroplane.* London: M. Parrish, 1961.

Reynaud, Marie-Hélène. *Marc Seguin: Du Pont de Tournon aux Premiers Chemins de Fer.* Paris: Éditions du Vivarais, 1986.

Robbins, Michael. *The Railway Age in Britain.* Harmondsworth, Middlesex, UK: Penguin Books, 1965.

Roberts, Gerrylyn K. "The Social and Cultural Significance of Science: The Royal Institution." *The British Journal for the History of Science* 13, no. 2 (1980): 154-57.

Rolt, L. T. C. *Victorian Engineering.* Harmondsworth, Middlesex, UK: Penguin Books, 1970.

Ross, Sydney. "John Herschel on Faraday and on Science." *Notes and Records of the Royal Society of London* 33, no. 1 (1978): 77–82.

Sinclair, Angus. *Development of the Locomotive Engine* (1907). Edited by John H. White, Jr. Cambridge, Mass: MIT Press, 1970.

Thomas, John Meurig. *Michael Faraday and the Royal Institution: The Genius of Man and Place.* Philadelphia: Adam Hilger, 1991.

Thomson, Thomas. *The History of Chemistry.* 2d ed. London: Henry Colbrun and Richard Bentley, 1830; reprint, New York: Arno Press, 1975.

Thornbury, Walter. *Old and New London.* London: Cassell, Petter, Galpin & Co., 1901.

Treneer, Anne. *The Mercurial Chemist: A Life of Sir Humphry Davy.* London: Methuen, 1963.

Wash, Howard M. "Culture and the Middle Classes: Popular Knowledge in Industrial Manchester." *Journal of British Studies* 27, no. 4 (1988): 375–404.

Weisburd, Stefi. "Hard Science." *Science News* 134 (9 July 1988): 24.

Whitt, L. A. "Atoms or Affinities? The Ambivalent Reception of Daltonian Theory." *Studies in History and Philosophy of Science* 21 (1990): 57–89.

Williams, L. Pearce. *Michael Faraday: A Biography.* New York: Basic Books, 1965.

———. "Science vs. Scientific Technology." *Science, Technology and Culture.* Edited by Henry J. Steffens and H. N. Muller III. New York: AMS Press, 1974.

Wilson, Leonard G. "Science by Candlelight." *The Mind and Art of Victorian England.* Edited by Josef L. Altholz. Minneapolis: University of Minnesota Press, 1976.

Wohl, Anthony. *Endangered Lives: Public Health in Victorian Britain.* London: J. M. Dent & Sons, 1983.

Young, C. F. T. *Steam Power on Common Roads.* London: John Murray, 1860.

Youngson, A. J. *The Scientific Revolution in Victorian Medicine.* New York: Holmes and Meier, 1979.

Index

Page numbers in **bold** type indicate illustrations.